Essays on Boredom
and Modernity

Critical Studies

Vol. 31

Amsterdam - New York, NY 2009

Essays on Boredom and Modernity

Edited by

Barbara Dalle Pezze
and
Carlo Salzani

Cover Image: Photo Philippe Sasso

Cover design: Pier Post

The paper on which this book is printed meets the requirements of "ISO 9706:1994, Information and documentation - Paper for documents - Requirements for permanence".

ISBN: 978-90-420-2566-0
©Editions Rodopi B.V., Amsterdam - New York, NY 2009
Printed in the Netherlands

CONTENTS

ACKNOWLEDGMENTS

As for any project, it would not have been possible to put together this collection of essays without the fortunate concurrence of many factors, the most important being the help and support of a number of persons whom we want to thank. In particular we wish to acknowledge the collaboration of Kevin Aho, Tobias Boes, Michael P Chaney, Chris Danta, William David Gartman, Graeme Gilloch, Espen Hammer, Graham Harman, Eugene W. Holland, Jeff Malpas, Adrian Martin, William McNeill, Max Penski, Lars Fr. H. Svendsen and Anthony Uhlmann.

The Delicate Monster:
Modernity and Boredom

Barbara Dalle Pezze and Carlo Salzani

The essay situates the phenomenon of boredom within the analysis of modernity and emphasises the strict interconnectedness of the two terms. Through a genealogical approach, it analyses the etymologies and the history of a number of terms related to modern boredom: *acedia, melancholy, ennui, spleen, Langeweile,* and finally the English *boredom.* If these terms are all related, the analysis shows that modern boredom is a recent and different phenomenon, as is demonstrated by the fact that the English term "boredom" dates only from the seventeenth century. Some of the causes of the "invention" of boredom are then briefly singled out in order to situate historically the crisis of the self and of human experience which are at the core of the modern epidemic of boredom. Finally, the essay explores the recent literature on the subject and summarises the contributions included in the collection.

> *C'est l'ennui! – l'oeil chargé d'un pleur involontaire,*
> *Il rêve d'échafauds en fumant son houka.*
> *Tu le connais, lecteur, ce monstre délicat,*
> *Hypocrite lecteur, – mon semblable, – mon frère!*
>
> [It is Ennui! – his eye swollen with unintentional tears,
> He dreams of scaffolds as he smokes his hookah pipe.
> You know him reader, that delicate monster,
> Hypocrite reader, – my fellow, – my brother!]
>
> Baudelaire, *"Au Lecteur"*

1.

Baudelaire's prefatory poem to *Les Fleurs du mal*, *"Au Lecteur,"* introduces the reader to a world of vice, error and sin, establishing the traits of that modernity which his merciless gaze will explore in the book. The counterpart of progress and modernisation – the idols of the nineteenth century – *"La sottise, l'erreur, le péché, la lésine"* [folly, error, sin, avarice] and *"le viol, le poison, le poignard, l'incendie"* [rape, poison, daggers, arson] characterise a modernity which coincides with moral exhaustion, decadence and evil.[1]

Baudelaire addresses a fellow connoisseur of this modern decay and summons the reader to a commonality of sin through the insistence on the pronoun "*nous*" (we) and the adjective "*nos/notre*" (our). The rhetorical game he plays with pronouns identifies the author and the narrator with the reader by including the formers into the crowd of modern sinners, but simultaneously establishes the distance of reflection from this identification, melding sympathy and contempt, irony and despair, solitude and multitude. This commonality does not revolve simply around sin and transgression, but is built also and foremost upon self-indulgence and spiritual failure: if these sins "*Occupent nos esprits et travaillent nos corps*" [occupy our minds and labour our bodies], nonetheless "*nous alimentons nos aimables remords, / Comme les mendiants nourrissent leur vermine*" [we feed our pleasant remorse / As beggars nourish their vermin]. A number on images insist on this point:

> *Nos péchés sont têtus, nos repentirs sont lâches;*
> *Nous nous faisons payer grassement nos aveux*
>
> [Our sins are obstinate, our repentance is faint;
> We exact a high price for our confessions]
>
> [...]
>
> *Aux objets répugnants nous trouvons des appas;*
> *Chaque jour vers l'enfer nous descendons d'un pas*
>
> [In repugnant things we discover charms;
> Every day we descend a step further towards Hell]
>
> [...]
>
> *Nous volons au passage un plaisir clandestin*
> *Que nous pressons bien fort comme une vieille orange.*
>
> [We steal as we pass by a clandestine pleasure
> That we squeeze very hard like a dried up orange.]

A multitude of *monstres* pursue the modern sinner and force him or her further into the hell of modernity: "*Satan Trismégiste*," "*le diable*" [the devil], "*Serré, fourmillant, comme un million d'helminthes, / Dans nos cerveaux ribote un peuple de demons*" [Serried, swarming, like a million maggots, / A legion of Demons carouses in our brains]; "*la mort dans nos poumons / Descend, fleuve invisible, avec de sourdes plaintes*" [Death, invisible river, / Descends into our lungs with muffled wails]; and then:

> *les chacals, les panthères, les lices,*
> *Les singes, les scorpions, les vautours, les serpents,*
> *Les monstres glapissants, hurlants, grognants, rampants*
> *Dans la ménagerie infâme de nos vices*

[the jackals, the panthers, the bitch hounds,
The apes, the scorpions, the vultures, the serpents,
The yelping, howling, growling, crawling monsters,
In the rotten menagerie of our vices].

However, within this multitude of at once hated and hailed tormentors,

Il en est un plus laid, plus méchant, plus immonde!
Quoiqu'il ne pousse ni grands gestes ni grands cris,
Il ferait volontiers de la terre un débris
Et dans un bâillement avalerait le monde;

[There is one more ugly, more wicked, more filthy!
Although he makes neither great gestures nor great cries,
He would willingly make of the earth a shambles
And, in a yawn, swallow the world;]

This demon of modernity is *ennui*, boredom, *"ce monstre délicat,"* [that delicate monster] which swallows everything – sin and remorse, confession and relapse, will and impotence, charm and repugnance – into the great yawn of indifference. Smoking the hookah pipe of forgetfulness, it embraces evil – though without the pomp or baldness of the great gesture, in a weak, self-indulgent, *delicate* way, as it were – and engulfs the world in destructive disillusion and defeat. This defeat is that of the modern subject, of the yearning for meaningfulness, self-realisation, self-fulfilment, generated by the Enlightenment utopia and fostered by the dreams of Romanticism.

As Elisabeth Goodstein notes, it is not simply that boredom crowns for Baudelaire the swarm of monsters and demons that disempower the modern subject; rather, it is itself the manifestation of its very failure, and thus a "synecdoche for the spiritual crisis" of modernity.[2] *"Au Lecteur"* can therefore be taken as a kind of manifesto of boredom, a banner which – implicitly – connects and intertwines the two terms: modernity and boredom. This connection must be made explicit, especially because boredom's nihilism tends to see itself as a timeless feature of the human soul and to efface its historicity.[3]

2.

As some of the more recent literature on boredom emphasises, the term and the concept have a history and present a whole genealogy of ancestors and forefathers, which can be only briefly sketched here. Reinhard Kuhn writes that the Greek had only one word that could occasionally be translated as boredom: άλυς (*àlus*). However, he notes that this term never occurs in the classical philosophy of the fourth century.[4] If Plato was concerned with μονοτονία (*monotonia, monotony*), this concept seems to characterize both divine bliss and hellish torment, but not a human condition.[5] In Latin, the

concept of *horror loci* can be associated to the genealogy of boredom, and
perhaps also that of *fastidium*,[6] but the term which was later taken as a
synonym of boredom is *taedium vitae*, to which Seneca devoted one of the
first philosophical investigations on boredom.[7] However, Kuhn concludes his
analysis of ennui in ancient literature arguing that, "if the ancient were aware
of ennui, they did not consider it a fit subject for literature. They carefully hid
it in the shadows."[8]

It is only with the inception of Christianity, Kuhn continues, that
boredom, or, better, *ennui*, under the name of *acedia*, took a central place as
intellectual and spiritual concern.[9] *Acedia* (*sloth* in English), is made up of
the Greek *κῆδος* (*kédos*), which means "care," "concern," "interest," and the
privative prefix *α-*. It thus denotes a lack of care or interest, a tiredness with
life, which the Christian Early Fathers in the desert beyond Alexandria
considered to be the worst sin and father (or mother) of all other sins.
Evagrius Ponticus (c. 345-399 A.D.), Lars Svendsen writes, considered
acedia to be demonic, the *daemon meridianus* ("*daemon qui etiam
meridianum vocatur*," the midday demon, or the demon of noontide[10]), which
attacks the monk in the stillness of the midday hour and empties the world of
any meaning. There are though fundamental differences between medieval
acedia and modern boredom: first and foremost, Svendsen notes, *acedia* was
a *moral concept* and not a *psychological state*, like modern boredom.[11] The
modern subject, Patricia Meyer Spacks glosses, *endures* or *suffers* boredom,
whereas the medieval monk *committed acedia* as a *sin*.[12] A misery of the
soul, a spiritual and moral apathy, it made the monk idle, alienated and
incapable of any spiritual work, and thus removed and turned him away from
the grace of God. However, it could be fought and avoided with effort, hard
work and prayers. Moreover, *acedia* was a marginal phenomenon, almost a
privilege, even a status symbol, reserved for monks and the upper echelons of
society, or the ones with the material basis required for it, whereas modern
boredom is certainly more "democratic," a mass phenomenon. There is even
a certain cultural prejudice – to which we will return later – that establishes a
connection between *acedia* and art, as if *acedia* created a privileged spiritual
condition for artistic creation. Kuhn for example writes: "Out of Sloth may
arise a beautiful and tempting chant. Dante uncovers a relationship between
art and ennui, which we will often encounter in later works. A certain
sensuality within monotony can give birth to a hauntingly lovely song whose
seductive melody can paralize the listener and prevent him from ever
reaching home."[13]

This connection was emphasised in High Middle Ages and especially in
the Renaissance, when *acedia* morphed into, or was superseded by,
melancholy.[14] The first point to underline is that the humanist naturalist
perspective transferred the emphasis from the soul to the body: whereas
acedia was a malady of the soul and had strong moral implications,

melancholy was believed to have physiological causes. Its etymology refers in fact to the Greek μέλαν-χολή (*mélan-kolé*), or black bile: *melancholy* was believed to be caused by an excess of black bile in the organism which provoked slowness, laziness, a certain sadness, and was related in astrology to Saturn, the planet of the slowest revolution. The "creative" side of *acedia* was also blown up in *melancholy*, which ambiguously combines illness and wisdom, passivity and creativity. It became in fact the malady of kings and philosophers and was attached as a label to the stereotype of the artist, the thinker, the "creator." The interest in the phenomenon gained huge proportions and endures to our times, as the enormous bibliography reveals – from Robert Burton's *Anatomy of Melancholy* (1621) to Julia Kristeva's *Soleil noir: Dépression et mélancolie* (1989). The "popularity," among intellectuals and academics, of a topic considered "noble" and worth of investigation, can also be judged as one of the reasons why, until quite recently, the more "democratic" and less dignified *boredom* was neglected and deemed unworthy of analysis.

Strictly related to *melancholy*, and constituting a sort of *trait d'union* with boredom, is the concept of *ennui*. The term entered the French language probably between the twelfth and thirteenth century and etymologically comes from the Latin *odium* and the late Latin expressions *inodiare*, "to hold in hatred," or *in odio esse*, "to be object of hate": it connotes thus a hatred of the world and of oneself, with a somewhat stronger tone than *acedia* and *melancholy* that brings it closer to modern boredom.[15] Today, albeit with many ambiguities, French still uses the term *ennui* for boredom, and so do Italian with the cognate *noia*, whereas the Spanish *enojo* (rage, anger) and even the English *annoy* retain a signification closer to the original connotation. (In Spanish boredom is expressed as *aburrimiento*, whose etymology – from the Latin *ab-horrere*, to hold in horror, to abhor – is close to *odium/ennui*.) *Ennui* came into English usage in the late seventeenth century to fill a void, the lack of a term to cover a concept for which *melancholy* was not always deemed appropriate. However, it entered English with a strongly dignified, almost metaphysical connotation: it became a category of the higher spirits and a literary topos, connotation that is conserved to a certain extent in contemporary usage and that inspired the first studies on it. Kuhn, in his analysis of *ennui* in Western literature, states that it "can and often does induce efforts to fill the void that it hollows out" and thus "can help us to explain the creative act" and "can be used as a critical tool for new and deeper interpretations of man's actions and of the expression that he gives to them through works of art."[16] As such, as Meyer Spacks notes, *ennui* is more closely related to *acedia* and *melancholy* than to modern boredom: "Ennui implies a judgement of the universe; boredom, a response to the immediate. Ennui belongs to those with a sense of sublime potential, those who feel themselves superior to the environment."[17]

It is curious and, Seán Desmond Healy writes, certainly ironic, that little after the English imported *ennui* into their language – perhaps regarding it as a particularly Gallic state of mind – Baudelaire imported the English *spleen* into French "to do justice to the exalted quality of his own ennui."[18] *Spleen* presents an evident connection to the etymology of *melancholy*, which came to be known as the "English Malady," and Baudelaire coloured it with the tones of his own romantic malaise: sickly sorrow, distaste for life, apathy and universal indifference.[19] We will return later to the importance of Romanticism for the development of the concept. To complete this short foray into etymology, let us briefly look at the German term for boredom, *Langeweile*: rather than refer to the cause of the mood (like *melancholy* or *acedia*), the German describes its effects on time. *Lange-weile*, which probably entered usage in the eighteenth century, literally means "a long whiling away of time": when we are bored time grows long and, Wolf Lepenies writes, "*Langeweile* appears to be eternal monotony, always the same, a gaping void."[20] Other terms became popular in the nineteenth century, like the more philosophical *Weltschmerz*, (which combines *Welt*, world, and *Schmerz*, pain), or *Schwermut* (which combines *schwer*, heavy, and *Mut*, mood, and is also an alternative translation for *melancholy*), but *Langeweile* affirmed itself as the most common translation for both the literary *ennui* and the simple, and less dignified, psychological state of *boredom*.

The English term in fact seems to be the most recent coin in the etymological family we are analysing: the verb *to bore* dates from the mid-eighteenth century; the noun *bore* as "a thing which bores" from the late eighteen century, as "a boring person" from the early nineteenth century; and the noun *boredom* would appear only in the second half of the nineteenth century. The etymology is not clear, although, Meyer Spacks writes, the *Oxford English Dictionary* "notes and dismisses efforts to connect it with the reiterative action of the bore as drill and with the French *bourre*, meaning padding."[21] Unlike its cousin *ennui*, *boredom* connotes a trivial emotion which trivialises the world, disempowers the individual and empties time, but is nonetheless quite difficult to categorise. The invention of a new term evidently was needed to represent and express a new form of malaise, which older or foreign terms were unable to cover. A new social, economical and political reality engendered a new psychological situation which needed a new terminology and a new representation. *Ennui, spleen* and even *melancholy* continued to be used, sometimes in concurrence with, or even as synonyms of, *boredom*; this created an ambiguity which confounds the analysis of boredom to our days, in the many attempts to clearly identify the different *nuances* and specific connotations of each term. This ambiguity can perhaps be cleared by reuniting, as Goodstein does, all these different gradations into a single *discourse*, which she calls the "modern discourse on boredom" and which, without claiming to erase the differences between the many terms, considers them as a whole in order to connote a phenomenon qualitatively different from all its ancestors and peculiar to modernity.[22]

Before trying to summarise the causes of this change and briefly describe its effects, a final note on etymology can be useful. The term *interesting*, in its current sense, appeared at the same time as *to bore*, in the late eighteenth century, and seems to be strictly related to it. Meyer Spacks explains that the original sense, now obsolete, centred on the idea of importance, whereas the modern definition designates "a set of responses by the observer: interest, curiosity, attention, emotion." The older meaning implied objectivity, the new one subjectivity and individualism, "centred on the uniqueness of every personal set of emotions." The personal response that lacks in the boring is what characterises the interesting, and thus "the interesting (in its modern version) and the boring imply one another. Without the concept of engagement, disengagement has no meaning. Interesting means not boring; the boring is the not interesting."[23]

3.

The consequence of the fact that boredom, as Goodstein notes, continues "to resonate with those older frameworks" – *horror loci, taedium vitae, acedia, melancholy, ennui, spleen* – is that the language of boredom remains ambiguous and this "constitutive ambiguity" gives rise to difficulties of interpretation.[24] Modern boredom undeniably resembles and echoes those older forms of malaise; however, "it can be identified with none of them." Each of the older forms of discontent is "embedded in a historically and culturally specific way of understanding and interpreting human experience," each one is a "construction" embedded in what she calls a "*rhetoric of reflection*," a language of self-understanding.[25] Attempts to identify modern boredom with *taedium vitae, acedia* or *melancholy* are simply anachronistic.

The "invention" of a new word is telling of the emergence of a new rhetoric of experience: "the experience of malaise cannot simply be abstracted from the language in which it is expressed."[26] This does not imply, Meyer Spacks glosses, that "boredom came into existence only when it was first named"; however, a new and different vocabulary was assigned to an emotion, and, she continues, if new feelings arguably never manifest themselves, "new concepts unequivocally do." The "invention" of the new concept of boredom in the eighteenth century allowed for the articulation of new ways of understanding the world.[27] To put it differently: the concept has not always been necessary, the new term was invented when and because it was needed, that is to say that, until the eighteenth century, "other categories of interpretation satisfied [people's] understanding of their own situations."[28]

Boredom was invented when and because a new experience demanded a new vocabulary and new forms of expression. Boredom, Meyer Spacks argues, "never constitutes an objective fact but is always a category of interpretation."[29]

What these and other authors want to emphasise is that boredom is not an inherent quality of the human condition, but rather it *has a history*, which began around the eighteenth century and embraced the whole Western world, and which presents an evolution from the eighteenth to the twenty-first century. It is evident then its strict and insoluble connection with *modernity*. It was modernisation that shattered the traditional forms of human experience and gave rise to new psychological and social forms which necessitated new forms of expression. Goodstein writes that boredom can thus be read as a "symptom" of modernity, and "appears as both cause and effect of this universal process – both as the disaffection with the old that drives the search for change and as the malaise produced by living under a permanent speed-up."[30] It is not, she specifies, that "boredom as such is the key to theorizing modernity, but rather that the problems of theorizing boredom are the problems of theorizing modern experience more generally.[31] Boredom is a modern phenomenon and, as such, is inherent to modernity, it is a determinant of the modern way of experiencing the world. In what follows we will attempt to briefly sketch causes and consequences that led boredom to occupy a central position in modernity. The picture will be necessarily rough, summary and simplified; moreover, all the causes listed below do not suffice as, nor claim to be, a total explanation. Our goal however is to make clear and emphasise the necessary connection between boredom and modernity.

A first cause for the invention of boredom can be identified in the Enlightenment revolution: the new, secular and materialist interpretation of human temporality displaced the faith in a divine order, coming redemption and transcendent meaningfulness, and substituted it with belief in human progress and earthly happiness. Max Weber famously called this process, which traverses and characterises modernisation, "disenchantment." This revolution meant also the fragmentation of the old traditional values, beliefs and forms of existence, based on a theological discourse. The Enlightenment created the new myth of rationality and universalised its scope, experiencing it – mythically – as the revelation of the ultimate meaningfulness of existence. However, the positive sceptical distance from the certainties of tradition and faith soon deteriorated into a nihilistic form of scepticism which showed the failure of this discourse to replace the old beliefs with a new meaningfulness. According to Goodstein, boredom is a new, disenchanted and secularised form of human discontent and thus "exemplifies the deterioration of Enlightenment into mythology."[32]

Simultaneously, the Industrial Revolution mechanised, fragmented, and ultimately emptied time. Technological industrialisation subjected everyday life to new temporal rhythms, altering thus the quality of human being in time. The temporality of modernity is the experience of an "empty, meaningless time" and boredom becomes an "index" of the decline of the traditional understanding of temporality.[33] As we have seen, the German word *Lange-weile* expresses the temporal context of boredom: as Lepenies writes, modernisation and mechanisation oriented subjective time to an objective parameter which he calls "*regular mechanical* time," based on precisely equal units and "embodied in the image of the clock." This sameness appears in boredom as eternal monotony, "always the same, a gaping void," which contradicts regular mechanical time. Modernity imprisons what Lepenies calls "*irregular natural time*" into the ratio of the frequency of events to mechanical time.[34] Boredom registers the costs of the Enlightenment vision of infinite rational progress and the inhuman demands of technologisation.[35] Under the push of speed and progress, the present becomes inexperianceable "in the face of historical acceleration into the unknown."[36] As Svendsen notes, "time, rather than being a horizon for opportunities, is something that has to be beguiled."[37] Moreover, urbanisation, mechanisation, modernisation, innovation subjected the modern self to a literal bombardment of new stimuli, disarranging the traditional parameters of experience. These stimuli become the only possible filling for empty meaningless time, a desire which is always renewed and never fulfilled.

The origins of the "interesting," the "thrilling," the "exciting," in their modern sense, are to be sought in this unfulfillable desire: the emptiness and meaninglessness of time is fought through the recourse to external stimulation. Hence a continuous call for novelty and innovation. The eighteenth and especially nineteenth century saw the proliferation of new forms of mass entertainment: boredom in fact arose at the same time of the new concept of "leisure" and is intimately connected with it. Division of labour and mechanisation in the development of the capitalist mode of production subjected human activity to sameness and repetition. Moreover, the high valuation of work in Industrial Revolution also involved a split between work and non-working time, and the invention and democratisation of leisure, a time to be filled with entertaining activities. The invention of the novel as literary genre can certainly be linked to this phenomenon and thus to boredom.[38]

Enlightenment rationalism called for a reaction in Romanticism, in which the desire for meaning was shifted to the "cultivation of the heart."[39] The Romantic aesthetic reaction identified in the subject the source of all meaning and value: from this moment in the development of the modern discourse on boredom dates in fact the idea of self-fulfilment and self-realisation, and the demand for life to be interesting. Svendsen insists that it is only with the advent of Romanticism that boredom "becomes [...] democratized and finds a broad form of expression."[40] He writes: "The conception of meaning that is particularly prevalent in the West from Romanticism onwards is that which conceives existential meaning as an individual meaning that has to be realized. It is this meaning that I refer to as a *personal meaning*, but I could also call it the *Romantic meaning*."[41] The discrepancies between the pursuit of this personal meaning and the opaque resistance of the world, between Romantic imagination and dull reality, exacerbated the discontent and transformed boredom into an all-engulfing phenomenon, which came to be known as the malaise of the nineteenth century, *la maladie du siècle*. In boredom the modern subject confronts the impossibility of realising the striving of the imagination, so that boredom as interpretation of human experience came to dominate psychological, sociological and metaphysical representations of the nineteenth century.

The Romantic emphasis on individual self-realisation points to a further cause for the invention of boredom: an increasing stress, in modernity, on subjectivity and individualism. As Meyer Spacks writes, "the rise of individualism [...] implies a concomitant increase in personal sense of entitlement": individual life is accorded more importance, and thus scrutiny on daily life intensifies, but constant evaluation evidences the lack of intensity, meaning and satisfaction in ordinary experience. "The inner life comes to be seen as consequential; therefore its inadequacies invite attention. The concept of boredom serves as an all-purpose register of inadequacy."[42] The increasing concentration on the self leads to a sense of victimisation; the crisis of experience and desire becomes a crisis of the self.[43] The crisis of the experience of the self and of the world is thus finally a crisis of *meaning*. All commentators agree that boredom involves a loss of meaning and can be metaphorically described, in Svendsen's words, as a "meaning withdrawal,"[44] or, in Kuhn's words, as "estrangement": "In the state of ennui the world is emptied of its significance. Everything is seen as if filtered through a screen; what is filtered out and lost is precisely the element that gives meaning to existence."[45] The whining of the collective meanings of tradition and the disillusion with the Romantic pretence of self-realisation led to what Goodstein calls the "democratization of scepticism in modernity."[46]

If the nineteenth century was obsessed by *ennui*, in the twentieth century boredom became the dominant theme of fictional evocations, partly, Meyer Spacks argues, "for reasons implicit in the common understanding of modernism, which posits an isolated subject existing in a secularized, fragmented world marked by lost or precarious traditions [...]. Boredom provides a convenient point of reference for the cultural psychic condition of those deprived alike of meaningful work and of pleasure in idleness. At once trivialized and magnified, boredom in its early twentieth-century representations alludes to the emptiness implicit in a life lacking powerful community or effective tradition."[47] In late-twentieth and early twenty-first century it has become an "all-purpose index of dissatisfaction," an "embracing rubric of discontent."[48]

4.

Being such an all-embracing and pervasive phenomenon, boredom presents a social significance which could not be left only to the lamentations of poets and the ruminations of philosophers, but called also for the analysis of physicians, psychoanalysts and social scientists. If philosophers began to focus on boredom at least with Pascal, and poets and writers of the late eighteenth and the whole of the nineteenth century made it one of their main themes, sociological, medical, and psychoanalytical accounts multiplied around the end of the nineteenth and the beginning of the twentieth century. Traditionally a much less popular topic of analysis than its cousin *melancholy*, boredom has attracted in recent years the interest of academia, resulting in a number of publications devoted to the phenomenon. The history of the scholarly discourse on boredom cannot be analysed here. Something must be pointed out though: scholarly analyses are not at all unanimous and concordant, in particular about the relation between boredom and modernity. This relationship is rather often ignored or deemed not essential. In what follows, we will attempt to give an overview of the most significative literature on boredom of the past forty years, grouping the texts according to the way boredom is understood, specifically in its relation to modernity. This classification, though, can only be superficial and approximate, and certainly fails to do justice to the complexities and sophistication of each work and analysis. However, it helps gaining a sense of the way the phenomenon is understood and represented.[49]

The medicalisation of boredom, especially in psychoanalysis, tends to reduce it to physiological categories: in very broad lines, boredom is explained as a *defence* from fears and desires which threaten the stability of the subject and thus lead to a *repression* that hinders the discharge of tension. In one of the first psychoanalytical analysis devoted entirely to boredom, Otto Fenichel argued that "boredom has a *physiological foundation*, namely that of the damming up of libido."[50] The problem with this explanation is that, as Healy writes, it fails to "explain the growth of the phenomenon in the last three hundred years.[51] In other words, the medicalisation of boredom lacks of any sense of history and fails to explain it as a social and historical phenomenon characteristic of modernity. It rather concentrates on social and personal *causes* and focuses on possible *cures*. Several recent examples can be mentioned. Mihaly Csikszentmihalyi analysed the concept within the frame of behaviour science in *Beyond Boredom and Anxiety: The Experience of Play in Work and Games* (1975), where he studied play and work as motivations against boredom and anxiety in order to improve the quality of life.[52] From a psychotherapeutical perspective come the analyses of Giovanni Carlo Zapparoli in *La paura e la noia* [*Fear and Boredom*, 1979][53]; René Digo's *De l'ennui à la mélancolie* [*From Boredom to Melancholy*, 1979][54]; the essays collected by Mark Stern in *Psychotherapy and the Bored Patient* (1988)[55]; Emilio Tiberi's *La spirale della noia* [*The Spiral of Boredom*, 1983] and *Misurazione della noia cronica* [*Measurement of Chronic Boredom*, 1990][56]; Carlo Maggini and Riccardo Dalle Luche in *Il paradiso e la noia* (*Paradise and Boredom*, 1991).[57] Adam Phillips' *On Kissing, Tickling, and Being Bored* (1993)[58] enjoyed popularity thanks to its opening language, style and analysis to a non-professional audience. Also on a level of popularisation, confining with pop-psychology, is Laurie Bekelman's *Boredom* (1995).[59] More recent examples of the psychological approach, inclusive of "recipes" on how to fight boredom, are Verena Kast's *Vom Interesse und dem Sinn der Langeweile* [*On Interest and the Sin of Boredom*, 2001][60] and Ulrike Zöllner's *Die Kunst der langen Weile* [*The Art of Boredom*, or *The Art of the Long While*, 2004].[61]

Sociological accounts tend instead to historicise the phenomenon and to comprehend it into materialist categories like *disenchantment* (Max Weber), *rationalisation*, *secularisation*. These sociological categories tend to claim the status of totalising explanation, but, again, they can only partially explain the invention of boredom. A list of recent sociological texts on boredom would include Orrin Klapp's *Overload and Boredom* (1986), an analysis of why and how the overload of information in contemporary society results in boredom[62]; Alfred Bellebaum's *Langeweile, Überdruss und Lebenssinn* [*Boredom, Weariness and the Meaning of Life*, 1990],[63] which, though briefly going into the history of the concept, focuses mainly on contemporary society; the witty account of Martin Doehlemann in *Langeweile?: Deutung eines verbreiteten Phänomens* [*Boredom?: Interpreation of a Widespread Phenomenon*, 1991][64]; and Anne Wallemacq in *L'ennui et l'agitation: Figures du temps* [*Boredom and Agitation: Figures of Time*, 1991].

Among the philosophical accounts, a constant trend adopts a theological approach, the roots of which can be found in Pascal's and Kierkegaard's treatment of boredom. This approach considers boredom as an evolution of *acedia* and thus a kind of "sin," which though can create a moment of self-analysis and can be redeemed. Bernard Forthomme combines historical analysis and theological frame in *De l'acédie monastique à l'anxio-dépression* [*From Monastic Acedia to Anxio-Depression*, 2000][65]; the same religious approach characterises Michael Raposa's *Boredom and the Religious Imagination* (1999),[66] and Richard Winter's *Still Bored in a Culture of Entertainment* (2002).[67] Other philosophical accounts tend, at least in the sixties and seventies, to neglect the historical development of the concept and to focus instead on the relation boredom-temporality, like in Vladimir Jankélévitch's *L'aventure, l'ennui, le sérieux* [*Adventure, Boredom, Seriousness*, 1963],[68] where boredom is read as part of his meditations on the relationships between psychological time (past and future) and what he calls "physical time," an unachievable present, instant suspended between two nothingness and which is characterised by boredom. Another contemporary, mainly a-historical approach is that of Antoine de La Garanderie in *La Valeur de l'ennui* [*The Value of Boredom*, 1968].[69]

When the history of the concept is recognised and traced, however, it is often taken as evidence of the permanence of boredom as a constant "quality" of the human condition: modern boredom is considered a variation of its ancestors *acedia, melancholy, ennui* and *spleen*, all expression of a metaphysical malady inherent to the fact of being human. This is obviously a gross generalisation, but variants of this approach characterise many analyses of boredom. An early example is Wolf Lepenies' *Melancholie und Gesellschaft* [*Melancholy and Society*, 1969][70]: Lepenies analyses melancholy in relation to society, and especially in relation to utopia or utopian desire. Boredom is a central feature in the book, but only as accompaniment or derivate of melancholy. The approach is historical (the development of modern society), but this is not the main point and melancholy is read as an a-historical feature of the human condition.

Often the author, trying to escape the rigid constrains of the psychological or sociological explanation, falls into the contradiction of treating boredom simultaneously as a socially and historically determined phenomenon, and as an indeterminate and malleable concept throughout the times. This is partially the case with Carlos Díaz's *Aburrimiento y sociedad* [*Boredom and Society*, 1970],[71] but especially with psychologist Michèle Huguet's two books on the topic, *L'ennui et ses discours* [*Ennui and its Discourses*, 1984][72] and *L'ennui ou la douleur du temps* [*Ennui or the Sufferance of Time*, 1987][73]; in particular in the second text, Huguet attempts to understand the "existentiality" of time as familiar and enigmatic sufferance emblematised by ennui, thus reducing even further the quasi-historical approach of the first book. Boredom is read with this ambiguity also in Benno Hübner's *Der de-projizierte Mensch: Meta-physik der Langeweile* [*The De-projected Man: Meta-physics of Boredom*, 1991][74] and Véronique Nahoum-Grappe's *L'ennui ordinaire: essai de phénoménologie sociale* [*Ordinary Ennui: Essay of Social Phenomenology*, 1995][75]: Nahoum-Grappe in particular focuses on a phenomenology of boredom in postmodern society, where boredom is read as an objective dimension, and thus as index of the moral status of a society deprived of ideologies and collective myths and stranded in the shallow waters of consumerism and media frenzy.

Where the question of boredom as "historical phenomenon or metaphysical malady?" is explicitly raised and analysed is in Roberto Garaventa's *La noia: esperienza del male metafisico o patologia dell'età del nichilismo?* [*Boredom: Experience of Metaphysical Evil or Pathology of the Age of Nihilism?*, 1997][76]: Garaventa asks the question whether boredom is an expression of a metaphysical – and thus a-historical, eternal – human discontent, or rather the epiphenomenon of the age of nihilism, characterised by the death of god and the hypertrophy of consciousness. He finally opts for the first option, analysing ancient, medieval and modern texts and bringing as evidence the a-temporality of human suffering and discontent, thus reuniting under the same label of "metaphysical evil" *acedia, melancholy, ennui, spleen* and modern/postmodern boredom. Garaventa is not alone in a historical approach which resolves into the ascertainment of the immutability of human discontent: Friedhelm Decher, in his *Besuch vom Mittagsdämon: Philosophie der Langeweile* [*The Visit of the Midday Demon: Philosophy of Boredom*, 2000],[77]: traces the history of boredom from Seneca to Russel to conclude that it is not a "quality" of modern society but rather an existential property of human life. The same approach is taken by historian Georges Minois in his ambitious *Histoire du mal de vivre: De la mélancolie à la dépression* [*History of the "Mal de Vivre": From Melancholy to Depression*, 2003][78]: Minois follows the history of the "*mal de vivre*" from antiquity to postmodernity, and finds a sort of continuity between *taedium vitae, acedia, tristesse, melancholy, ennui, spleen, nausea,* and *depression,* all expression of a metaphysical and immutable "*mal de vivre*," identified with the human condition *tout court.*

This approach is retained in a number of literary studies, which analyse boredom – or, better, *ennui* – as a literary *topos*. One of the first examples is Guy Sagnes' *L'Ennui dans la littérature française de Flaubert à Laforgue, 1848-1884* [*Ennui in French Literature from Flaubert to Laforgue*, 1969].[79] Other studies embrace the whole history of Western literature, like Madeleine Bouchez's *L'ennui, de Sénèque à Moravia* [*Ennui from Seneca to Moravia*,1973],[80] which reads the evolution of the literary representations of *ennui* as the manifestations, through history, of one immutable phenomenon. A text that stands out for research, erudition and influence over the subsequent literature is Reinhard Kuhn's *The Demon of Noontide: Ennui in Western Literature* (1976)[81]: Kuhn presents a literary overview of the concept of *ennui* from the ancient Greeks to the twentieth century, using the terms *acedia, melancholy, spleen,* and *boredom,* as surrogates, translations or subdivisions of the literary concept of *ennui*. Kuhn's major claim, though, is that only *ennui,* among the various manifestations of existential alienation and disaffection also classed as boredom, plays a significant role in the development of the human spirit.[82] This universalist and elitist argument is accompanied by a total disregard for the relation boredom-modernity.

Another study *à la* Kuhn is Frantz-Antoine Leconte's *La tradition de l'ennui splénétique en France de Christine De Pisan à Baudelaire* [*The Tradition of Splenetic Ennui in France from Christine De Pisan to Baudelaire*, 1995][83]: Leconte eruditely undertakes an exploration of metaphysical ennui in French philosophy and literature from the Middle Ages to late nineteenth century, identifying boredom with a metaphysical – that is, a-historical – malady of the human condition. The same does Norbert Jonard in *L'Ennui dans la littérature européenne. Des origines à l'aube du 20e siècle* [*Ennui in European Literature, from the Origins to the Dawn of the Twentieth Century*, 1998],[84] interpreting *ennui* as a recurrent phenomenon in human history that manifests itself in moments of crisis and ideological change.

However, a certain trend, which usually combines the philosophical, the literary and at times the sociological approach – though obviously giving predominance to one or the other – focuses on the peculiar relationship between boredom and modernity. We have embraced this thesis and have thus used mostly these works for this introduction. Ludwig Völker began an analysis of the history of the concept in *Langeweile: Untersuchungen zur Vorgeschichte eines Literarischen Motivs* [*Boredom: Analyses of the Pre-history of a Literary Motif*, 1975].[85] This book investigates the pre-history of the term and concept in mostly German and European literature and focuses on how the word originated and came into common use. One of the first serious philosophical analysis of the concept is Seán Desmond Healy's *Boredom, Self, and Culture* (1984)[86]: Healy analyses the history of modern philosophy and literature to show how modern boredom (which he calls "hyperboredom") is generated by the collapse of meaning in Western thought. The approach is historical and focused on the peculiarity of the modern phenomenon, though the analysis is limited to philosophy, and social, political and economical con-causes are overlooked. Christopher Schwartz contributes to the historicisation of the phenomenon with his analysis of boredom in German Romanticism, *Langeweile und Identität* [*Boredom and Identity*, 1993][87]: the study approaches boredom and its relation to the changes in identity perception – and construction of identity – in German Romanticism. The disintegration of the traditional social structures and the narcissistic emphasis on the "I" lead to the disintegration of psychic structures: boredom is thus read as a modern identity crisis. Schwartz's analysis focuses mostly on literature but also dwells on the philosophical implications of the argument.

An important contribution to the analysis of the concept is Patricia Meyer Spacks' *Boredom: The Literary History of a State of Mind* (1995).[88] The analysis here dwells mostly on British eighteenth-century women's literature from a feminist perspective, though at times reaches out to modernism and postmodernism. Meyer Spacks importantly puts the emphasis on the "invention" of the concept and its differences from its ancestors *acedia*, *melancholy, ennui and spleen.* The analysis highlights the necessary relation between the invention of the concept and the epochal changes in modernity which made the invention of a new interpretative category necessary. Gender-oriented investigations are also to be found in Rosa de Diego's and Lydia Vázquez's *Taedium feminae* (1998),[89] which analyses feminine boredom as literary topic and bored women as writers in European literature from the eighteenth to the twentieth century; and, partially, in Martina Kessel's *Langeweile* (2001), where the reading of the gender dynamics in the evolution of the concepts is part of the analysis of the development of its discursive meanings, mostly in Germany, between the end of the eighteenth century and WWI.[90] Gabriele Planz's *Langeweile* (1996)[91] focuses on the critical years of the nineteenth-century's *fin de siècle* and the early years of the twentieth century and connects boredom to the decadence characteristic of the cultural identity crisis of the time. Valentin Mandelkow, in *Der Prozess um den "ennui" in der französischen Literatur und Literaturkritik* [*The Trial on "ennui" in French Literature and Literary Critique*, 1999],[92] explores the ways *ennui* was represented in literary criticism. Also focusing on literary *ennui* within a historical approach, mostly in North American literature, is Camille La Bossière's *The Progress of Indolence* (1997).[93]

A study which enjoyed popular reception, and was thus translated into many languages, is *Kjedsomhetens filosofi* [*A Philosophy of Boredom*, 1999],[94] by Lars Svendsen. Svendsen emphasises the connection between modernity and boredom and identifies the latter as the whining of meaning typical of the last three centuries; he then gives a basically Heideggerian reading of some literary and pop-culture texts. The work combines philosophical analysis with accessibility for a larger, non-academic audience, without simplifying the philosophical complexities of the phenomenon. A more ambitious, but philosophically less acute, study is Ian Irvine's *The Angel of Luxury and Sadness* (2001)[95]: Irving traces the rise to cultural power over the last two centuries of what he calls "normative ennui" and identifies a "new alienation" (also "postmodern ennui") in modernity, linked to social and cultural trends such as hypercapitalism, spiritual disenchantment, globalization, mediatisation, and so on. Boredom as effect of a meaning withdrawal is identified also in Genrich Krasko's *This Unbearable Boredom of Being: A Crisis of Meaning in America* (2004)[96]: boredom is here described as the effect of a movement of historical decadence, from a sociological-moralistic perspective. The same motif of decadence and meaninglessness, this time in Europe, is to be found in the more philosophical Arnaud Codjo Zohou's *Les vies dans l'ennui: insinuations* [*Lives in Boredom: Insinuations*, 2002].[97]

The most thorough and complete philosophical investigation of boredom to date is however Elizabeth Goodstein's *Experience Without Qualities: Boredom and Modernity* (2005), which we have widely used for this introduction.[98] Analysing in depth the previous literature on the phenomenon, Goodstein's ambitious work combines the sociological, philosophical and literary perspectives[99] and attempts to embrace all the new social, cultural and political factors which provoked the epochal change of modernity and relates them to a change in the parameters of human experience that transformed it into what, with a Musilian wink, she calls an "experience without quality." She thus emphasises that the very social and cultural changes that characterise modernity are the same that led to the "democratisation" of boredom: modernity and boredom are shown to inextricably connected and inseparable.

5.

The aim of the present collection is to contribute to the body of literature on boredom with a number of essays which focus on particular texts, authors, or aspects of the phenomenon. The approach is multidisciplinary and the collection is indeed quite heterogeneous, putting together philosophers of cognition, literary critics, psychologists and political scientists; if the main approach is philosophical, the essays reflect also on literature, film, new media and psychology. There is, at a first sight, no connection between a behaviourist approach to the question of boredom as a kind of mind disorder, and the analysis of the notion of boredom in Heidegger, Benjamin or Beckett. However, what finally holds these essays together and makes for the cohesiveness of this collection is in fact the pervasiveness of the phenomenon in many aspects of our lives, cultures and societies, and in a number of scholarly discourses: "boredom" is a category used today in the most diverse disciplines, from philosophy to literature, from psychoanalysis to media studies, from sociology to behaviourist psychology, and is therefore quite difficult – and limiting – to define it univocally and unambiguously. A collection focusing only on one aspect of the phenomenon or on one disciplinary approach would perhaps have produced a more "harmonious" picture, but also a more partial and circumscribed one. Our intention, rather, is to put the emphasis on the centrality of boredom as a general interpretive category and to stress, not only its significance for the comprehension of contemporary society, but also its presence in various and heterogeneous scholarly discourses. The genealogical approach used in this first chapter seemed to us the appropriate way to introduce the topic; however, the aim of the collection is to add some pieces to a much larger mosaic, to a composite image that is necessarily diversified and multivocal, and requires therefore a multidisciplinary approach. The different perspectives from which the present essays depict the phenomenon thus integrate and complete each other to compose a fragment of the new "discourse on boredom" that underlines both its actuality and its pervasiveness.

This point constitutes also the rationale of the book: to our knowledge, there is no collection of essays approaching the phenomenon of boredom from a multidisciplinary perspective. This volume provides selective and punctual takes on the subject, which, on the one hand, restrict the focus and thus allow to go deeper than a more general analysis, but, on the other, taken together, give a more round picture of the pervasiveness of boredom and also of the academic interests in it. These interests, as we have emphasised, are extremely diversified and result in heterogeneous, and often discordant and contrasting, representations. However, the interest is nonetheless constantly growing and producing original and innovative interpretations, which testify for the importance of thinking about boredom today. On the one hand, we would like to make a strong case for connecting boredom as an interpretive category to the umbrella-concept of modernity, and embrace therefore that quite recent trend in the literature – and mostly in the literature in English – which pursues this argumentative line; in this sense, boredom becomes today a privileged analytical tool to read and understand the modern and postmodern crisis of experience. On the other hand, this conviction opens up multiple accesses to the understanding of the crisis, which connect psychic and spiritual life to historical and social changes, to literary and philosophical creation, to mass-culture strategies and media policies, to politics and governance in the age of the boring. The *fil rouge* that guides these readings, and the proposal that this volume, though in a partial and highly selective way, puts forward, is therefore to think seriously – and from a multiplicity of perspectives – about boredom today.

In keeping with the genealogical approach of this introduction, in the first essay of the volume Isis Leslie traces the historical manifestations of boredom in the West from Attic Greece to the modern age. The essay examines the decline in political participation through a wide historical lens, and attributes it to a transformation in Western culture that began under the Roman Empire. It identifies an externalization of responsibility for self-cultivation and management that began to occur in the period between the classical Greek era and the imperial culture of Rome and its mandate of obedience. The Imperial externalization of authority was magnified in the context of the emergence of pastoral power in the hierarchies of the early Church and later with the rise of industrial society. The essay traces thus a cultural transformation that, Leslie argues, leaves moderns, and, specifically, contemporary Americans, bored. Leslie defines boredom as a sense of emptiness that is accompanied by mad pursuit of and/or passive waiting for trivial, insubstantial stimulations and distractions that are ultimately unfulfilling. The essay is not intended to be an exhaustive treatment of the subject; rather, it aims to provide a theoretical framework within which to understand a large scale, historical and cultural transformation in the West that gives foundation to the modern phenomenon of boredom. The essay also underscores the political nature and significance of the modern phenomenon of boredom.

In a more specific and punctual take, William McDonald analyses Kierkegaard's demonic boredom. Kierkegaard diagnoses modern boredom as both a social phenomenon and as an individual malaise. He focuses on a distinctive second-order form of boredom, "demonic boredom," in which the reflective aesthete affects boredom in order to overcome it through irony. Modern boredom is construed as an aesthetic and psychological problem, which consists in a lack of resources to make life "interesting." Its antidotes are taken to be distraction, by means of entertainment, gossip, the press, and immersion in popular opinion (for first-order boredom), or the subjective injection of "the interesting," by means of irony and of "poeticizing" actuality (for demonic boredom). The construal of boredom as aesthetic and psychological, and the conception of its antidotes in terms of distraction and "the interesting," distinguish modern boredom from its predecessor concept, *acedia*. Kierkegaard argues that the modern conceptions of boredom and its antidotes are flawed, since they ignore the spiritual dimensions of *acedia*. Demonic boredom is a mood, rather than an emotion, and fails to seek its only real antidote in the passion of faith, which can be ignited through spiritual exercises, heartfelt concern for others, temporal reorientation of the self towards eternity, and through finding the "fullness of time" in the life of Christ.

Continuing on the philosophical line, Matthew Boss examines the phenomenological analysis of the mood of boredom due to Martin Heidegger. The essay shows why this analysis has as its primary concern, not the psychological or anthropological investigation of a mood as something "merely subjective," but the fundamental philosophical questions that are traditionally the province of metaphysics. Heidegger's analysis takes boredom not as a "subjective experience" whose possible causes might be a matter of interest to psychology but as a phenomenon with an essentially temporal character. For boredom is a mood in which time becomes suddenly conspicuous. Heidegger distinguishes three different forms of boredom which make time manifest in different ways. The mood's relevance to the questions of metaphysics – such as the traditional ontological problem of the categories – is in the kind of time revealed by "deep" boredom in distinction from the "clock-time" of everyday life. It is Heidegger's basic philosophical position that our understanding of being (and so, too, all metaphysical inquiry) always has an inner connection to time through its relation to human temporality. The essay shows how his investigation of boredom is an attempt to demonstrate this relationship between time and metaphysics, and to do so concretely – that is, by the application of the phenomenological method of philosophy.

James Phillips draws from this Heideggerian interpretation, and from a different reading made by Adorno, in order to reflect on Beckett's boredom. Beckett, he argues, is sometimes conspicuously tedious. The conspicuousness warns against interpreting the boredom of the audience or reader as a response to a shortcoming in the author's artistic ability. For Beckett, boredom is not simply something to be avoided. Beckett is not alone in twentieth-century art in questioning, even embracing that which the good taste of previous eras judged negatively. He can therefore be seen as belonging to a tradition in modern art that wishes more to provoke than to please the public. Philosophically, however, Beckett's new relationship to boredom can be profitably compared to Heidegger's account of boredom as revelatory. Boredom, as a kind of anti-sublime that presents the subject not with the "too much" of magnitude and power (as in Kant's "Analytic"), but with the "too little" of hackneyed meanings, is revelatory of the absence of wonder. For Heidegger, boredom is a revelation from which the subject is shut off. In this light, the boredom in Beckett's work can be seen not as a judgement on the world, but as the world's judgement on the subject. Adorno, who speaks of the spiritualization of Beckett's art, is similarly not insensitive to the insignificance of the boring because for him spirit is self-questioning and not the contradictory reification of a spirit distinct from the boring. Heidegger's and Adorno's philosophical analyses help to situate the ways in which Beckett's work involves a redefinition of art's revelation and its relationship to metaphysics.

A different philosophical interpretation – Walter Benjamin's reading of the phenomenon – informs the three following essays and opens up passages to the analysis of art, film and the new media. Carlo Salzani situates the meaning of boredom within Benjamin's project of "redemptive critique." In particular, the article relates the analysis of boredom, especially in convolute "D" of the *Arcades Project* ("Boredom, Eternal Return"), to Benjamin's critique of experience – a connection that Benjamin never explicitly made – and thus to a number of central concepts in his work, like *ennui*, *spleen* and *melancholy*. The argument revolves around the difference between *Erlebnis* and *Erfahrung*. *Erfahrung* is the term Benjamin used to designate pre-modern experience, characterised by connectedness and durability which implied a relation to memory and community, whereas *Erlebnis* designates modern experience, broken, immediate, limited and disconnected from memory and community. In the notes for the *Arcades Project* and the Baudelaire book, boredom can be related to *Erlebnis*: it is the "malady" that accompanies the disintegration of the traditional forms of experience, which Benjamin called the "atrophy of experience." Boredom is thus related to the notions of overstimulation, shock, repetition, the reification and mechanisation of time, the eternal return of the same, novelty, and so on, and is an inescapable feature of modern life. Melancholy and spleen are the results of this atrophy of experience, but, thanks to their connection to allegory, also play a fundamental role in Benjamin's revolutionary project: the melancholy gaze of the allegorist reduces the historical event to ruin, showing its *facies hippocratica*, its "death mask," thus exposing the naked truth of the demise of experience. This is the dialectical potential of allegory and thus of spleen. The final section attempts, as a way of conclusion, to outline the "constructive" potentiality that Benjamin found in boredom through a reading of Convolute "D."

Rachel Torbett focuses her analysis on a different – though strictly related – aspect of Benjamin's work: his "theory of cinema" and the relation between the cinematic experience and the demise of experience. Modernity, she writes, is never flat. Defined by negativity, destruction, and revolution, modernity's art forms no longer stand over and above time. No longer boring, art is a matter of moments, and with these moments is borne a new kind of spectator, one that Benjamin calls "distracted." In his famous essay, "The Work of Art in the Age of Mechanical Reproduction," Benjamin describes the cinema as having revolutionary potential in virtue of this distracting effect. Not only does the cinematic image mimic the structure of the modern world, its mimicry is destructive, tradition is dismantled, and the spectator is freed from the shackles of "auratic" time and experience. While this reading of Benjamin's essay is most probably the strongest, it is not necessarily conclusive: there is an ambivalence in Benjamin's philosophy of time and experience, one that is most often articulated in commentaries on the return of the "auratic" in Benjamin's philosophy. The essay describes the ambiguity of Benjamin's aura through the cinema of Werner Herzog. Like Baudelaire's poetry, Herzog's cinema both destroys the aura, and evokes its return. As auratic artworks, Herzog's films side with the time of boredom, but they do so within an art form arrested by distraction. Timeliness makes a return to the cinema, but cinema does not return to tradition; time returns to Herzog's cinema ambiguously, and ferociously, in the rubble of tradition. Cinematic experience is neither entirely distracting, nor is it strictly boring either; like Baudelaire again, something "lived through" is given the "weight of experience."

Marco van Leeuwen applies an interpretation of Benjamin's aura to an analysis of digitally-induced boredom in modern information societies. According to Benjamin, the acceleration of urban life around the end of the 19th century had profound consequences for the ways in which people were able to experience the world. In his analysis, deep and singularly meaningful experiences were forced out by droves of repeated, superficial ones, *Erlebnis* ("momentary experience") thus replacing *Erfahrung* ("momentous experience"). Today, the increased (and still increasing) availability of information is claimed by some to have a similar effect on the value of *social exchange*: the profound connection one can feel in a face-to-face encounter is more and more often replaced by convenient and quick, but phenomenologically shallow information-transfer via e-mail. This lack of an embodied connection in *mediated social interaction* has the added downside of allowing a "do-it-yourself normativity," an underdetermination of ethical constraints in on-line interaction. Van Leeuwen uses Benjamin, Dilthey and Nietzsche to support the idea that, in some ways, these modern forms of communication are not necessarily inferior to traditional embodied and direct forms of interaction. Instead, the essay claims that in mediated interaction there might even be room for certain *auratic* qualities, in a way close to Benjamin's use of the word.

Finally, Joseph Boden examines the trait of boredom proneness within a behaviourist approach. The experience of boredom has been linked to a wide range of impulsive and destructive behaviours, including criminal activity, violence, compulsive gambling and sexual activity, as well as other maladaptive behaviours. Research also suggests that individuals who engage in these maladaptive behaviours often share a certain personality trait in common: boredom proneness. The essay reviews the range of emotional states and behaviours that have been linked to boredom proneness, such as depression, anxiety, interpersonal sensitivity, obsessive-compulsive behaviour, somatization, anger and aggression, and procrastination. Further, the essay examines research that locates the trait of boredom proneness within established models of personality structure, and in particular links between boredom proneness and the major personality traits of neuroticism and extraversion. In addition, the links between boredom proneness and cognitive and neuropsychological phenomena are examined, including time perception, task absorption, and attention control. Finally, the essay examines possible causal pathways by which boredom proneness is linked to maladaptive behaviour, with a focus on poor behavioural choices that may stem from attempts at regulating the aversive state of boredom, cognitive distortions engendered by the effects of boredom, and impaired social relationships amongst those high in boredom proneness.

NOTES

[1] Charles Baudelaire, *Les Fleurs du mal*, Oeuvres Complètes, Claude Pichois ed., vol. 1 (Paris: Gallimard, 1975), pp.5-6; the translation is our own.
[2] Elisabeth S. Goodstein, *Experience without Qualities: Boredom and Modernity* (Stanford, CA: Stanford UP, 2005), p. 223ff.
[3] Ibid., p. 4.

[4] Reinhard Kuhn, *The Demon of Noontide: Ennui in Western Literature* (Princeton, NJ: Princeton University Press, 1976), p. 16.

[5] Ibid.

[6] Cf. Ibid., p. 25ff.

[7] Ibid., p. 31.

[8] Ibid., p. 35.

[9] Ibid., p. 376.

[10] Quoted in Ibid., p. 43.

[11] Lars Svendsen, *A Philosophy of Boredom*, trans. John Irons (London: Reaktion, 2005), pp. 49-52.

[12] Patricia Meyer Spacks, *Boredom: The Literary History of a State of Mind* (Chicago and London: The University of Chicago Press, 1995), p. 11.

[13] Kuhn, *The Demon of Noontide*, p. 58. On *acedia* cf. the whole chapter two of Kuhn's book (pp. 39-66), but especially Siegfried Wenzel, *The Sin of Sloth: Acedia in Medieval Thought and Literature* (Chapel Hill: The University of North Carolina Press, 1960).

[14] A number of Latin terms coexisted with, and covered the same semantic fields of, *acedia* and initially also *melancholy*, but had lesser posthumous fortune: *siccitas, tristitia, inertia, aegritudo, desidia, pigritia, otium, tepiditas, mollitia, somnolentia, dilatio, tarditas, negligentia, remissio, dissolution, penuria, incuria*. Cf. Kuhn, *The Demon of Noontide*, pp. 39-41.

[15] On the etymology of *ennui* cf. Goodstein, *Experience without Qualities*, pp. 109ff.

[16] Kuhn, *The Demon of Noontide*, p. 378.

[17] Meyer Spacks, *Boredom*, p. 12.

[18] Seán Desmond Healy, *Boredom, Self, and Culture* (London and Toronto: Associated UP, 1984), p. 29.

[19] Goodstein, *Experience without Qualities*, pp. 116ff.

[20] Wolf Lepenies, *Melancholy and Society*, trans. Jeremy Gaines and Doris Jones (Cambridge, MA & London: Harvard UP, 1992), p. 87.

[21] Cf. Meyer Spacks, *Boredom*, p. 13. Cf. also Goodstein, *Experience without Qualities*, pp. 107ff.

[22] Goodstein, *Experience without Qualities*, p. 3n.

[23] Meyer Spacks, *Boredom*, pp. 113-16. Cf. also Healy, *Boredom, Self, and Culture*, p. 22ff.

[24] Goodstein, *Experience without Qualities*, p. 102.

[25] Ibid., p. 4, emphasis in the original.

[26] Ibid.

[27] Meyer Spacks, *Boredom*, p. 28.

[28] Ibid., p. 10.

[29] Ibid., p. 70.

[30] Goodstein, *Experience without Qualities*, pp. 1-2.

[31] Ibid., p. 407.

[32] Ibid., pp. 3-4.

[33] Ibid., p. 3. Cf. also p. 18.

[34] Lepenies, *Melancholy and Society*, pp. 87-8.

[35] Goodstein, *Experience without Qualities*, p. 124.

[36] Ibid., pp. 122-3.

[37] Svendsen, *A Philosophy of Boredom*, p. 23.

[38] And so does the invention of tourism and many other mass entertainments. Cf. Meyer Spacks, *Boredom*, p. 60. On the democratisation of leisure cf. also Goodstein, *Experience without Qualities*, p. 168ff.

[39] Ibid., p. 127.

[40] Svendsen, *A Philosophy of Boredom*, p. 21.

[41] Ibid., p. 30.

[42] Meyer Spacks, *Boredom*, p. 23.

[43] Goodstein, *Experience without Qualities*, p. 157.

[44] Svendsen, *A Philosophy of Boredom*, p. 30.

[45] Kuhn, *The Demon of Noontide*, p. 12.

[46] Goodstein, *Experience without Qualities*, p. 112.

[47] Meyer Spacks, *Boredom*, p. 219.

[48] Ibid., pp. 249. 251.

[49] We will here very briefly mention a number of works dealing specifically with boredom as a cultural, social, artistic or philosophical phenomenon. Works which only partially deal with the phenomenon, or which focus on the treatment of boredom by a specific author, are not mentioned. For the same reason, we look only at studies in book form, and not at the myriad of articles and essays that have been published in journals or collections.

[50] Otto Fenichel, "On the Psychology of Boredom," *The Collected Papers of Otto Fenichel*, Hannah Fenichel and David Rapaport eds., vol. One (London: Routledge & Kegan Paul, 1954) p. 302; emphasis added.

[51] Healy, *Boredom, Self, and Culture*, p. 52.

[52] Mihaly Csikszentmihalyi, *Beyond Boredom and Anxiety: The Experience of Play in Work and Games* (San Francisco: Jossey-Bass, 1975).

[53] Giovanni Carlo Zapparoli, *La paura e la noia: Contributo alla psicoterapia analitica degli stati psicotici* (Milan: Il saggiatore, 1979).

[54] René Digo, *De l'ennui à la mélancolie: Esquisse d'une structure temporelle des états dépressifs* (Toulouse: Privat, 1979).

[55] E. Mark Stern, ed., *Psychotherapy and the Bored Patient* (New York and London: Haworth, 1988).

[56] Emilio Tiberi, *La spirale della noia: saggio sul rapporto tra il deterioramento di sistemi motivazionali normali e l'attivazione di un sistema motivazionale perverso* (Milan: Franco Angeli, 1983) and *Misurazione della noia cronica* (Milan: Giuffrè, 1990).

[57] Carlo Maggini and Riccardo Dalle Luche, *Il paradiso e la noia* (Turin: Bollati Boringhieri, 1991).

[58] Adam Phillips, *On Kissing, Tickling, and Being Bored: Psychoanalytic Essays on the Unexamined Life* (Cambridge, MA: Harvard UP, 1993). Cf. also Adam Phillips, *On Flirtation* (Cambridge, MA: Harvard UP, 1994).

[59] Laurie Beckelman, *Boredom* (Parsippany, N.J.: Crestwood House, 1995).

[60] Verena Kast, *Vom Interesse und dem Sinn der Langeweile* (Düsseldorf: Walter, 2001).

[61] Ulrike Zöllner, *Die Kunst der langen Weile: Über den sinnvollen Umgang mit der Zeit* (Stuttgart: Kreuz, 2004).

[62] Orrin E. Klapp, *Overload and Boredom: Essays on the Quality of Life in the Information Society* (New York: Greenwood Press, 1986).

[63] Alfred Bellebaum, *Langeweile, Überdruss und Lebenssinn: Eine geistesgeschichtliche und kultursoziologische Untersuchung* (Opladen: Westdeutscher Verlag, 1990).

[64] Martin Doehlemann, *Langeweile?: Deutung eines verbreiteten Phänomens* (Frankfurt am Main: Suhrkamp, 1991).

[65] Bernard Forthomme, *De l'acédie monastique à l'anxio-dépression: Histoire philosophique de la transformation d'un vice en pathologie* (Paris: Sanofi-Synthélabo, 2000).

[66] Michael L. Raposa, *Boredom and the Religious Imagination* (Charlottesville: UP of Virginia, 1999).

[67] Richard Winter, *Still Bored in a Culture of Entertainment: Rediscovering Passion and Wonder* (Downers Grove, ILL: InterVarsity Press, 2002).

[68] Vladimir Jankélévitch, *L'aventure, l'ennui, le sérieux* (Paris: Aubier, 1963).

[69] Antoine de La Garanderie, *La Valeur de l'ennui* (Paris: Editions du Cerf, 1968).

[70] Wolf Lepenies, *Melancholie und Gesellschaft* (Frankfurt am Main: Suhrkamp, 1969). English translation *Melancholy and Society*, trans. Jeremy Gaines and Doris Jones (Cambridge, MA & London: Harvard UP, 1992).

[71] Carlos Díaz, *Aburrimiento y sociedad* (Madrid: Zero, 1970).

[72] Michèle Huguet, *L'ennui et ses discours* (Paris: Presses universitaires de France, 1984).

[73] Michèle Huguet, *L'ennui ou la douleur du temps* (Paris: Masson, 1987).

[74] Benno Hübner, *Der de-projizierte Mensch: Meta-Physik der Langeweile* (Wien: Passagen Verlag, 1991).

[75] Véronique Nahoum-Grappe *L'ennui ordinaire: Essai de phénoménologie sociale* (Paris: Austral, 1995).

[76] Roberto Garaventa, *La noia: Esperienza del male metafisico o patologia dell'età del nichilismo?* (Rome: Bulzoni, 1997).

[77] Friedhelm Decher, *Besuch vom Mittagsdämon: Philosophie der Langeweile* (Lüneburg Klampen, 2000).

[78] Georges Minois, *Histoire du mal de vivre: De la mélancolie à la dépression* (Paris: Editions de La Martinière, 2003). "*Mal de vivre*" could be translated as something like "Listlessness of Life," but the sense of a cosmic, metaphysical suffering that the French expression carries would be lost in the English translation.

[79] Guy Sagnes, *L'Ennui dans la littérature française de Flaubert à Laforgue, 1848-1884* (Paris: A. Colin, 1969).

[80] Madeleine Bouchez, *L'ennui, de Sénèque à Moravia* (Paris: Bordas, 1973).

[81] Reinhard Kuhn, *The Demon of Noontide: Ennui in Western Literature* (Princeton, NJ: Princeton University Press, 1976).

[82] The more recent literature in English usually attacks Kuhn's work; Goodstein devotes interesting pages to the critique of his approach, method and arguments. Cf. Goodstein, *Experience without Qualities* pp. 45ff.

[83] Frantz-Antoine Leconte, *La Tradition de l'ennui splénétique en France de Christine de Pisan à Baudelaire* (New York: Peter Lang, 1995).

[84] Norbert Jonard, *L'ennui dans la litterature europeenne. Des origines a l'aube du XXe siecle* (Paris: Champion, 1998).

[85] Ludwig Völker, *Langeweile: Untersuchungen zur Vorgeschichte eines literarischen Motivs* (Munich: Wilhelm Fink, 1975).

[86] Seán Desmond Healy *Boredom, Self, and Culture* (London and Toronto: Associated UP, 1984).

[87] Christopher Schwarz, *Langeweile und Identiät: Eine Studie zur Entstehung und Krise des romantischen Selbsgefühls* (Heidelberg: Unviversitätsverlag C. Winter, 1993)

[88] Patricia Meyer Spacks, *Boredom: The Literary History of a State of Mind* (Chicago and London: The University of Chicago Press, 1995).

[89] Rosa de Diego and Lydia Vázquez, *Taedium Feminae* (Bilbao: Desclée de Brouwer, 1998).

[90] Martina Kessel, *Langeweile: Zum Umgang mit Zeit und Gefühlen in Deutschland vom Späten 18. bis zum frühen 20. Jahrhundert* (Göttingen: Wallstein, 2001).
[91] Gabriele Planz, *Langeweile: Ein Zeitgefühl in der deutschsprachigen Literatur der Jahrhundertwende* (Marburg: Tectum, 1996).
[92] Valentin Mandelkow, *Der Prozess um den "ennui" in der französischen Literatur und Literaturkritik* (Würzburg: Königshausen & Neumann, 1999).
[93] Camille R. la Bossière, *The Progress of Indolence: Readings in (Neo)Augustan Literary Culture* (Toronto: York Press, 1997).
[94] Lars Fr. H. Svendsen, *Kjedsomhetens Filosofi* (Oslo: Universitetsforlaget, 1999); English translation *A Philosophy of Boredom*, trans. John Irons (London: Reaktion, 2005).
[95] Ian Irvine, *The Angel of Luxury and Sadness (Vol. 1): The Emergence of the Normative Ennui Cycle* (North Charleston, SC: BookSurge, 2001).
[96] Genrich L. Krasko, *This Unbearable Boredom of Being: A Crisis of Meaning in America* (New York: iUniverse, 2004).
[97] Arnaud Codjo Zohou, *Les vies dans l'ennui: Insinuations* (Paris, Budapest, Turin: l'Harmattan, 2002).
[98] Elisabeth S. Goodstein, *Experience without Qualities: Boredom and Modernity* (Stanford, CA: Stanford UP, 2005).
[99] The second part of the study is divided into three major chapters respectively on Simmel (sociology), Heidegger (philosophy) and Musil (literature).

WORKS CITED

Beckelman, Laurie. *Boredom*. Parsippany, N.J.: Crestwood House, 1995.

Bellebaum, Alfred. *Langeweile, Überdruss und Lebenssinn: Eine geistesgeschichtliche und kultursoziologische Untersuchung*. Opladen: Westdeutscher Verlag, 1990.

Bouchez, Madeleine. *L'ennui, de Sénèque à Moravia*. Paris: Bordas, 1973.

Csikszentmihalyi, Mihaly. *Beyond Boredom and Anxiety: The Experience of Play in Work and Games*. San Francisco: Jossey-Bass, 1975.

Decher, Friedhelm. *Besuch vom Mittagsdämon: Philosophie der Langeweile*. Lüneburg Klampen, 2000.

Díaz, Carlos. *Aburrimiento y sociedad*. Madrid: Zero, 1970.

Diego, Rosa de and Lydia Vázquez. *Taedium Feminae*. Bilbao: Desclée de Brouwer, 1998.

Digo, René. *De l'ennui à la mélancolie: Esquisse d'une structure temporelle des états depressifs*. Toulouse: Privat, 1979.

Doehlemann, Martin. *Langeweile?: Deutung eines verbreiteten Phänomens*. Frankfurt am Main: Suhrkamp, 1991.

Fenichel, Otto. "On the Psychology of Boredom." *The Collected Papers of Otto Fenichel*. Hannah Fenichel and David Rapaport ed. Vol. One. London: Routledge & Kegan Paul, 1954. 292-302.

Forthomme, Bernard. *De l'acédie monastique à l'anxio-dépression: Histoire philosophique de la transformation d'un vice en pathologie*. Paris: Sanofi-Synthélabo, 2000.

Garaventa, Roberto. *La noia: Esperienza del male metafisico o patologia dell'età del nichilismo?* Rome: Bulzoni, 1997.

Goodstein, Elisabeth S. *Experience without Qualities: Boredom and Modernity*. Stanford, CA: Stanford UP, 2005.

Healy, Seán Desmond. *Boredom, Self, and Culture*. London and Toronto: Associated UP, 1984.

Hübner, Benno. *Der de-projizierte Mensch: Meta-Physik der Langeweile*. Wien: Passagen Verlag, 1991.

Huguet, Michèle. *L'ennui et ses discours*. Paris: Presses universitaires de France, 1984.

———. *L'ennui ou la douleur du temps*. Paris: Masson, 1987.

Irvine, Ian. *The Angel of Luxury and Sadness (Vol. 1): The Emergence of the Normative Ennui Cycle*. North Charleston, SC: BookSurge, 2001.

Jankélévitch, Vladimir. *L'aventure, l'ennui, le sérieux*. Paris: Aubier, 1963.

Jonard, Norbert. *L'ennui dans la litterature europeenne. Des origines a l'aube du XXe siecle*. Paris: Champion, 1998.

Kast, Verena. *Vom Interesse und dem Sinn der Langeweile*. Düsseldorf: Walter, 2001.

Kessel, Martina. *Langeweile: Zum Umgang mit Zeit und Gefühlen in Deutschland vom späten 18. bis zum frühen 20. Jahrhundert*. Göttingen: Wallstein, 2001.

Klapp, Orrin E. *Overload and Boredom: Essays on the Quality of Life in the Information Society*. New York: Greenwood Press, 1986.

Krasko, Genrich L. *This Unbearable Boredom of Being: A Crisis of Meaning in America*. New York: iUniverse, 2004.

Kuhn, Reinhard. *The Demon of Noontide: Ennui in Western Literature*. Princeton, NJ: Princeton University Press, 1976.

La Bossière, Camille R. *The Progress of Indolence: Readings in (Neo)Augustan Literary Culture*. Toronto: York Press, 1997.

La Garanderie, Antoine de. *La valeur de l'ennui*. Paris: Editions du Cerf, 1968.

Leconte, Frantz-Antoine. *La tradition de l'ennui splénétique en France de Christine de Pisan à Baudelaire*. New York: Peter Lang, 1995.

Lemoine, Patrick. *S'ennuyer, quel bonheur!* Paris: A. Colin, 2007.

Lepenies, Wolf. *Melancholie und Gesellschaft*. Frankfurt am Main: Suhrkamp, 1969.

———. *Melancholy and Society*. 1969. Trans. Jeremy Gaines and Doris Jones. Cambridge, MA & London: Harvard UP, 1992.

Maggini, Carlo and Riccardo Dalle Luche. *Il paradiso e la noia*. Turin: Bollati Boringhieri, 1991.

Malpique, Cruz. *Psicologia do tédio: Ensaio*. Porto: Livraria Ofir, 1963.

Mandelkow, Valentin. *Der Prozess um den "Ennui" in der französischen Literatur und Literaturkritik*. Würzburg: Königshausen & Neumann, 1999.

Meyer Spacks, Patricia. *Boredom: The Literary History of a State of Mind*. Chicago and London: The University of Chicago Press, 1995.

Minois, Georges. *Histoire du mal de vivre: De la mélancolie à la dépression*. Paris: Editions de La Martinière, 2003.

Nahoum-Grappe, Véronique. *L'ennui ordinaire: Essai de phénoménologie sociale*. Paris: Austral, 1995.

Phillips, Adam. *On Flirtation*. Cambridge, MA: Harvard UP, 1994.

———. *On Kissing, Tickling, and Being Bored: Psychoanalytic Essays on the Unexamined Life*. Cambridge, MA: Harvard UP, 1993.

Planz, Gabriele. *Langeweile: Ein Zeitgefühl in der deutschsprachigen Literatur der Jahrhundertwende*. Marburg: Tectum, 1996.

Rabinbach, Anson. *The Human Motor: Energy, Fatigue, and the Origins of Modernity*. New York: BasicBooks, 1990.

Raposa, Michael L. *Boredom and the Religious Imagination*. Charlottesville: UP of Virginia, 1999.

Sagnes, Guy. *L'ennui dans la littérature française de Flaubert à Laforgue, 1848-1884*. Paris: A. Colin, 1969.

Schwarz, Christopher. *Langeweile und Identiät: Eine Studie zur Entstehung und Krise des romantischen Selbsgefühls*. Heidelberg: Unviversitätsverlag C. Winter, 1993.

Stern, E. Mark, ed. *Psychotherapy and the Bored Patient*. New York and London: Haworth, 1988.

Svendsen, Lars. *A Philosophy of Boredom*. Trans. John Irons. London: Reaktion, 2005.

Svendsen, Lars Fr. H. *Kjedsomhetens Filosofi*. Oslo: Universitetsforlaget, 1999.

Tiberi, Emilio. *La spirale della noia: Saggio sul rapporto tra il deterioramento di sistemi motivazionali normali e l'attivazione di un sistema motivazionale perverso*. Milan: Franco Angeli, 1983.

——. *Misurazione della noia cronica*. Milan: Giuffrè, 1990.

Völker, Ludwig. *Langeweile: Untersuchungen zur Vorgeschichte eines literarischen Motivs*. Munich: Wilhelm Fink, 1975.

Wallemacq, Anne. *L'ennui et l'agitation: Figures du temps*. Bruxelles: De Boeck Université, 1991.

Wenzel, Siegfried. *The Sin of Sloth: Acedia in Medieval Thought and Literature*. Chapel Hill: The University of North Carolina Press, 1960.

Winter, Richard. *Still Bored in a Culture of Entertainment: Rediscovering Passion and Wonder*. Downers Grove, ILL: InterVarsity Press, 2002.

Zapparoli, Giovanni Carlo. *La paura e la noia: Contributo alla psicoterapia analitica degli stati psicotici*. Milan: Il saggiatore, 1979.

Zohou, Arnaud Codjo. *Les vies dans l'ennui: Insinuations*. Paris, Budapest, Turin: l'Harmattan, 2002.

Zöllner, Ulrike. *Die Kunst der langen Weile: Über den sinnvollen Umgang mit der Zeit*. Stuttgart: Kreuz, 2004.

CHAPTER 2

From Idleness to Boredom:
On the Historical Development of Modern Boredom

Isis I. Leslie

The essay traces the historical manifestations of boredom in the West from Attic Greece to the modern age, examining the decline in political participation through a wide historical lens, and attributing it to a transformation in Western culture that began under the Roman Empire. It identifies an externalization of responsibility for self-cultivation and management that began to occur in the period between the classical Greek era and the imperial culture of Rome and its mandate of obedience. The Imperial externalization of authority was magnified in the context of the emergence of pastoral power in the hierarchies of the early Church and later with the rise of industrial society. The essay traces thus a cultural transformation that leaves moderns, and, specifically, contemporary Americans, bored. Boredom is defined as a sense of emptiness that is accompanied by mad pursuit of and/or passive waiting for trivial, insubstantial stimulations and distractions that are ultimately unfulfilling. The essay also underscores the political nature and significance of the modern phenomenon of boredom.

1. Introduction

Michel de Montaigne and Ralph Waldo Emerson, inspired by him, speak of idleness as a moral failing.[1] They conceive and censure idleness on the basis of classical moral ideals of the virtues of political participation and the classical idea that self-cultivation is a universal obligation (albeit an obligation only of the exclusive social group that the Greek citizenry constitute) to contribute to the social, political, and moral improvement of the worlds to which one owes one's existence. In the classical ethos, one forms one's identity through this contribution.[2]

But from the Ancients to Montaigne to the time of the Emersonian nineteenth century, a conceptual transformation occurred regarding the notion of individual responsibility to participate in politics. This change resulted from a gradual redefinition of the public and private domains and, particularly relevant to the emergence of the modern phenomenon of boredom, involved a dissipation of the notion in the West that the private sphere is, in a primary capacity, a realm for self-cultivation for political life. This reconception of the private domain began in the Roman context of empire, and continued as an integral component of the popularization of Christianity. But industrialization ultimately produced the contemporary, once American, but now transnational culture where the idea of an obligation to cultivate the self for the social good, in the ancient sense, has largely been lost. I want to suggest that the loss of a political ethic of private self-cultivation is the basis of the nineteenth-century emergence of boredom as a widespread, culturally recognizable phenomenon in the Western world.

In this formulation, the phenomenon of boredom is the consequence of an externalization in Western culture of responsibility for self-management. Michel Foucault traces the externalization of responsibility for "self-care," also referred to as "the art of existence," from the early admonition, to "[s]pend your whole life learning how to live," that is consistently reiterated in the classical era by Stoics, Epicureans, Platonists and Aristotelians alike, to the Christian and finally modern era where no such injunction prevails.[3] The rise of the Christian church marks the beginning of an unprecedented relocation of responsibility for self-management from the individual person to "pastoral power," or the priesthood, institutions, and hierarchies of the church.[4] However, the externalization of responsibility for self-management that state-sanctioned Christianity effected in the West began to take shape in Rome prior to the popularization of Christianity in the context of empire, when the Roman state began to demand and enforce universal conformity to its laws, including for example tax laws and mandates to sacrifice to Roman divinities, for example.[5] The relocation of self-management from the contemplative life to mere compliance with the dictates of the imperial government of the state that such laws represent brought with it a revaluation of political and private standards of self-cultivation. Particularly, the value of obedience was elevated above that of self-cultivation.

And subsequently, Christianity's separation of the spiritual from the worldly, the "this-worldly" from the "other-worldly," made new forms of personal dislocation possible, specifically the emergence of a new concept and experience of boredom. By contrast, for the ancients knowledge unerringly directed the will, as Plato argues in *Protagoras* and Book IV of *The Republic*, where he concludes that *akrasia*, or acting against the good, can only be the result of ignorance.[6] The Stoics and Epicureans likewise maintained that wisdom produces virtue.[7] In the classical conception, the cure of any undesirable state of mind was simply better knowledge through reflection and/or dialogue. The Christian notion of original sin, however, introduces the possibility, in fact the inevitability, of a divided self, divided against itself in its sinful and divinity-seeking components. A discourse thus developed in the Christian world, more voluminous to be sure in the monasteries of the Eastern parts of the empire, about how best to manage the corrupt will.

St. Augustine's discussion in Book 8 of *Confessions* of his own divided will is exemplary here, as are the extended discussions of *acedia*, variously translated as boredom, sloth and idleness, of Evagrius and John Cassian in the fourth century A.D.[8] *Acedia* is one possible vice (of seven) of the corrupted will. Evagrius describes *acedia* as a "lack of care,"[9] where Cassian writes of a "listlessness" of the desert that is the "noonday demon [...] mentioned in the ninetieth Psalms," under the sway of which a monk becomes "exhausted," "anxious," "disengaged and blank," "confused" and longs for "far-off and distant monasteries," convinced that "[e]verything that lies at hand [...] is harsh."[10] And knowledge will not necessarily help here, as it would the ancients in any unpleasant mental state. But one must faithfully persevere nonetheless. Centuries later, St. Ignatius of Loyola would develop his Spiritual Exercises to combat the vices, including *acedia*, to better approach to the divine. However, Loyola asserts that there can be no certainty that *acedia* will be overcome, because there may be mysterious, divine purposes for one's discomfort.[11]

Nonetheless, despite the extraordinary number of peasants who joined the Eastern monasteries in the late days of the empire – Peter Brown, for instance, notes that in 418 A.D., the Patriarch of Alexandria alone could count six hundred monks he could call on for social service – the experience of Augustine, Loyola and the Eastern monks, was still exceptional.[12] The discourse of boredom in the West was primarily limited to the professional classes that monastic education produced. It was not until the context of industrialization that the language of boredom became common parlance and was understood in the modern, secular sense to be a common experience.

2. Modern Boredom

In English, the term "boredom" came into common usage during the industrializing nineteenth century.[13] But it has only been in the last few years that research on boredom has become popular in the discipline of psychology. This research however has significant weaknesses.[14] Some of its principle weaknesses include a lack of definitional consensus, a lack of rich theoretical constructs that account for the varied manifestations of boredom, its etiology and social context. For instance, studies in psychology on boredom have not systematically differentiated situational from dispositional boredom, or either from boredom that has lack of meaning as a key feature, which has been a central aspect of boredom as it is defined in the sociological literature, discussed below. And while studies using a number of psychometrics of boredom have found interesting correlations between boredom in a number of theorizations and other affective and attentional states, a meta-theory has not been developed that can account for these correlations.[15] For example, studies using the most recent and comprehensive psychometric of boredom, the Boredom Proneness Scale (BPS), have found correlations between boredom and depression (low energy and anhedonia) and between boredom and introspection. However, while the bored tend to be introspective, they also tend to lack insight into their internal states, or "lack self-awareness." Interestingly, boredom seems to be coextensive with a kind of "blind" introspection. But, notwithstanding this seemingly potentially rich insight, mainstream American psychology has failed to offer a robust analysis of the apparently blind introspection of the bored.

I would suggest that an exclusively psychological approach is inadequate to understand the phenomenon of boredom in the modern world. Instead, political, sociological, and historical theoretical approaches to its study are necessary as well. Moreover, social theorists have already offered a set of promising insights into the nature of boredom in modern Western social and political life.

Of modern boredom, George Simmel wrote that the accelerated pace of modern technological life, time pressures and over-stimulation make it nearly impossible to devote the time necessary to develop value systems adequate to leading fulfilling lives. In his reasoning, urban life fosters boredom because it precludes taking the time necessary to make the kinds of value distinctions that meaningful commitments rely on, and that make life satisfying. For Simmel and his followers, a certain numbness prevails in modern societies because of lack of time in which to make meaningful moral commitments. People compensate for their lack of moral value by seeking intense, but fleeting, experiences.[16]

In a less psychological analysis, Emile Durkheim argued in *The Division of Labor in Society* that modern society is characterized by a proliferation of functional specializations which has not been accompanied by a parallel elaboration of procedural "rules of conduct" that govern relations between the specialized component parts of the increasingly complex social system.[17] Durkheim refers to this lack of social rules as lawlessness, or anomie. Durkheim also discusses this anomie in a psychological rather than a functional register. In *Suicide*, he defines a *nomos* as a dominant meaning system, or symbolic order, in a given society by which individuals interpret, understand, structure and give meaning to their experiences and social relationships. Elaborating this idea, Peter Berger argues that the primary function of a *nomos* is to provide legitimation to the realities of suffering, evil, and death. Society – its ritual and political practices and its institutions provide significance to individual lives,

> despite the recurrent intrusions into individual and collective experience of the anomic, (or if one prefers, demonizing) phenomena of suffering, evil, and above all, death. [...] The anomic phenomena must not only be lived

through, they must also be explained – to wit, explained in terms of the *nomos* established in the society in question.[18]

In Durkheim's view, however, modern society, in its every increasing complexity, has begun to fail to fulfil its nomic psychological function. In my reading, the absence of meaning that defines anomie provides the ground for modern boredom. Martin Heidegger similarly held that the modern preoccupation with technological innovation and newness detracts not only from attentive engagement with the world and the people in it, but also from authentic thought, which has led to the new status of boredom (*Langeweile*) as "the basic mood" (*Stimmung*) of the age.[19] For Heidegger, in the modern age, a generalized mood of boredom characterizes modern culture. This non-subjective, but general mood, precedes thought, and preceding it, infuses modern thought. In a similar vein, Orrin Klapp argues that the advertising industry in the information age is best characterized by its public relations campaigns, or spin, that claims substantively identical consumer goods are unique.[20] Such goods include movies, books, sporting events and even political candidates. In Klapp's assessment, the result of a discursive world in which public discourse cannot be trusted is that, as we recognize the decreasing likelihood of reliable or meaningful messages in the noise that fills our airwaves and social worlds, we stop listening, and finally become bored. Klapp argues that, as a consequence of our boredom, "social placebos" proliferate, such as self-help books, lotteries, and Who Wants to Be a Millionaire?-style game shows that promise to cure the condition of mass, profound boredom that the information age fosters.

Philip Cushman too shares significant conclusions with Durkheim, Heidegger, Simmel, and Klapp, particularly regarding boredom as an indelible characteristic of modern life.[21] More specific than Klapp's examination of the "information age," Cushman situates his study within a broader examination of Western culture, but focuses specifically on conceptions of selfhood in the United States. Cushman argues that individualism as it emerged during the Enlightenment era flattened the socially embedded relations of community and tradition that once characterized social and political life in the West, replacing those once vibrant social networks with

> a landscape in which relatedness usually shows up either as the result of a social profit-loss calculus, as the product of the isolated parent-child dyad (and later in the life, the romantic dyad), or as part of the impression management and personnel manipulations of the workplace [...]. Isolation and dissatisfaction have become a taken-for granted way of life.[22]

For Cushman, members of the middle-classes, especially, consequently suffer from a prevalent subjective experience of emptiness which consumer culture exploits and exacerbates through its relentless promises of fulfilment it can never provide. Instead of fulfilment in consumption, the middle-classes struggle "with feelings of unreality, hopelessness, low self-esteem, and despair." Echoing Heidegger, for whom boredom and the condition of being bored (*sich langweilen*) are the "basic mood[s]" of our time, for Cushman, "the empty self has become the predominant configuration of our era" – where by "empty," Cushman means "a subjective experience of interior lack, absence, [and] emptiness."[23] If emptiness and lack are defining features of boredom, Cushman's empty self is bored. Like social theorists before him, Cushman's study of boredom returns to an analysis of the conditions of late industrial life. Cut off from traditional social networks, citizens in the modern world demonstrate a "desperate yearning to be [...] soothed, and made whole by filling up the emptiness." They seek relief by consuming ever larger quantities of the same goods whose marketing Klapp argues itself led to the collapse of the discursive universe, which is the principal cause of modern boredom in the first place.

I want to suggest that the vacuity of the inner worlds of modern subjects cannot be understood without examining the collapse of the discursive universe that began in the West with the Roman abandonment of earlier Greek understandings of identity formation as a public achievement. With the expansion of empire, even when classical forms of public identity persisted, they took on different social functions. Peter Brown notes, for instance, that training in Greek philosophy was eventually reduced entirely in Rome to a mere status marker for noble families across the empire.[24] The collapse of the classical Greek discursive universe was followed by the Imperial and Christian elevations of ideals of obedience and authority, and an attendant externalization of personal responsibility for self-management.

Jürgen Habermas traces a re-establishment of a public sphere in eighteenth-century Europe that is based in the autonomy from coercion that private property provided the bourgeois in a secular environment.[25] However, Habermas notes too that industrialization, the concentration of wealth it produced, and the expansion of welfare-statism required by industrialism ultimately eliminated what autonomy the bourgeois once had by restructuring the professions and the nature of work and leisure, marking a new collapse of public discourse in the modern West.

The rise of the mass media and the ascension of the image, where static, iconic modes of public communication replace discourse, bring us to the present day. In this connection, the contemporary cultural phenomenon of boredom should be understood to be the product of a culture that produces obedient citizens who externalize responsibility for self-management, and therefore no longer prioritize self-cultivation. The modern citizen-subject is also alienated from language, prioritizing instead the visual, iconic.

In his *Comments on the Society of the Spectacle*, Guy Debord notes that "the spectacle has spread itself to the point where it now permeates all reality."[26] The most highly developed spectacular society, which Debord located in US culture, is recognizable by the coextension of five principal qualities that include the "incessant technological renewal" that is so central to Heidegger's analysis of boredom, "integration of the state and economy, generalized secrecy; unanswerable lies [and] an eternal present."[27] An "eternal present" is accomplished through what Debord views as an eradication of historical knowledge in general, beginning with the most recent past, and replacement of history with rumours. Debord writes,

> Spectacular domination's first priority was to eradicate historical knowledge in general, beginning with just about all rational information and commentary on the most recent past. The evidence for this is so glaring it hardly needs further explanation.

> Media/police rumours acquire instantly – or at worst after three or four repetitions – the indisputable status of age old historical evidence.[28]

By dissolving history in media images, power becomes a matter of reputation. Thus, in the spectacular society:

> we can see the profound truth of the Sicilian Mafia's maxim, so well appreciated throughout Italy: "When you've got money and friends, you can laugh at the law." [...] the laws are asleep; because they were not made for the new production techniques, and because they are evaded in distribution by new types of agreement. (70-71)

These new types of agreement include the media production of public opinion by reporting opinion polls, for instance, Nielsen ratings, etc. As Debord writes further:

> What the public thinks, or prefers, is of no importance. This is what is hidden by the spectacle of all these opinion polls, elections, modernizing restructurings. No matter who the winners are, the faithful customers will get the worst of it, because that is exactly what has been produced for them. (70-71)

The society of the spectacle thus marks the expiration of deliberative, discursive democracy. Correspondingly, the notion of the legal state, for Debord, is a mere relic from the era of the founding the nation states. The illusion of the continuation of democracy is but another production of the society of the spectacle, a society in which reduction to the passive consumption of images leaves the public largely bored. In this context, particularly in the US, corporate power has prevailed while at the same time distracting the public from the workings of its own power through maintenance of a lack of transparency and promotion of commodity fetishism. We see a Roman obedience that can only be challenged if the economy begins to too obviously fail.

The following section of this essay more closely traces the transformation of ideals of selfhood from the ancients to the present that I argue suggest have in part led to this modern predicament.

3. Classical Selfhood

For the Ancients, political responsibility and self-cultivation were inseparable. Thus in an argument for social and moral obligation to subordinate merely personal to political concerns, Plato argues in the *Crito* for the indefensibility of civil disobedience. The famous passage, where the personified laws condemn Socrates for hypothetical disobedience, makes this point clear. To the suggestion that Socrates illegally abscond to avoid execution, the laws respond that he owes his life, and therefore obedience, to them:

> Come now, what charge do you bring against us and the State, that you are trying to destroy us [by your disobedience]? Did we not give you live in the first place? was it not through us that your father married your mother and begot you? [...] Then since you have been born and brought up and educated [by us], can you deny, in the first place, that you were our child and servant [...] Do you expect to have such license against your country and these laws that if we try to put you to the death in the belief that it is right to do so, you on your part will try your hardest to destroy your country and us its Laws in return? [...] you must do whatever your city and your country commands, or else persuade it in accordance with universal justice; but violence [through disobedience] is a sin even against your parents.[29]

Plato's assertion, here, of the obligation to accept punishment proceeds by standard Socratic elenchus.[30] Crito suggests Socrates abscond, Socrates, speaking as the laws, obtains agreement to a series of indirectly related premises. Socrates then argues, and his interlocutor agrees, that the stated premises are incompatible with the original suggestion, whereupon Socrates asserts that it has been proven that the initial idea was a bad one. Crito concludes: "Yes." The laws are right. Citizens owe their existence to law and are therefore obliged to obey. The Platonic devaluation of the merely personal is evident too throughout *The Republic*, for instance, in Plato's discussion of political leadership. Those best fit to rule, the philosopher-kings, have the most highly cultivated character of all citizens, but as such, they are never inclined to rule. They are not power-seekers, but rule only out of civic duty.[31]

The Platonic emphasis of political obligation over personal preference, however, does not come at the expense of self-cultivation. The philosopher-kings are distinctive precisely for their knowledge, knowledge is necessary to the fulfilment of political obligation and self-cultivation is necessary to attaining knowledge. On this point, Plato writes:

> When he has quieted both spirit and appetites, he arouses his third part in which wisdom resides and thus takes his rest; you know that it is then that he best grasps reality.[32]

Through self-discipline, subduing desires and foregoing immediate gratification, one cultivates the qualities needed to fulfil the duties of political participation. Here, the failure to cultivate one's inner world, or "idleness," is at once a betrayal of self and society.

Self-cultivation as a virtue and political obligation is also a central aspect of Aristotelian ethics. As *zoon politikon*, what distinguishes the essence of the human from the base animal is political life.[33] And since, for Aristotle, every citizen is obliged to participate in public life alternatively as ruler and ruled, all citizens are obliged to cultivate the virtues that leadership demands.[34] In this formulation, the retreat from public life that idleness entails becomes more than just vice; it is an abnegation of the human. As noted above, the stoic philosophers also took this position, although they advocated a cosmopolitan notion of identity rather than a national one. The prevalent ideal in the classical world was that political obligation was a natural and moral feature of human life.

4. Roman Selfhood

The classical Greek notion of the inseparability of self-cultivation and political participation persisted in Rome, but was challenged and ultimately transformed with the expansion of empire. Marcus Tullius Cicero (106-43 B.C.), like the Greeks, viewed philosophy as "the richest, the most bounteous, and the most exalted gift of the immortal gods to humanity."[35] For Cicero, too, self-cultivation through education sustains philosophy. It enables one to realize the highest virtue of humanity, a virtue Cicero identifies with politics. He writes:

> The existence of virtue depends entirely upon its use; and its noblest use is the government of the state.[36]

In keeping with classical Greek ideals of political obligation, Cicero characterizes political participation as a duty: "For in truth," he asserts,

> our country has not given us birth and education without expecting to receive some sustenance, as it were, from us in return; nor has it been merely to serve our convenience that she has granted to our leisure a sage refuge and for our moments of repose a calm retreat.[37]

Still and again, the solitude of self-cultivation and reflection is inseparable from political life. Cicero appropriates the Greek notion of humanity as definitively and fundamentally social, asserting that a "certain social spirit [...] has [been] implanted in the nature of man," and that man is not a "solitary or unsocial creature."[38] But already in Rome, such ideas did not go unchallenged.

The Epicurean school, for instance, against whom Cicero often directed his arguments, maintained that virtue requires that "[w]e [...] free ourselves from the prison of affairs and politics."[39] Presaging the Rousseauan concern for the distractions from virtue that public life could present, the Epicureans encouraged withdrawal from politics. The Epicurean advocacy of political withdrawal was increasingly well-accepted by the Roman elite and political participation correspondingly became less important to them.[40] This change represents a transformation under the Roman Empire of the Greek identification of self-cultivation and political obligation. This transformation can be accounted for, at least in part, by the structure of empire.

In contrast to the centripetal, participatory structure of Greek political life that produced the idea that identity is formed through public life, the centrifugal nature of empire demanded new modes of social organization and management of citizens. The Roman census represents the emergence of new theoretical constructs and methods to identify, account for, and control individuals in the context of empire that, importantly, linked individual identity to property rather than communicative political action. Modelled on the Egyptian census that was conducted every fourteen years, from approximately A.D. 33 to 257, the Roman census was primarily a means of collecting taxes, where taxes due were determined by property owned. A standard Roman census report, took the following form:

> To the census officers of Isieum Panga from Aurelius Anicetus son of Plutarchys, ex-magistrate in charge of the conveyance of oxen, councilor of the city of the Oxyrhynchites. In accordance with the orders issued by Aurelius Basileus the ex-prefect, I register for the house-by-house census [...] the quarter share of vacant lots belonging to me in the village of Usueynm Oabga [...] And I swear the oath customary among the Romans that I have not made a false declaration. Year two of Imperator Caesar Marcus Iulius Phillipus Pius Felix [...] I, Aurelius Anicetus son of Plutarchus, have submitted the return and sworn the oath.[41]

Conducting the census required the establishment of an imperial bureaucracy that demanded obedience. Carried out by regional magistrates throughout the empire, the entire population was required to participate or be liable to punishment. Citizenship thus took on a new meaning in the Empire that was modelled not on substantive discursive participation, as the Greeks understood politics and political identity, but on juridical obedience.

The census also laid the infrastructural groundwork for a new kind of concern with the private lives of Roman citizenry. The organization of the census made access to the private domains of the citizenry possible, which in turn enabled new social controls, such as that represented by the edict the emperor Trajan Decius, issued in A.D. 249, which required all citizens throughout the empire to honour the Roman gods through sacrifice and libation. Using the infrastructure that census taking established, the government could now not only keep records of the economic activities of individual citizens, but also, monitor (prescribe and proscribe) private behaviour. And, significantly, reports of compliance with the edict took a very similar structural form to the census reports that preceded the edict:

> To the commission in charge of the sacred victims and sacrifices of the city. From Aurelius [...], son of Theodore and Pantonymis, his mother of the same city. I have always and without interruption sacrificed and poured libations to the gods, and now in your presence in accordance with the decree I have poured a libation, and sacrificed, and partaken of the sacred victims, together with my own son Aurelius Dioscorus and my daughter Aurelia Lais. I request you to certify this form me below. Year one of Imperator Caesar Gaius Messius Quintus Traianus Decius Pius Felix Augustus.[42]

Rome thus saw an elevation of obedience as a political value and a subordination of the value of political speech as a means of public identity formation.[43]

The imperial superimposition of publicly sanctioned practices in individual homes marks a transformation of the classical Greek ideal of self-cultivation of virtue for and through political participation, contemplation and dialogue, for obedience now became a significant element of proper political behaviour. And the appearance of obedience as a public value set the stage for monotheistic religion, Christianity, and the Catholic Church, which in turn, brought further transformations to prevalent ideals of selfhood, the private domain and internal life.

5. Christian Selfhood

Consistent with the new imperial Roman precedent of obedience, the rise of Christianity replaced the contemplative model of virtue with an ideal of virtue defined in significant part by an obedience that Abraham demonstrates in his willingness to sacrifice his son, Isaac, in blind faith. The Catholic Church concretizes this Abramaic value of obedience by relocating authority and responsibility for self-management in pastoral power. In contrast to the classical ideal of contemplative self-discipline, Catholicism rendered many individuals in fact incapable of self-management. Laypersons could not directly access the revelation of the New Covenant. In this way, the Church simultaneously elevated the value of obedience and further separated identity formation from discursive practices that were foundational to identity formation.

The meaning of the political domain changed dramatically during this period. Identity was no longer primarily established through political speech and participation, but now through one's relation to the divine, which itself was mediated by the priesthood. The good Christian leaves what is Caesar's to Caesar, as Paul states, a point St. Augustine's distinction between divine and human cities also expresses. The good Christian looked to sacred texts through the interpretive lens of the pastoral class and toward the afterlife for self-definition.[44] In the Christian understanding of the highest good – that is, salvation – political action is irrelevant to the common person, beyond disinterested charity and contributions to the church. Not politics, but piety is the primary mode of identity formation. It is for this reason that Rousseau like Machiavelli warns against a Christian citizenry. Christianity does not produce engaged nationalists who are prepared to sacrifice themselves for their nations, but an otherworldly *populus* who will sacrifice itself only for Christ.

Thus, in contrast to the appearance in public that is the foundation of classical identity formation, Jesus of Matthew 6: 1-18 warns that open displays of piety, the most important aspect of Christian identity, are hypocritical because sincere and pious devotion cannot "appear unto men." Divinity "seethe in secret."[45] Arendt therefore concludes that Christianity is hostile to public identity formation. Matthew's admonition against public displays of piety is an admonition against pride as impiety. In this formulation, Christianity is hostile to the public domain in its classical conception, for its injunction against pride and also because the Christian values of equality and modesty are in tension with the classical agonistic ideal of politics where the public is an arena in which individuals can establish superiority and unique individuality.

Montaigne's writings capture the transition in Western culture from the classical conception of personal virtue as inseparable from political participation to the Christian ideal of personal piety. In a condemnation of idleness, Montaigne writes:

> Unless you keep [minds] busy with some definite subject that will bridle and control them, they throw themselves in every direction in disorder hither and yon in the vague field of imagination. Like a runaway horse [... the idle mind] gives itself [...] trouble [...] and gives birth to so many chimeras and fantastic monsters one after another without order or purpose.[46]

Observing his own mind, Montaigne asserts:

in order to contemplate [the] ineptitude and strangeness [of my own thoughts] at my pleasure, I have begun to put them in writing, hoping in time to make my mind ashamed of itself.

Idleness, in Montaigne's formulation, is a vice of solitude that emerges when one's fantasies are left unchecked. By contrast, solitude should involve a stoical self-discipline that "forge[s] the soul" for the public good.[47] Ashamed of his idle fancy, Montaigne hopes to control his imagination through self-examination. Solitude in his understanding should involve a diligent self-examination that prepares one for re-entry into the political realm. Thus Montaigne writes:

> [Solitude] seems to me to be more appropriate and reasonable for those who have given to the world their most active and flourishing years. [...] It is time to untie ourselves from society, *since we can contribute nothing to it*. And he who cannot lend, let him keep from borrowing. Our powers are failing us; let us withdraw them and concentrate them on ourselves.[48]

For Montaigne, as Francis Heck states:

> the rapport between solitude and society [is] a "natürlicher Rhythmus", a harmony, a natural rhythm.[49]

One's powers for public involvement will intermittently lapse, but

> [s]olitude produces the *vertu* of the humanist who begins with himself and then expands his sphere to all men, imparting to them the benefits he has derived from solitude. Individually men benefit and society profits from the individual.[50]

This condemnation of idleness and understanding of solitary retreat to self-examination as a necessary element of political participation recapitulates the classical ideal of self-cultivation as a public obligation. However, although enamoured with classical ideas, Montaigne was also a devout Roman Catholic.[51] In this connection, it is not surprising that Montaigne's condemnation of idleness echoes Luke's disdainful description in *Acts* 17:21-23 of the Athenians, where Luke writes:

> For all the Athenians and strangers which were there spent their time in nothing else, but either to tell, or to hear some new thing. Then Paul stood in the midst of Mars' hill, and said, Ye men of Athens, I perceive that in all things ye are too superstitious. For as I passed by, and beheld your devotions, I found an altar with this inscription, TO THE UNKNOWN GOD. Whom therefore ye ignorantly worship.

In Luke's construal, the Athenians lack the discipline that submission to divine revelation provides, and therefore, due to a lack of faith, are ignorant. Notice the inversion here of the relationship between knowledge and submission. The Greeks submitted only to knowledge. Christians submit to faith to receive it.

Moreover, as Montaigne identifies idleness with unbridled fantasy, Luke's Athenians are "too imaginative," lacking the direction and structure that submission to divine authority grants. Their minds are consequently preoccupied with ill-formed ideas of fabricated idols and "an unknown god." For Luke, distracted from the pursuit of reliable truth by idle talk and the search for "some new thing" – an unceasing quest for novelty – (an idea that we have seen return in discussions of modern boredom) the idle, undisciplined minds of the Athenians become "too superstitious," overrun by fantasy.

However, as *Proverbs* 15:19 states, idleness will produce its own punishment:

> The way of the sluggard is hemmed in as with thorns, but the path of the diligent is a highway. Idleness its own punishment and diligence is its own reward.

Idleness is sinful because it expresses disobedience to divine intent and, as such, causes suffering. But rather than political, the consequences of idleness in the Christian view, for Luke if less so for Montaigne, primarily involve individual well-being, in this life and the next.

Protestantism returned significant authority and responsibility for self-management from canonical legalism and pastoral authority to the individual and promoted literacy and the idea of universal equality in community. In doing , Protestantism inaugurated the rise of democracy in the Western world.[52] But the political domain largely remained external to ideals of selfhood. Moreover, paradoxically, with industrialization and, subsequently, secularization, the Protestant relocation of the site of truth to the individual ultimately led to a loss of individual authority and impoverishment of subjective interior worlds that set the stage for the modern phenomenon of boredom.

6. Protestant Selfhood

The Protestant rejection of papal authority and canonical law and the popularization of Christian sacred texts through translation into vernacular languages meant not only a loss of clear rules by which to interpret the texts but also a loss of clear rules by which to govern the self. Indeed, Martin Luther's rejection of the idea that good works led to salvation led to the more radical Antinomian idea that if good works will not guarantee salvation, neither would "bad" ones necessarily hinder it, which in turn created profound uncertainty about ideals of self-conduct. At the same time, as Colin Campbell argues in his deeply Weberian text, *The Romantic Ethic and the*

Spirit of Modern Consumerism, the Protestant elevation of the values of asceticism and industry contributed to the emergence of capitalism, the progressive rationalization of modern society, and the disenchantment of the modern world. But, another Protestant ethic also found expression.[53] The Protestant rejection of papal and clerical authority and attendant attribution to the individual of a capacity for direct communion with the divine increased the cultural emphasis and value placed on the internal lives of individuals. The Protestant relocation of the primary domain of religious experience to the individual, who no longer required priestly mediation and validation, ushered in an elevation of the faculty of imagination that has persisted in Western culture. This elevation of the faculty of imagination is particularly important in contemporary industrial society as regards the ascension of the image, the collapse of discourse, and the consequent emergence of boredom as a widespread cultural phenomenon.

Campbell observes that the unmooring of the Protestant imagination leaves it vulnerable and therefore the self vulnerable in the new context of urban, industrial society. In this analysis, the contemporary prevalence of advertising and consumer culture is due precisely to the aggressive appeal of the advertising industry to the unmoored Protestant imagination. Consumer culture is so successful because it appeals to the yearnings of an imagination no longer anchored by traditional forms of religion and community. The constant striving for greater things that once characterized aspiration toward the divine now finds expression in incessant consumption, producing subjects who are, in fact, profoundly dependent on unceasing pursuit and acquisition of new consumer goods. The modern phenomenon of boredom must be understood in the context of this new unanchored selfhood.

7. Industrialization

The impact of industrialization on the reconfiguration of selfhood and emergence of boredom as a mass phenomenon cannot be overemphasized. In the United States, industrialization saw millions of young men and women move alone to Northern industrial centres in response to the demands of the new economy. In a context of mass urban relocation, the moral functions traditional communities had once played in monitoring the individual could no longer be effective. The traditional doctrine of original sin according to which, without the guidance of community, the individual was doomed to fall victim to temptation, left many condemned to live lives of moral corruption. The doctrine of original sin in its traditional form therefore no longer served a functional role, and indeed became oppressive in a world that demanded self-promotion – a world in which production and profit became the highest values, even over human life.[54] Indeed, in the industrial context, the very public speech and action that defined valuable action and grounded classical identity are themselves denounced as idle. On this point, Arendt writes that industrial society

> will incline to denounce speech and action as idleness, idle busybody-ness and idle talk, and generally will judge public activities in terms of their usefulness to supposedly higher ends.[55]

In this connection, Christianity was inadequate to the moral demands of an industrial society. A new moral scheme was needed that allowed the individual to believe in his moral rectitude despite social isolation. In a world where production and profit had become the only recognizable realms of value, public speech was deemed superfluous, Christian modesty had become incompatible with economic and social goals; Protestantism had elevated the faculty of imagination and obedience, now to economic forces, which took precedence, as the image and the visual emerged as the primary means of public being.

As Philip Rieff notes, in modern political culture

> [t]he aesthetics of rhetoric is largely displaced by the aesthetics of spectacle. Seeing, as in an earlier period of authoritarianism, is believing.[56]

William Ellery Channing's "self-culture" movement and Ralph Waldo Emerson's idea of "self-reliance" both emerged in the context of the new cultural uncertainty about self-management of a secularized Protestant, industrializing world. Both offered systems of self-governance appropriate to the isolation that characterized this new world. Both rejected the idea of original sin, replacing it with an idea of the inherent goodness of humanity, thus removing the burdens in a market society of a moral demand for virtuous modesty and the fear of moral collapse that living outside traditional communities engendered.[57] But Emerson best expresses the passive receptivity and priority of vision that characterizes the modern American stance.

The priority Emerson gives to vision is evident, for example, in his famous declaration that in his highest moments of being he is a "transparent eyeball."[58] Likewise, his advocacy of withdrawal from the active worlds of commerce and politics reiterate the passive mode of being that is the foundation of modern boredom. Although, in a classical gesture, Emerson condemns idleness, he also encourages withdrawal from public life, advising each person to "go alone," away from society, "taking the way [away] from man not to man."[59] Emerson warns:

> [f]riend, client, child, sickness, fear, want, charity, all knock at thy closet door and say, – "Come out unto us." But keep thy state; come not into their confusion [for ... if] any man consider the present aspects of what is called by distinction society, he will see the need of these ethics.[60]

The ideal man for Emerson elevates himself above the chaos and corruptions of market society and politics to live in the rarefied domain of solitude. Emerson's solitary retreat from public life represents a secularized, Protestant conception of identity that sets the stage for the modern cultural phenomenon of mass boredom.

Although deeply influenced both by the Ancients and by Montaigne, Emerson reiterates the Protestant separation of self-cultivation from political life.[61] Despite his celebration of Platonism, Emerson's condemnation of idleness reflects a secular, Christian, rather than Greek influence that grows out of his grounding in the Unitarian tradition of American Protestantism. Emerson's declares in "Self-Reliance," for instance:

> Do your work, and I shall know you. Do your work, and you shall reinforce yourself.[62]

This proclamation expresses a Protestant ethic of diligence as the basis of publicly recognizable identity. But in contrast to Montaigne's idea of solitary self-cultivation as a periodic, but temporary, retreat from the public realm, Emerson advocates a retreat from the public domain that involves a radical rejection of society.

In contrast to the classical view, the Emersonian admonition against idleness is configured in a modern context, where the private domain and, with it, private life, have been truncated. The ancients understood "the private" to be not only the ground of family and intimacy, to meet and protect one from the demands of physical necessity, but also and more importantly, to provide a place for the cultivation of the virtues needed for political action through complex strategies of self-care that involved contemplation, physical activity and meditation. At times, Emerson presents an ideal private domain that is absolutely untouched by public life. He writes:

> What I must do is all that concerns me, not what the people think. [...] It is easy in the world to live after the world's opinion; it is easy in solitude to live after our own; but the great man is he who in the midst of the crowd keeps with perfect sweetness the independence of solitude.[63]

However, one does not communicate or participate in democracy in solitude and communicative discourse is the foundation of deliberative democracy. Although numerous critics, such as Frederick Douglass, Herman Melville, and Orestes Brownson were vocal about the ethical, moral and political limitations of Emersonian thought, Emersonianism superseded the traditional doctrine of original sin and its constitutive idea of the moral dependence of the individual on the community and went on to dominate the cultural terrain of nineteenth-century Northern and eventually after the Civil War, the entirety of America.

A product of the nineteenth century, Emerson wanted to escape the new, incessant demands for action which market society places on its members. It is for this reason that Emerson idealizes receptivity, as when he writes in *Experience* "All I know is reception,"[64] and celebrates an identification with vision as a receptive sense. However, as Rieff has written:

> [i]t is precisely the emptying of discursive values and their replacement by aesthetic [imagistic ones] that is one of the chief problems of politics in our time.[65]

In contrast to the active, productive and generative, discursive occupation that characterizes rhetorical engagement, the reception of images is significantly passive. And in this passive stance, a new imaginative, but "empty," malleable, and externally oriented mode of selfhood is born. As Rieff argues, this passive mode of selfhood is the bane of modern democracy, but it is also the foundation of modern boredom.

8. Conclusion

A recent *New Yorker* article notes that the amount and frequency that Americans read has declined precipitously, in fact, to a twenty year low.[66] If reading rates are rightly taken as one measure of public discursive engagement, it seems a primarily visual mass media has in fact largely replaced discursive engagement as the primary means of American cultural engagement. This is problematic for public culture not only because images are readily received in perfect solitude, but their dispersal is significantly one-sided, not discursive, even if Nielsen ratings do determine what is re-broadcast.

Arendt noted that a progressive transformation of classical political ideals has led not only to the decline of the public domain and devaluation of civic duty, but also altered the structure and formation of individual identity. She points out that where the ancients established identity through political speech and action, modern individuals are increasingly alienated and isolated from one another in activities of labour, production, and consumption, and find that identity formation is not anymore in any significant way a political accomplishment. As Alexis de Tocqueville and Karl Marx both feared, no longer driven by association, obligation, or attachment to the public domain, modern Western subjectivity has been increasingly confined to a private sphere which, rather than the foundation of public life it once was, is instead defined as an escape from the demands of the marketplace and the incessant pursuit of status. But for Arendt, as for Aristotle, the highest development of humanity depends on political participation. The self can only be "disclosed," not only to others, but also to the self, in public speech and action.[67] Indeed, for Arendt, our identities, but more, our very feeling for reality depends utterly upon the existence of a public realm into which things can appear out of the darkness of sheltered existence, even the twilight which illuminates our private and intimate lives is ultimately derived from the much harsher light of the public realm.[68]

In this conception, a robust selfhood, sense of the world and one's place in it, even one's demarcation of the private domain, depend on public self disclosure.

In this analysis, without public lives, we cannot have private ones. This idea is also consistent with intersubjective psychoanalytic accounts of the formation of selfhood.[69] Without a life in speech, in books, in language, of engagement with others, we cannot have internal monologues, or even imaginary dialogues. We become empty selves. We become bored. And in the visual context the mass media creates, instead of conversation, we pursue more images, whether through plastic surgery, or photographs of iconic but discursively empty celebrities. And as importantly, our participation in political life and democracy will suffer along with our identities, unless and until we can find a way to reengage with one another in public speech.

NOTES

[1] Cf. Michel de Montaigne, "On Idleness," *Essays*, trans. Donald M. Frame (Stanford, CA: Stanford University Press, 1973); Ralph Waldo Emerson, "Self-Reliance," *Selected Essays* (London: Penguin, 1984).

[2] Cf. for instance Plato's discussion of political responsibility in the *Republic*, Aristotle's discussion in the *Politics*, and the Stoic mandate to cosmopolitan citizenship.

[3] Michel Foucault, *The Care of the Self: The History of Sexuality, Volume Three* (New York: Vintage, 1988), pp. 43, 48. Cf. R.W. Sharples, *Stoics, Epicureans, and Sceptics: An Introduction to Hellenistic Philosophy*. (London and New York: Routledge, 1996).

[4] Michel Foucault, "The Subject and Power," *Power: Subjectivity and Truth*, ed. Paul Rabinow, trans Robert Hurley and others, v.3 of *The Essential Works of Michael Foucault, 1954-1984*, (New York: The New Press, 2000), p. 33.

[5] J.B. Rives, "The Decree of Decius and the Religion of Empire," *The Journal of Roman Studies*, Vol. 89. (1999), pp. 135-154.

[6] Plato, *Protagoras*, trans. Benjamin Jowett. (London: Dodo, 2007); *The Republic*, trans. Allan Bloom. (New York: Basic Books, 1991).

[7] Michael Trapp, *Philosophy in the Roman World* (Burlington, VT: Ashgate, 2007), pp. 98-109.

[8] Scott MacDonald, "Augustine and Platonism: The Rejection of Divided-Soul Accounts of Akrasia," in eds. Jorge Garcia and Jiyuan Yu, *Uses and Abuses of the Classics* (Burlington, VT: Ashgate, 2007), pp. 75-88; John Cassian, *The Institutes* (New York: Newman Press, 2000), pp. 217-238; Michael Raposa, *Boredom and the Religious Imagination* (Charlottesville: University Press of Virginia, 1999), pp. 11-40.

[9] Raposa, *Boredom and the Religious Imagination*, p. 21.

[10] Cassian, *The Institutes*, pp. 219-221.

[11] Raposa, *Boredom and the Religious Imagination*, pp. 27-29.

[12] Peter Brown, *The World of Late Antiquity* (New York: Harcourt and Brace, 1971), pp. 96-114.

[13] Sean Desmond Healy, *Boredom, Self, and Culture* (Cranbury, N.J.: Dickenson University Press, 1984), pp. 15, 60.

[14] Stephen J. Vodanovick, "Psychometric Measures of *Boredom*: A Review of the Literature," *Journal of Psychology: Interdisciplinary and Applied*, 137.6 (November 2003), pp. 569-95.

[15] The most popular psychometrics that measure boredom are: the Boredom Proneness Scale (BPS), the most comprehensive and detailed metric; the Job Boredom Scale (JBS), the Boredom Coping Scale (BC), the Boredom Susceptibility Scale (BS), the Leisure Boredom Scale (LBS), the Freetime Boredom Scale, and the Sexual Boredom Scale (SBS). Cf. Vodanovick, "Psychometric Measures of *Boredom*."

[16] Kevin Aho, "Simmel on Acceleration, Boredom and Extreme Aesthesia," *Journal for the Theory of Social Behaviour* 37.4 (December 2007), pp. 447-62.

[17] Martin Olsen, "Durkheim's Two Concepts of Anomie," *The Sociological Quarterly* 6.1. (Winter 1965), pp. 37-44.

[18] Peter Berger, *The Sacred Canopy: Elements of a Sociological Theory of Religion* (New York: Anchor Books, 1990), p. 53.

[19] Leslie Paul Thiele, "Postmodernity and the Routinization of Novelty: Heidegger on Boredom and Technology," *Polity* 29.4 (Summer 1997), pp. 489-517.

[20] Orrin E. Klapp, *Overload and Boredom: Essays on the Quality of Life in the Information Society* (Westport, CT: Greenwood Publishers, 1986).

[21] Philip Cushman, *Constructing the Self, Constructing America: A Cultural History of Psychotherapy* (Reading, MA: Addison-Wesley , 1995).

[22] Ibid., p. 245.

[23] Ibid.

[24] Peter Brown, *Power and Persuasion in Late Antiquity* (Madison: University of Wisconsin, 1992), pp. 35-70.

[25] Jürgen Habermas, "Further Reflections on the Public Sphere," in ed. C. Calhoun, *Habermas and the Public Sphere* (Cambridge, MA: MIT Press, 1992), pp. 421-462.

[26] Guy Debord, *Comments on the Society of the Spectacle*, trans. Malcolm Imril (London: Verso Classics, 1990), p. 9.

[27] Ibid., p. 11.

[28] Ibid., pp. 13-14, 55.

[29] "Socrates in Prison: *Crito*," 50a-51c, in Plato, *The Last Days of Socrates* (London: Penguin, 1969), pp. 90-91.

[30] Gregory Vlaston, "The Socratic Elenchus," *The Journal of Philosophy*, 79.11 (November 1982), pp. 711-14.

[31] Plato, *The Republic*, VII, 473.

[32] Ibid., IX, 572a-b.

[33] Aristotle, *The Politics,* trans. Ernest Barker. (Oxford: Oxford University Press, 1962), 1252b:9 – 1253a9.

[34] Aristotle, *The Politics*, 1288a: 12-15.

[35] *Laws*, I. 58. (Cambridge, MA: Harvard University Press, 1928), cited in "Marcus Tullius Cicero," *History of Political Philosophy*, ed. Leo Strauss and Joseph Cropsey (Chicago: University of Chicago, 1987), p. 156.

[36] Cited in ibid., p. 159.

[37] Ibid.

[38] Ibid.

³⁹ Ibid.

⁴⁰ Brown, *The World of Late Antiquity*, pp. 115-26.

⁴¹ Rives, "The Decree of Decius and the Religion of Empire," p. 149.

⁴² Ibid., p. 148.

⁴³ A consideration of the new avenues that Roman imperial infrastructure established for the circulation of authority sheds a corrective light on Michel Foucault's genealogy of "governmentality." Foucault argues that as opposed to the centralization of power that characterized political power in the early-modern, Machiavellian and classical Athenian states, in late-modernity, political power and methods of socialization are dispersed throughout society. In his analysis, urbanization, industrialization and the increasingly complex systems of social organization attendant to them transformed the nature of political authority by generating a requirement that citizens be taught to conduct themselves in conformity with the new demands of the economy. For Foucault, the complexity of modern society engendered a proliferation of discourses and institutions that produced increasingly complex methods of individual conduct formation, the central aim of which is to cultivate specific characteristics in citizens, dictating their internal lives, for the state interest. Political power, thus begins to function explicitly, Foucault writes, "at the level of the consciousness of each individual who makes up the population," thus marking "the birth of a new art, or at any rate a range of absolutely new tactics and strategies of control." Certainly, the Edict of Decius was concerned with citizens' behaviour, rather than their internal lives. It merely demanded that citizens *practice* Roman sacrifice, not believe in it. But the Edict of Decius nonetheless underscores the continuity between ancient and modern modes of public regulation of private life in contrast to the discontinuity that Foucauldian periodization stresses. Michel Foucault, "Governmentality," in *The Foucault Effect: Studies in Governmentality,* eds. Graham Burcell, Colin Gordon, and Peter Miller (Chicago: University of Chicago, 1991), pp. 87-104. Cf. Colin Gordon's Introduction to *The Foucault Effect*, p. 13; Gerhard Oestreich, *Neostoicism and the Early Modern State*, trans. D. McClintock (Cambridge: Cambridge University Press, 1983), p. 157, cited in Colin Gordon's Introduction to *The Foucault Effect*, p. 13.

⁴⁴ Cf. Foucault, "The Subject and Power."

⁴⁵ Hannah Arendt, *The Human Condition* (Chicago: University of Chicago Press, 1998), p. 75.

⁴⁶ Montaigne, "On Idleness," p. 20.

⁴⁷ Ibid., p. 21.

⁴⁸ Montaigne, "Of Solitude," *Essays*, p. 178, emphasis added.

⁴⁹ Francis S. Heck, "The Meaning of Solitude in Montaigne's 'Essays'," *The Bulletin of the Rocky Mountain Modern Language Association* 25.3 (December 1971), p. 96.

⁵⁰ Ibid., p 97.

⁵¹ Cf. Montaigne, "Of Prayer," in *Essays*, pp. 229-236.

⁵² Cf. Steve Bruce, "Did Protestantism Create Democracy?," *Democraticization* 11.4 (2007), pp. 3-20.

⁵³ Colin Campbell, *The Romantic Ethic and the Spirit of Modern Consumerism* (New York: Writersprintshop, 2005).

⁵⁴ Cf. Andrew Delbanco, *The Death of Satan: How Americans Lost a Sense of Evil* (New York: Noonday Press, 1996).

⁵⁵ Arendt, *The Human Condition*, p. 208.

⁵⁶ Philip Rieff, "Aesthetic Functions in Modern Politics," *World Politics* 5.4 (July 1953), p. 481.

[57] Mary Cayton, "The Making of An American Prophet: Emerson, His Audiences, and the Rise of the Culture Industry in Nineteenth-Century America," *The American Historical Review*, 9.3 (June 1987), pp. 597-620.

[58] Emerson writes: "In the woods, we return to reason and faith. There I feel that nothing can befall me in life, – no disgrace, no calamity, (leaving me my eyes,) which nature cannot repair. Standing on the bare ground, – my head bathed by the blithe air, and uplifted into infinite space, – all mean egotism vanishes. I become a transparent eye-ball; I am nothing; I see all; the currents of the Universal Being circulate through me; I am part or particle of God. The name of the nearest friend sounds then foreign and accidental: to be brothers, to be acquaintances, – master or servant, is then a trifle and a disturbance. I am the lover of uncontained and immortal beauty. In the wilderness, I find something more dear and connate than in streets or villages. In the tranquil landscape, and especially in the distant line of the horizon, man beholds somewhat as beautiful as his own nature," "Nature," in *Selected Essays*, p. 39.

[59] Emerson, "Self-Reliance," p. 192.

[60] Ibid.

[61] Of Montaigne, Emerson writes: "The personal regard which I entertain for Montaigne may be unduly great. […] A single odd volume of Cotton's translation of the Essays remained to me from my father's library, when a boy. It lay long neglected, until, after many years, when I was newly escaped from college, I read the book, and procured the remaining volumes. I remember the delight and wonder in which I lived with it. It seemed to me as if I had myself written the book, in some former life, so sincerely it spoke to my thought and experience," "Montaigne: the Skeptic," *Selected Essays*, p. 321.

[62] Emerson, "Self-Reliance," p. 181.

[63] Ibid.

[64] Emerson "Experience," in *Selected Essays*, p. 309.

[65] Rieff, "Aesthetic Functions in Modern Politics," p. 480.

[66] Caleb Crain, "Twilight of the Books," *The New Yorker*, December 24th, 2007.

[67] Arendt, *The Human Condition*, p. 180.

[68] Ibid., p. 51.

[69] Cf. Robert Stolorow, *Psychoanalytic Treatment: An Intersubjective Approach.* (Hillsdale, NJ: The Analytic Press, 1987).

WORKS CITED

Aho, Kevin. "Simmel on Acceleration, Boredom and Extreme Aesthesia." *Journal for the Theory of Social Behaviour* 37.4 (December 2007). 447-62.

Arendt, Hannah. *The Human Condition.* Chicago & London: The University of Chicago Press, 1998.

Aristotle, *Politics.* Trans. Ernest Barker. Oxford: Oxford University Press, 1962.

Berger, Peter. *The Sacred Canopy: Elements of a Sociological Theory of Religion.* New York: Anchor Books, 1990.

Brown, Peter. *The World of Late Antiquity*. New York: Harcourt and Brace, 1971.

———. *Power and Persuasion in Late Antiquity*. Madison: University of Wisconsin, 1992.

Bruce, Steve. "Did Protestantism Create Democracy?" *Democraticization* 11.4 (2007). 3-20.

Burcell, Graham, Colin Gordon, and Peter Miller (eds.). *The Foucault Effect: Studies in Governmentality*. Chicago: University of Chicago Press, 1991.

Campbell, Colin. *The Romantic Ethic and the Spirit of Modern Consumerism*. New York: Writersprintshop, 2005.

Cassian, John. *The Institutes*. New York: Newman Press, 2000.

Cayton, Mary. "The Making of An American Prophet: Emerson, His Audiences, and the Rise of the Culture Industry in Nineteenth-Century America." *The American Historical Review* 9.3 (June 1987). 597-620.

Crain, Caleb. "Twilight of the Books." *The New Yorker*, December 24, 2007.

Cushman, Philip. *Constructing the Self, Constructing America: A Cultural History of Psychotherapy*. Reading, MA: Addison-Wesley, 1995.

Debord, Guy. *Comments on the Society of the Spectacle*. Trans. Malcolm Imril. London: Verso, 1990.

Delbanco, Andrew. *The Death of Satan: How Americans Lost a Sense of Evil*. New York: Noonday Press, 1996.

Emerson, Ralph Waldo. *Essays: First and Second Series*. New York: Vintage/Library of America, 1990.

———. *Complete Works*, Volume I: Nature, Addresses & Lectures. Cambridge: Riverside Press, 1903-04.

Foucault, Michel. *The Care of the Self: The History of Sexuality*, Volume Three. New York: Vintage, 1988.

———. *Power: Subjectivity and Truth*. Vol. 3 of *The Essential Works of Michael Foucault, 1954-1984*. Ed. Paul Rabinow. Trans Robert Hurley and others. New York: The New Press, 2000.

Habermas, Jürgen. "Further Reflections on the Public Sphere." In *Habermas and the Public Sphere*. Ed. C. Calhoun. Cambridge, MA: MIT Press, 1992.

Healy, Sean Desmond. *Boredom, Self, and Culture*. Cranbury, NJ: Dickenson University Press, 1984.

Heck, Francis S. "The Meaning of Solitude in Montaigne's 'Essays'." *The Bulletin of the Rocky Mountain Modern Language Association* 25.3 (December 1971).

Klapp, Orrin E. *Overload and Boredom: Essays on the Quality of Life in the Information Society*. Westport, CT: Greenwood Publishers, 1986.

MacDonald, Scott. "Augustine and Platonism: The Rejection of Divided-Soul Accounts of Akrasia." in *Uses and Abuses of the Classics*. Eds. Jorge Garcia and Jiyuan Yu. Burlington, VT: Ashgate, 2007.

Montaigne, Michel de. *Essays*. Trans. Donald M. Frame. Stanford, CA: Stanford University Press, 1973.

Olsen, Martin. "Durkheim's Two Concepts of Anomie." *The Sociological Quarterly* 6.1. (Winter 1965). 37-44.

Plato. *Protagoras*. Trans. Benjamin Jowett. London: Dodo, 2007.

——. *The Republic*. Trans. Allan Bloom. New York: Basic Books,1991.

——. *The Apology, Phædo and Crito*. Trans. Benjamin Jowett. New York: P.F. Collier & Son, 1909–14.

Rives, J.B. "The Decree of Decius and the Religion of Empire." *The Journal of Roman Studies* 89 (1999). 135-154.

Rieff, Philip. "Aesthetic Functions in Modern Politics." *World Politics* 5.4 (July 1953). 478-502.

Sharples, R.W. *Stoics, Epicureans, and Sceptics: An Introduction to Hellenistic Philosophy*. London and New York: Routledge, 1996.

Raposa, Michael. *Boredom and the Religious Imagination*. Charlottesville: University Press of Virginia, 1999.

Stolorow, Robert. *Psychoanalytic Treatment: An Intersubjective Approach*. Hillsdale, NJ: The Analytic Press, 1987.

Strauss, Leo and Joseph Cropsey (eds.). *History of Political Philosophy*. Chicago: University of Chicago Press, 1987.

Thiele, Leslie Paul. "Postmodernity and the Routinization of Novelty: Heidegger on Boredom and Technology." *Polity* 29.4 (Summer 1997). 489-517.

Trapp, Michael. *Philosophy in the Roman World*. Burlington, VT: Ashgate, 2007.

Vlaston, Gregory. "The Socratic Elenchus." *The Journal of Philosophy* 79.11 (November 1982). 711-14.

Vodanovick, Stephen J. "Psychometric Measures of Boredom: A Review of the Literature." *Journal of Psychology: Interdisciplinary and Applied* 137.6 (November 2003). 569-95.

CHAPTER 3

Kierkegaard's Demonic Boredom

William McDonald

Kierkegaard diagnoses modern boredom as both a social phenomenon and as an individual malaise. He focuses on a distinctive second-order form of boredom, "demonic boredom," in which the reflective aesthete affects boredom in order to overcome it through irony. Modern boredom is construed as an aesthetic and psychological problem, which consists in a lack of resources to make life "interesting." Its antidotes are taken to be distraction or the subjective injection of "the interesting." Kierkegaard argues that the modern conceptions of boredom and its antidotes are flawed, since they ignore the spiritual dimensions of *acedia*. Demonic boredom is a mood, rather than an emotion, and fails to seek its only real antidote in the passion of faith, which can be ignited through spiritual exercises, heartfelt concern for others, temporal reorientation of the self towards eternity, and through finding the "fullness of time" in the life of Christ.

> The demonic is the vacuous, the boring ...
> the vacuous, the boring signify in turn the self-enclosed
>
> Vigilius Haufniensis[1]

1. Boredom in Modernity

Boredom is not a universal feature of human life, but arises as a distinctive malady of modernity in epidemic proportions. This epidemic is accompanied by a burgeoning of discourse about boredom in the nineteenth century, which both mirrors the epidemic and helps to propagate it. The modern concept of boredom is distinct from the medieval concept of *acedia* in belonging to a different discourse, which is produced by different institutions; it is conceived as a psychological malady, a social malaise, or an aesthetic challenge, rather than as a sin; its antidotes are conceived as either distraction by means of "busyness" or by craving "the interesting," or as transfiguration of experience through intensification of the imagination, rather than as spiritual discipline, patient devotion or penance; and it is conceived in purely human, secular terms, rather than in religious terms.

As a widespread phenomenon, whose causes are rooted in profound social and economic changes, modern boredom seems closer to the ancient

Roman *taedium vitae* than to *acedia*. Both ancient Romans and post-industrial Europeans suffered from changes to the temporal structure of experience, caused by urbanization and the artificial administration of time, which rendered the individual's sense of time empty and meaningless.[2] The reaction in both cases was to seek distraction from tedium – in *panis et circenses* [bread and circuses][3] – or, in the case of the "cultured" in modernity, to embrace boredom as an aesthetic fashion. It is this latter phenomenon that Kierkegaard diagnoses as *demonic boredom*.[4]

Demonic boredom is an affliction of the leisured classes, epitomized by "the English tourist"[5] and the travelling member of "a spleen club."[6] The latter description aligns boredom with the theory of humours, in which the spleen is the source of the black bile that causes melancholy.[7] Those of melancholic humour are predisposed to mournful reflection, in which they become isolated from other people and "from a true understanding of themselves."[8] It is this melancholic lack of self-understanding, because of emotional and spiritual isolation, which lies at the root of modern boredom, for Kierkegaard, and which therefore demands an emotional and spiritual remedy. Demonic boredom arises when the melancholic aesthete affects boredom in an ironic pose to distance himself from the mundane busyness of modern life. Unfortunately, his feelings of boredom paralyse him emotionally and his aesthetic irony isolates him spiritually, so that he becomes self-enclosed. But rather than despair at his paralysis and isolation, the bored aesthete revels in them defiantly and seeks to become psychologically autarchic, by manipulating memory and forgetfulness, and by the prudent rotation of moods.[9]

The demonic aesthete himself diagnoses boredom as a failure of imagination. This failure is a product of industrial, urban temporality, with its acceleration of the tempo of life into a mechanized busyness, and the levelling of values in mass society. The demonic aesthete asserts that all people are boring, but they may be divided into two classes: those who bore others and those who bore themselves. "Those who bore others are plebians, the crowd, the endless train of humanity in general; those who bore themselves are the chosen ones, the nobility."[10] The demonic aesthete, of course, assigns himself to the latter class, who in boring themselves tend to entertain others.[11]

However, for Kierkegaard, demonic boredom is more radical – and evil[12] – than immediate "plebeian" feelings of the emptiness of time. Demonic boredom is a reflective form of consciousness, which has a developed capacity for freedom and self-determination. However, it misuses this freedom in selfish pursuit of (cerebral) pleasure, and in doing so becomes prey to chance and fate. It also suffers from secular hubris in the wake of the anthropological turn, after which human beings think they can become selves, and understand themselves, with human resources alone.[13] Demonic boredom springs from a misrelation in the constitution of the self, between the elements of temporality and eternity, from a misrelation between self and other, and from a failure to acknowledge the role of God in the constitution of the self. The individual fails to give sufficient weight to the eternal in the task of becoming a self, so that everything becomes unbearably light. Without the *gravitas* of eternal salvation to give direction, temporal existence degenerates into a series of arbitrary "nows" which are only distinguished by relative intensity of mood. The aesthete caught up in the distractions and busyness of modernity only finds purpose in pursuit of "the interesting" and its converse, flight from boredom. The bored aesthete, however, fails to connect to other people through concerned emotions, and therefore sinks back into moody self-enclosure.

Kierkegaard categorizes boredom as a *mood* [*Stemning*][14] – along with the related moods of irony, melancholy, anxiety and despair. Moods lack determinate objects, and are pervasive (if ephemeral) states of mind which condition the individual's whole orientation to existence.[15] These moods are unhappy attunements to aimless subjectivity, and border on solipsism in isolating the individual from empathetic and emotional connection with other people. Moods are capricious, influenced by circumstance and chance, and detract from the individual's capacity for self-determination – even when that capacity has been developed through self-reflexive consciousness. The ultimate antidote to these moods is to choose to become a (religious) self; but the path to selfhood requires the integration of character through building up dispositions to positive emotions, such as patience, perseverance, hope, faith, love and joy.

While Kierkegaard regards boredom as a problem which the afflicted individual must address, he also sees it as a social problem generated by a culture of narcissistic reflection, superficial distraction, gossip, busyness, and secularity. The age lacks passion and seriousness, and the task of the individual to become a religious self in this context is thereby made more difficult. Because modernity prefabricates opinions, social dispositions, attitudes, values, and even the facsimile of faith (through the institutions of Christendom), modern individuals are increasingly unaware that they even have the achievement of selfhood as a task. Yet the best hope for awakening awareness of this task lies in the suffering inherent in the afflictive moods themselves.

Although boredom is a malaise specific to modernity, on Kierkegaard's view, it is continuous with the medieval sin of *acedia*, or spiritual sluggishness, which distracts from devotional practices such as prayer and meditation.[16] *Acedia*, according to Aquinas, is a refusal of the joy [*gaudium*] that comes from God's love.[17] For Kierkegaard, the refusal of God's love is a refusal to open oneself in faith to the absolute other; yet openness and faith are prerequisites for selfless love of any person – and are prerequisites for becoming a (spiritual) self. As a refusal of love, *acedia* is either a passive despair or a defiant despair – both forms of "the sickness unto death," which is a sin, whose only cure is the passion of faith.[18] Even the etymology of *"acedia"* provides a clue about the spiritual problems it poses. *"Akēdia"* is the ancient Greek for lack of *"kēdos* which means care, concern, trouble, sorrow, and affliction, and which comes from the verb *kēdomai*, meaning to be anxious over or about."[19] *Acedia*, then, is the sin of not caring for, troubling oneself with, or being bothered about others (or anything) – which is ultimately derived from one's lack of concern for God. It is precisely this lack of concern which envelops Kierkegaard's aesthete as a mood:

> I couldn't be bothered doing anything [*Jeg gider slet ikke*]. I couldn't be bothered riding – the motion is too powerful; I couldn't be bothered walking – it's too tiring; I couldn't be bothered lying down, for either I would have to stay down, and I couldn't be bothered doing that, or I would have to get up again, and I couldn't be bothered doing that either. *Summa Summarum*: I couldn't be bothered.[20]

Robert C. Roberts defines an emotion as a "serious concern-based construal." That is, an emotion is an evaluative cognition, based on an attitude of concern or care, which construes aspects of events in such a way that they appear true for the perceiver.[21] The problem with Kierkegaard's bored aesthete is that he is emotionally numb and therefore doesn't care about anything. He is transfixed by a mood, an attunement to his own emptiness, which prevents him from relating with concern to anything. He is not serious about anything, so that to every possibility he is equally indifferent – even to "all the glories of the world or all the torments of the world."[22] Although this resembles *acedia*, and ultimately has a spiritual solution in faith and love, in the modern context it is misconceived as primarily a psychological affliction, to be addressed by prudential self-management. Like *acedia*, aesthetic boredom results in neglect of spiritual practices such as prayer and meditation; but the practices alone are no antidote. What is required is inward transformation of the individual, by the choice of ethical-religious existence and by acknowledgement of sin (understood as that which dirempts human beings absolutely from the divine), together with faith in God's forgiveness of sin and Christ as the sign of atonement. The ultimate antidote to modern boredom is the passion [*Lidenskab*] of faith, which is a focussed suffering [*Lidelse*] capable of opening the self to God's gift of forgiveness and a new state of being. The propædeutic to faith is the cultivation of ethical and religious emotions and dispositions, in which the individual becomes inwardly concerned for the welfare of others.

Acedia is ambivalent, since it is both a sin and is capable of awakening "dreaming spirit" to self-consciousness through sin-consciousness. It can usher in "the dark night of the soul," as a necessary stage in the journey to mystical enlightenment.[23] The mystic needs to exercise patience and perseverance during this spiritual trial, and to maintain faith that God's light will ultimately disperse the darkness. Modern individuals have forgotten the potential of *acedia* for spiritual transformation, because they are in too much of a hurry to avoid suffering. They have lost faith in Providence, have lost their religious understanding of *acedia* as a sin, and have converted it into the all-too-human psychological problem of boredom. The modern reaction is, hubristically and impatiently, to stifle boredom with the purely secular means of frenetic activity.[24] However, none of the new distractions of the city, from the consumption of images in peepshows, vaudeville, the *camera obscura* and the wax museum, to the opinion-mongering gossip of the popular press or the busyness of modern life, can distract the aesthete from the despair that underlies boredom.[25]

The modern age, on Kierkegaard's view, has disconnected reflection from passion.[26] Reflection alone is unable to transform a self which is narcissistically preoccupied with self-image. Reflection can only multiply this false self-image in empty simulacra. For self-transformation to occur, the self must engage emotionally with others, in a manner which entails personal risk. In order to transfigure the despair of boredom, reflection must be grounded in passionate concern for others, be guided by earnest faith in the eternal, and be strengthened by perseverance in suffering – rather than escape habitually into sensuous pleasure.

The first step on the path to selfhood is to respond to the suffering of boredom by choosing to take responsibility for one's feelings. The aesthete initially does this by developing his "rotation method" of moods, through the cultivation of the arts of recollection and forgetfulness.[27] He uses irony as a means of distancing himself negatively from what he finds boring, and creates an aesthetic film over mundane actuality by "poeticizing" it in his imagination. He also takes "the interesting" [*det Interessante*] as the object of desire, rather than taking *interest* [*inter-esse*] in others for their own sakes. Interest is conceived by Kierkegaard as consciousness in its role as actively concerned intermediary in relating "ideality" to "actuality"[28] – and amounts to something like serious concern-based construal.

The path to selfhood and the avoidance of boredom have many byways and cul-de-sacs. Moods, emotions and cognitions are related dialectically to one another, with each movement becoming the basis for the next – and with each stage also being a potential point of stasis or misdirection. Demonic boredom is one such point, attained when the reflective aesthete has failed to use irony, melancholy, poetic imagination and despair to achieve escape velocity from self-absorption. Instead, the demonic individual mistakes self-enclosure for inwardness, and defiantly locks out heterogeneity – to become demonically bored.

In order to understand Kierkegaard's analysis of boredom, and its cure, we need to place it in the context of his views on: (i) the stages or spheres of existence, especially from the immediate aesthetic to the ethical-religious; (ii) the constitution of consciousness as that which inserts itself between "ideality" and "actuality" to map language and ideas seriously and truthfully onto what is the case, and to act freely to realize ideas in action; (iii) the role of emotions, as opposed to moods, in establishing continuity of character and connection with others; (iv) the ontology of the self and its constitution through relation to the other; (v) the relationship between time, eternity and human temporality; and (vi) contemporaneity and the fullness of time, in the moment of divine atonement when eternity intersects time. These views apply both to Kierkegaard's analysis of the task confronting individuals in their quest for existential purpose (which has the power to banish boredom), and to his analysis of the social malaise of his era, which produces individuals prone to boredom.

2. Existential Spheres

Kierkegaard is often represented as dividing human existence into three separate spheres: the aesthetic, the ethical, and the religious. The existential spheres or stages are also taken to be related in a simple progression, so that the reader moves from the lower to the higher by absorbing the lessons of Kierkegaard's authorship. This is a gross simplification, which fails to take into account the stages within the aesthetic, the *confinia* [border regions] of irony and humour which lie between existential spheres, moods like anxiety and despair which can pervade different spheres, and divisions within the religious, such as that between immanent and paradoxical religiosity.[29] Most of these distinctions are not meant to be absolute, and different elements of each individual's behaviour might be relegated to different "spheres" – but every version of Kierkegaard's theory of existential spheres identifies the same major break in the journey toward selfhood: that between the aesthetic and the ethical-religious. This is the divide marked by the famous "either/or" – *either* choose the ethical-religious *or* remain in some form of aestheticism.

The choice to commit oneself to the ethical-religious life is non-cognitively motivated.[30] Kierkegaard devotes much of his authorship to examining forms of non-cognitive motivation, which might prompt his readers to abandon the self-deception and despair of the "present age" in order to embrace ethical-religious life. Only if one chooses the ethical-religious life, with inward passion, is there any chance of becoming a self. Boredom – like melancholy, irony, and anxiety – stands as both an obstacle and a potential aid to motivating this choice.

Boredom has various forms, from that epitomized by the English tourist, and ironic member of a spleen club, through the aesthete who bores himself while amusing others, to the guilt-obsessed Quidam, who is "a demoniac character in the direction of the religious."[31] Each form of boredom is characterized by meaningless repetition, which empties time of eternal significance, and which fails to enrich each moment spiritually with selfless concern for others.

The journey to selfhood, both in Kierkegaard's account and in the Hegelian account he parodies, begins with immediacy. Immediacy is sometimes contrasted with reflection, either in the form of innocence or in the form of immersion in sensate experience or erotic desire. But there are also forms of reflective immediacy, in which a person's self-relation is unmediated by concern for others, and even a "higher immediacy" conferred by God's grace. The immediacies of innocence and desire preclude boredom, since they lack reflective awareness of the meaninglessness of their own activities. Higher immediacy also precludes boredom, since grace has imbued every moment with "the fullness of time." The domain of boredom, then, is reflective immediacy. In order to understand this category, we need to examine its contrasts with innocent and sensate immediacy and with higher immediacy. We also need to examine Kierkegaard's analysis of the role of language in reflective immediacy.

The life filled by desire, sensate experience and corporeal drives is illustrated in "The Immediate Erotic Stages or The Musical-Erotic."[32] Characters from Mozart's operas are presented as exemplars of these stages, which culminate in the figure of Don Giovanni, who epitomizes sexual desire as a force of nature. Don Giovanni is incapable of changing his behaviour by means of self-reflection, since he is totally immersed in desire.[33] He is quintessentially musical, and as such, is swept along in the tempo imposed by the musical key. But in this immediate immersion in sensate experience, Don Giovanni is immune to boredom, despite his meaningless repetition of seduction (1003 in Spain alone).[34] There is no room in his experience for emptiness, since his whole nature is replete with sensuous desire.

Mozart's Don Giovanni, as an incarnation of the immediacy of music, expresses the idea of the sensuous more perfectly than any literary representation, including those of Byron, Molière, and Heiberg.[35] Language, by its very nature, is "mediacy."[36] Consciousness consists in the opposition between the "ideality" of language, and the "actuality" which language purports to represent. Consciousness is also that which relates "ideality" and "actuality" to one another.[37] In a speech act, the speaker substitutes language for actuality, and thereby creates a space for the reflexive self-awareness of *how* one relates sign and signified. Into this space crawl the possibilities of contradiction, doubt, and boredom. Contradiction and doubt arise when one becomes aware that one has failed, or might have failed, to map ideality accurately onto actuality.[38] Boredom arises when consciousness has no serious concern for mapping representations truthfully onto actuality.

Boredom, then, presupposes reflection. It is a mood that infects the space of consciousness between the ideal and the actual.

The epitome of boredom is the English tourist, that "heavy, inert woodchuck whose total resource of language consists of a single monosyllable, an interjection with which he indicates his highest admiration and his deepest indifference."[39] The English tourist fails to use language to differentiate his concern, because he lacks all concern. His language is almost musical in its paucity of reflection, but is also unmusical in its lack of modulation and passionate immediacy. His interjection falsifies by superimposing a uniform expression on the manifold of actuality, and he fails to relate actuality and ideality actively in consciousness. Language is reduced to a bare grunt, and consciousness approaches its limit of passive indifference. The English tourist has so little concern or capacity for differentiating how he maps ideality onto actuality, that the lack of concern itself signifies an empty consciousness.

But boredom can also infect more reflective consciousness. In literary representations of Don Juan, Faust, and Johannes the seducer,[40] we find illustrations of the modern, reflective seducer. The reflective seducer, unlike the English tourist, uses language actively and modulates its use in carefully calculated differentiation of its likely effects. He uses the potential in language and consciousness for contradiction and doubt, to deceive and manipulate his victims, who in the stories considered by Kierkegaard's aesthete, are initially immersed in innocent immediacy.[41] The primary aim of the reflective seducer in deceiving is to generate "interesting" effects in his victims, including the effect of corrupting their innocent immediacy by making them reflective. The victims, however, ultimately become reflective by means of their suffering and thereby begin the journey to selfhood, while the seducers remain immured in their own selfishness. The dialectic of seducer and victim parallels Hegel's dialectic of master and slave, in which the master remains locked in self-serving desire, while the slave gains the capacity for objective reflection on himself by means of the work he carries out for the master.[42]

On one level, the reflective seducer's pursuit of the interesting by means of deceit and manipulation succeeds in dispelling boredom. On another level, he is stuck in an ultimately meaningless repetition of serial deceit, in which he continually fails to relate to the victim as a person worthy of moral respect and genuine love. His machinations do not map ideality onto actuality, but manipulate actuality to fit his preconceived ideas. The seducer regards the victim as merely an instrument to titillate his own mood – as Johannes does with Cordelia.[43]

The reflective aesthete is immersed in "immediacy" in another sense, since he doesn't mediate his personal freedom with reflection. Rather than choose a form of life which delivers him from emotional vicissitude, he relies on chance, fate and contingency to deliver him from boredom. He tries to establish an autarchy of moods, through the control of recollection and forgetfulness, in order to generate "the interesting" and divert himself from boredom,[44] but this only leads to demonic self-enclosure and despair. The attempt to manipulate his moods to avoid boredom, by controlling what he recollects and forgets, relies on confounding "the interesting" [*det Interessante*] with "interest" [*inter-esse*]. The word "interest" is derived from the Latin words for "to be" [*esse*] and "between" [*inter*]. Interest is the work of consciousness, to insert itself between actuality and ideality, so as to relate them to one another with serious concern for the eternal truth. Without this concern to orient the relating of ideality to actuality, interest degenerates into the interesting – or whatever distracts the subject from boredom. The capacity to recollect and to forget is dependent on one's initial awareness in paying attention, and that awareness in turn is dependent on the emotion that motivates interest in the object of attention. For example, if one has paid attention "with the speed of hope," a person "will recollect in such a way he will be unable to forget."[45] If one fails to reflect with genuine interest, one does not really insert consciousness between ideality and actuality, but merely redoubles ideality tautologically, in empty fantasy.[46]

The aesthete muses on tautology in *Either/Or*,[47] in a way which amounts to an ironic critique of himself, and also to a parody of Hegel's definition of the essence of reflective immediacy. Hegel says in the *Science of Logic*:

> 1. Essence is simple immediacy as sublated immediacy. Its negativity is its being; it is self-equal in its absolute negativity, through which otherness and relation-to-other has vanished in its own self into pure equality-with-self. Essence is therefore simple identity-with-self.

> 2. This identity-with-self is the *immediacy* of reflection. It is not that equality-with-self that *being* or even *nothing* is, but the equality-with-self that has brought itself to unity, not a restoration of itself from an other, but this pure origination from and within itself, *essential* identity.[48]

By implication, the essence of the immediacy of reflection, for Hegel, is tautological self-identity without a constitutive role for anyone or anything outside itself. Kierkegaard's aesthete embodies just this principle, to become a human tautology. His egotistical self-absorption originates from within himself, and fails to reach beyond the immediacy of his own reflection. Being a human tautology is tantamount to being empty of heterogeneous content, a condition which characterizes both the experience of boredom and being demonic.[49] Even a space of reflection developed by sophisticated imagination, then, is prone to boredom – at least insofar as its sole motivation is to avoid boredom, and the sense of its own emptiness, by pursuing "the interesting."

But the ethical-religious life begins neither with nothing (contra Hegel), nor does it spring fully formed from the head. It is not achieved by reflection, irony or anxiety, though these can motivate the initial existential choice to live ethically. The ethical-religious life begins with the individual choice to evaluate one's actions, with earnest inward passion, primarily in the categories of good and evil.[50] This choice consolidates the personality, purifies the inner being, and brings the individual into "an immediate relationship with the eternal power that omnipresently pervades all existence."[51] Ethical-religious life also entails concern for others.

Real freedom, for Kierkegaard, consists in choosing the ethical-religious life, since it is only by making this choice that one willingly becomes responsible for one's own actions. Having made the commitment to the ethical-religious life, the individual is on the path to becoming an eternally valid self – or spirit. Through decision, resolve, devotion and spiritual practice the ethical-religious individual builds character, in the form of dispositions to emotional concern. The aesthete, on the other hand, is driven by luck, fate, chance and contingency – and never takes responsibility for his or her own actions. While the ethical-religious individual nurtures a capacity for spiritual growth, the aesthete wallows in self-satisfied complacency. The only disturbances to this spiritual stasis are caused by boredom, irony, melancholy and anxiety.

When the concept of the ethical-religious is introduced in the second volume of *Either/Or*, it is understood in terms of cognitive normative ethics, since it entails commitment to abide by ethical norms regarded as true. These normative ethics, moreover, connect the individual with other individuals in a community of concern. The main exponent of these ethics is Judge William, the epitome of civic virtue. He champions openness and transparency in continuity with others in one's community, especially through the institutions of marriage and the law. This is in contrast to the aesthetic author of the first volume of *Either/Or*, who writes aphorisms *ad se ipsum* [to himself], who manipulates, deceives and seduces others, and who is primarily concerned to avoid boredom, and to cultivate moods which support the inflation of the whole of reality with "the interesting."

While the choice of the ethical is the choice to strive to act for the sake of the good, goodness is initially conceived as civic virtue. This entails acknowledgement of a community of interest, which in turn requires openness and transparency in communication, in order to facilitate mutual understanding and cooperation. Ethical judgments must be intelligible within the axiological framework of the community and justifiable by public reason. Within this framework, the individual is strictly subordinate to the "universal" demands of the ethical community.

These demands, if taken seriously, prove too difficult to fulfil. Even the most conscientious individual will find himself or herself guilty of either transgressing or falling short of civic duty. This might be something relatively trivial, such as failure to be perfectly open and honest in every human interaction, or something abhorrent enough to be punishable by law. Human beings are fallible, frail, egocentric and in process of development. This goes as much for human communities as for human individuals. But if human communities are ethically imperfect, then their civic virtues and correlative public reason must also be open to doubt. This is where religion comes in as a transcendent source of values, which can trump empirical civic virtues. The second volume of *Either/Or* concludes with a sermon by an anonymous pastor, on the topic "The Edification That Lies In The Thought That Against God We Are Always In The Wrong."

Guilt-consciousness is not enough to propel someone into religious consciousness. Ultimately the individual must attain sin-consciousness, to be elevated from the realm of psychology to the realm of spirit. In order to do this, they need help from outside themselves. This is where Christ as teacher and savior enters the picture, bringing both the eternal truth with him and the condition for learning that truth.[52] That condition is sin-consciousness, which is the *sine qua non* of Christian faith, which in turn is the only antidote to despair. Despair is the spiritual equivalent of what boredom is in the realm of the psyche.

3. Moods and Emotions

Central to Kierkegaard's understanding of boredom is his identification of it as a mood. While moods and emotions are often conflated, Kierkegaard distinguishes them primarily in terms of their intentional objects. Moods lack a determinate object, while emotions are expressions of concern for, or interest in, determinate objects. Whereas emotions enable consciousness to relate "ideality" and "actuality" to one another with passion and interest, moods merely attune the subject reflexively to its own subjectivity.

The four main moods Kierkegaard examines in his dialectic of existential stages are: melancholy, boredom, irony and anxiety. Each mood is a form of suffering, though it is not always *felt* as suffering by its subject. Insofar as it is felt as suffering, the mood has the potential to motivate the sufferer by repulsion. On the other hand, each mood also has the potential to fascinate the subject into perverse attraction, to the point of demonic self-absorption. For example, the melancholic can fall in love with his own unhappy mood and descend into depression and even suicide. The ironist can negate everything, in a universal scepticism which undermines all bases for action and belief.[53] The anxious person can become addicted to uncertainty, and hover endlessly in possibilities. The bored person can demonically embrace boredom, as the last resort of imagination, to defy reliance on anything beyond its own subjective resources – in order to "kill time" rather than submit to "eternity."[54]

Another figure Kierkegaard uses to signify the empty doubling of oneself, in existential tautology, is the Romantic ironist. While trying to create a reflective distance from the world with the affectation of bored irony, the Romantic ironist loses all continuity of character except for boredom itself.[55] He also loses touch with the actual world, and instead of being interested in mapping ideality truthfully onto actuality, or in actualizing the ideal, he projects his own emptiness onto everything with as little discrimination as the English tourist. By contrast, Socratic irony has ethical seriousness and motivating power. Socratic irony is defined as "infinite absolute negativity,"[56] and Socrates himself is characterized as "the nothing from which the beginning must nevertheless begin."[57] Socratic irony was construed by Hegel as the midwife at the birth of reflective self-awareness.[58] Irony functions in the space of reflective consciousness, between the ideal and the actual, by negating the given actuality or placing it in suspension. It stings consciousness into self-awareness and confronts it with the possibility of actively relating ideality and actuality with passionate interest in truth, rather than slump lazily into received wisdom or convention and to be prone to boredom.

But Romantic irony lacks the ethical passion of Socratic irony. It does not negate the actual in a way that clears a space for a new positivity, or that serves truth and reason. Instead, Romantic irony negates actuality in a way that leaves room only for bored attunement to its own vacuity. Romantic irony, reduced to boredom, has only negative motivating power through repulsion.[59] But as an affectation it is chosen as a fashionable character trait, as though it is in some way attractive, which cancels its power to motivate even by repulsion.

Anxiety, like boredom and Romantic irony, is a mood. Anxiety has an intentional object, but its object is "nothing" – or more accurately, anxiety has an indeterminate intentional object, which is nothing *actual*. This allows *possible* future states to be intentional objects of anxiety. Boredom is an adumbration of anxiety insofar as it has "nothing" as its content, but it lacks the modality of possibility.[60] To be able to imagine possible future states is necessary for the exercise of freedom, including the freedom to choose the ethical-religious life. The most life-affirming emotional orientation to possibility is hope, which is absent in boredom.[61] But even the vertiginous *feeling* of anxiety – momentous and unsettling, expectant with dread – has a direction towards action which the monotony of boredom lacks. Whereas anxiety draws one toward the future, boredom moves one, if at all, only by repulsion. Anxiety, then, heralds the possibility of freedom, while boredom at most repels towards anxiety.

For Kierkegaard, the path to spiritual selfhood requires the individual to cultivate ethical-religious emotions rather than aesthetic moods. In particular, the individual needs to build up emotions which construe the world in terms of concern for the welfare of others. These include kindness, generosity, magnanimity, sympathy, hope, faith, and of course love, which subsumes all spiritual emotions.[62] Kierkegaard wrote a series of "Edifying Discourses" [*Opbyggelige Taler*][63] to accompany his aesthetic writings, precisely to build up spiritual emotions. Their purpose was to speak to the heart of "that single individual" – his reader – in order to strengthen the reader's capacity for construing the world in terms of concern for others.

Emotions do not exist in isolation, but form constellations in the spirit. So Kierkegaard's edifying discourses try to build up emotions such as patience, hope, perseverance, faith, and humility, which do not on the surface appear to be necessarily concerned with the welfare of others. However, each of these emotions, when taken in a Christian sense, is other-regarding, even if only by virtue of being subordinated to love of God, who is taken to be the absolute other. Hope, for example, seems as though it could have something purely selfish as its intentional object – like winning the lottery. But this is "earthly hope." Eternal hope, by contrast, is understood as "hope against hope," when all earthly hope has vanished. It is a steadfast, patient religious passion,[64] and a specification of the spirit, rather than a mere psychological longing.[65]

Ultimately, all spiritual emotions can be subsumed under Christian love, understood as *agape* – self-sacrificing, other-regarding concern for the eternal happiness and well-being of others.[66] It is only the cultivation of this type of love, and the constellation of emotions that support it, which can serve as antidotes to boredom, demonic boredom, and the despair that underlies both.

4. Ontology of the Self

The most explicit discussion of the ontology of the self is found in the first chapter of *The Sickness Unto Death*, where the pseudonymous author Anti-Climacus asserts that a human being is composed of the following sets of opposites: finitude/infinitude, temporality/eternity, and freedom/necessity.[67] Elsewhere in Kierkegaard's *oeuvre* we also find the opposites: body/soul,[68] possibility/necessity,[69] and ideality/actuality.[70] The human being as such is not yet a self, according to Anti-Climacus. The self is *spirit*, which is the "third" in the relation between these opposites. The role of spirit is to relate the opposites to one another and to the self, which consists in this process of self-relating, as well as in relating one's self to God, the absolute other who establishes and maintains the very ground of being of the self.[71]

Each individual has the task of becoming a self, even though selfhood cannot be attained without ultimate dependence on God. Selfhood consists in finding the appropriate equilibrium between the constituent opposing elements within oneself as a human being. That equilibrium is attained by relating the opposites to one another, and to the self as a unity, by adopting the right emotional attitude and by cultivating faculties which govern components of the self. For example, imagination is the faculty for possibility; intuition is the faculty for infinity;[72] will is the faculty for freedom. The proper emotions with which to relate the present time to eternity (construed for temporal beings in terms of the future) are patience and hope.[73] The proper emotion with which to relate to God as the ground of our being is faith. The proper emotion with which to relate possibility to necessity is humility. The means to integrity of character and action is to will one thing, *through the heart*, that is, through the passion of love.[74]

As we have seen, the problem with boredom and the other moods is that, while they have a certain capacity to move the individual psychologically, they also have a capacity to return "tautologically" into mere reverberations of the subject with itself. Spirit requires the acknowledgement of otherness even within the constitution of the self. Each set of constitutive polarities of the self marks a potential self-difference, which requires the spirit to relate itself to itself appropriately; and also to relate itself to the absolute otherness of God. The appropriate means for spirit to relate itself to itself and to God is through passionate concern, fired by the idea that upon this activity depends one's eternal salvation. Boredom is not a passionate concern. It is a self-enclosed indifference to otherness, including the otherness implicit in the oppositional structure of the human being and the otherness of God. Boredom fails as a form of consciousness, which consists of the opposition between ideality and actuality, since it erases the opposition by retreating into its own ideality and ignoring actuality (or by transfiguring it into fantasy, or by negating it with Romantic irony). It also fails as a form of consciousness that relates ideality and actuality appropriately to one another, since if it relates them at all, it does so without passionate concern or interest.

5. Time, Temporality, Eternity and the Moment

One of the principal axes of the self is temporality, in which spirit strives to hold time and eternity in equilibrium. For temporal experience, the main problem is to come to grips with the "parts of time," viz. past, present, and future. The ideal for a Christian is to grasp the past through recollection, the future through hope, and the present through the repetition [*Gjentagelse*] of faith. The latter consists in repeating "the moment" [*Øieblikket*] in which eternity intersects time – so that the present instant is replete with meaning ("the fullness of time").[75] That is, the Christian strives to grasp again, with subjective passion, the significance of eternity in every moment of temporal existence. This imbues life with ethical-religious seriousness and eternal significance. The aesthete, however, tries to manipulate the experience of past and future by means of selective memory and expectation, and fails to relate the present moment to eternity at all. That renders the present an arbitrary and meaningless series of "nows" – a temporal orientation which lies at the root of boredom. In order to avoid the feeling of emptiness in the face of an endlessly recurring present, the aesthete seeks distraction in the new, or in the intensity of mood in the now.

For the aesthete (as for Plato), the present is a purely abstract division between past and future. For Plato (and the aesthete), the present is a "vanishing moment" – the temporal equivalent of a spatial point, which has no extension. On Plato's spatial analogy, the now occupies no place, since the being which occupied a place in the past is annulled in order to occupy its place in the future, and this process passes through the non-place of the now.[76] Plato's analysis of time is meant to underpin his analysis of change, understood as the movement of becoming, which is from non-being to being. The reflective aesthete, too, is in search of movement, to escape the vacuity of boredom and to be renewed in the interesting. However, from Kierkegaard's point of view, the reflective aesthete fails to imbue the present with sufficient intensity to renew himself, since he fails to relate it with existential earnestness to eternity. The reflective aesthete refers the moment to his own subjective feelings, and thereby returns to the boring self-enclosure of the demonic. This is a variation on the Platonic doctrine of *anamnesis*, in which eternal truth is always already there and merely has to be recollected.[77] The aesthete assumes that he is always already in possession of the truth of existence, and merely has to pay attention selectively, by manipulating memory and expectation, in order to remain in this "truth" – conceived as subjective satisfaction in mood. This assumption leaves no room for radical change in the nature of the self, and so on Kierkegaard's view, excludes the possibility of being "born again" as spirit.

According to Kierkegaard, *contra* Plato, a self has not always been itself in a retrospective eternity, but must become itself in its eternal validity by means of an act of freedom undertaken in time. Becoming a self is an event, which requires a change of state of one's self from potential (or "dreaming") spirit to self-conscious spirit.[78] It is a pathos-filled transition, in which the individual appropriates his or her spiritual identity through resolution, in earnest inwardness before God and with consciousness of eternity. In this process of change, a new self is born and everything is transfigured (for consciousness). The self is changed qualitatively from an earlier self to a new self by grounding in an absolute present (the eternal) conceived in terms of choosing contemporaneity with Christ. That is, for the Christian every moment has eternal ethical-religious significance, since the Christian resolves with the passion of faith to grasp each moment as an occasion for striving to imitate Christ, to emulate the "fullness of time" signified by Christ as the temporal incarnation of the eternal.[79] In the moment of faith, the Christian relates to Christ as revealed truth and as saviour. Christ offers the forgiveness of sins, and therefore atonement with the eternal in time. Insofar as the moment is transformed into "an atom of eternity"[80] intensively, "inwardness is [...] eternity or the constituent of the eternal in man."[81]

Christ represents the fullness of time, since he is the temporal incarnation of the eternal. Each moment of life in Christ is replete with absolute meaning. The fullness of time is the antithesis of both boredom (the emptiness of time), and of the demonic (the vacuous). The passion of faith is the human conduit to this fullness of time. The primary expression of Christian faith is striving to imitate Christ, and this is manifest in reaching out with loving concern to "the neighbour" or the one in need, in every moment. Here love is conceived as *agape* – or selfless, self-sacrificing love for the sake of others, which is the antithesis of demonic self-enclosure and of the egotistical desire of the seducer.[82] The reflective aesthete is motivated solely by selfish desire, whether positively in pursuit of "the interesting" or negatively in repulsion from the suffering of boredom. He fails to suffer (boredom or anything else) for the sake of others, and therefore fails to transfigure his despair into joy,[83] or his demonic self-absorption into spiritual enlightenment.

Selfish desire is dubbed "the flesh" in Christianity, and is excluded as the epitome of sin.[84] Therefore, the only real antidote for boredom, and for the demonic despair which the reflective aesthete substitutes for boredom, is to embrace oneself as spirit. That means to be motivated primarily by concern for others.[85] It also means to relate oneself to oneself with ethical-religious seriousness and passionate concern, while acknowledging the ultimate ground of this conscious self-mediation to be the eternal God, and to take Christ in faith to be the atonement for sin, in the fullness of time when eternity intersects time.

Kierkegaard's analysis of demonic boredom as a sin, whose antidote is faith and love, is tantamount to conceiving of boredom as *acedia*.[86] However, because demonic boredom occurs in a secular context, and is (mis)conceived as a social and psychological problem with prudential solutions, it requires more indirect means to motivate its sufferers to change than was required for *acedia* in the monastic setting. Moreover, the changes in the experience of temporality fostered by the industrial revolution, by urbanization, and by mass communication, mass consumption, and mass entertainment, require an ironic distance from this "given actuality" if the individual born in the modern age is to be free to find the antidote to demonic boredom in spiritual practices and passions.[87]

NOTES

[1] Søren Kierkegaard, *The Concept of Anxiety: Kierkegaard's Writings VIII*, translated by Reidar Thomte (Princeton, N.J.: Princeton University Press, 1987), pp. 132-133 (translation modified).

[2] Despite the similarities, modern boredom is distinct from *taedium vitae* insofar as the former depends on a post-Enlightenment conception of historical time as linear and progressive. Modern boredom also assumes that boredom is an artefact of the tedium of the world, rather than a defect in the bored subject, although Kierkegaard criticizes the modern aesthete for making that assumption. Cf. Elizabeth S. Goodstein, *Experience without Qualities: Boredom and Modernity* (Stanford University Press, 2005), pp. 35, 402-403.

[3] Cf. Søren Kierkegaard, *Either/Or Part I: Kierkegaard's Writings III*, translated by Howard V. Hong & Edna H. Hong (Princeton, N.J.: Princeton University Press, 1987), p. 286.

[4] While there have been many attempts at typologies of boredom, one of the most illuminating is that of Martin Doehlemann, who distinguishes: (i) situative boredom; (ii) the boredom of satiety; (iii) existential boredom, which is characterized by lack of content; and (iv) creative boredom, which drives one to make something new. Kierkegaard's notion of demonic boredom is equivalent to Doehlemann's "existential boredom," though it also has the potential to drive one to creativity. See Martin Doehlemann, *Langeweile? Deutung eines verbreiteten Phänomens* (Frankfurt am Main: Suhrkamp Verlag, 1991), pp. 22-23. Cf. also Lars Svendsen, *A Philosophy of Boredom*, translated by John Irons (London: Reaktion Books, 2005), pp. 41ff.

[5] Kierkegaard, *Either/Or Part I*, p. 290.

[6] Søren Kierkegaard, *The Concept of Irony: Kierkegaard's Writings II*, translated by Howard V. Hong & Edna H. Hong (Princeton, N.J.: Princeton University Press, 1989), p. 285.

[7] Wolf Lepenies, *Melancholy and Society*, translated by Jeremy Gaines & Doris Jones (Cambridge, MA & London: Harvard University Press, 1992), pp. 69-70.

[8] Harvie Ferguson, *Melancholy and the Critique of Modernity: Søren Kierkegaard's Religious Psychology* (London & New York: Routledge, 1995), p. 10.

[9] Kierkegaard, *Either/Or Part I*, pp. 281-300.

[10] Ibid., p. 288.

[11] Ibid., p. 289.

[12] Ibid., p. 285. Although it is the demonic aesthete who wittily asserts that "boredom is the root of all evil," Kierkegaard ironically regards the self-enclosure that characterizes the demonic personality, with its selfish lack of concern for the well-being of others, and with its refusal to acknowledge the constitutive role of God in becoming a self, to be the real roots of all evil.

[13] Carl Henrik Koch, *Kierkegaard og "Det interessante"* (Copenhagen: C.A. Reitzels Forlag, 1992), pp. 7-8. Cf. Michel Foucault's analysis of the birth of "man" or "the subject" as definitive of the modern *episteme*, in which the human being displaces God as the ultimate explanatory concept in the social sciences. On Foucault's analysis, the human subject is conceived in modernity as finite, but this very finitude is taken to provide the conditions for grounding objective knowledge. Cf. Michel Foucault, *The Order of Things: An Archaeology of the Human Sciences* (London: Tavistock, 1970), especially Chapter 9, "Man and his doubles," pp. 303-343. Kierkegaard, by contrast, takes the human being to be a composite of finitude and infinitude, and wants to return to a conception of the self as dependent for its very constitution on God. Cf. Søren Kierkegaard, *The Sickness Unto*

Death: Kierkegaard's Writings XIX, translated by Howard V. Hong & Edna H. Hong (Princeton, N.J.: Princeton University Press, 1980), pp. 13-14.

[14] The Danish word "*Stemning*," like its German counterpart "*Stimmung*," means "mood," "attunement," "atmosphere," or "ambience." It is cognate with the word for voice, "*Stemme*," and the verb "to tune" – "*at stemme.*"

[15] Vincent A. McCarthy, *The Phenomenology of Moods in Kierkegaard* (The Hague: Martinus Nijhoff, 1978), pp. 124-126.

[16] Michael L. Raposa, *Boredom and the Religious Imagination* (Charlottesville & London: University Press of Virginia, 1999), p. 7.

[17] Goodstein, *Experience without Qualities*, p. 36.

[18] Kierkegaard, *The Sickness Unto Death*, pp. 42-75.

[19] Patrick Bigelow, "The Ontology of Boredom," *Man & World* 16.3 (1983), p. 258.

[20] Kierkegaard, *Either/Or Part I*, p. 20 (translation modified).

[21] Robert C. Roberts, "What An Emotion Is: A Sketch," *The Philosophical Review* 97 (1988), pp. 187-191.

[22] Kierkegaard, *Either/Or Part I*, p. 37.

[23] Raposa, *Boredom and the Religious Imagination*, p. 2.

[24] Søren Kierkegaard, *Søren Kierkegaard's Journals and Papers*, Vol. 1, A-E, edited and translation by Howard V. Hong & Edna H. Hong with the assistance of Gregor Malantschuk (Bloomington & London: Indiana State University Press, 1967-1978), p. xxvii.

[25] Cf. George Pattison, *Religion and the Nineteenth-Century Crisis of Culture* (Cambridge: Cambridge University Press, 2002), Chapter 1.

[26] Søren Kierkegaard, *Two Ages: Kierkegaard's Writings XIV*, translated by Howard V. Hong & Edna H. Hong (Princeton, N.J.: Princeton University Press, 1978), pp. 60ff.

[27] Kierkegaard, *Either/Or Part I*, pp. 281-300.

[28] Søren Kierkegaard, *Johannes Climacus: Or, De Omnibus Dubitandum Est*, translated by T.H. Croxall (Stanford: Stanford University Press, 1967), pp. 148-149.

[29] Cf. Stephen Dunning, *Kierkegaard's Dialectic of Inwardness: A Structural Analysis of the Theory of Stages* (Princeton, N.J.: Princeton University Press, 1985), chapter 1. The construal of the stages as a simple progression from aesthetic, through ethical, to religious stages also ignores Kierkegaard's parody of the *scala paradise*, especially the version implicit in Hegel's *Encyclopedia of the Philosophical Sciences*. Cf. William McDonald, "Retracing the Circular Ruins of Hegel's *Encyclopedia*," in Robert L. Perkins (ed.), *International Kierkegaard Commentary Volume 12: Concluding Unscientific Postscript to "Philosophical Fragments"* (Macon: Mercer University Press, 1997), pp. 227-245.

[30] Poul Lübcke, "An Analytical Interpretation of Kierkegaard as Moral Philosopher," *Kierkegaardiana 15* (Copenhagen: C.A. Reitzel, 1991), pp. 93-96.

[31] Quidam is a character who is likely to bore others. Cf. Søren Kierkegaard, *Stages On Life's Way: Kierkegaard's Writings XI*, translated by Howard V. Hong & Edna H. Hong (Princeton, N.J.: Princeton University Press, 1988), pp. 231, 398.

[32] Kierkegaard, *Either/Or Part I*, pp. 47-135.

[33] Ibid., p. 108.

[34] Ibid., p. 192.

[35] Ibid., pp. 103-115.

[36] Kierkegaard, *Johannes Climacus*, pp. 148-149.

[37] Ibid., p. 149.

[38] This is also true of frivolity [*Letsindighed*], which is the polar opposite of depression [*Tungsindighed*]. Frivolity is often used to distract from heaviness of mind, in similar fashion to the use of novelty to drive away boredom.

[39] Kierkegaard, *Either/Or Part I*, p. 290.

[40] Cf. "The Seducer's Diary," in ibid., pp. 301-445.

[41] Cf. the aesthete's discussions of Marie Beaumarchais, from Goethe's *Clavigo*, Donna Elvira from Laurids Kruse's translation and adaptation of Mozart's *Don Giovanni*, and Margarete from Goethe's *Faust*, in ibid., pp. 176-215.

[42] G.W.F. Hegel, *Phenomenology of Spirit*, translated by A.V. Miller (Oxford: Oxford University Press, 1977), pp. 111-119.

[43] Cf. Kierkegaard, *Either/Or Part I*, p. 445, where Johannes speculates "whether or not one could poeticize oneself out of a girl in such a way as to make her so proud that she imagined it was she who was bored with the relationship. It could be a very interesting epilogue, which in and by itself could have psychological interest..."

[44] Ibid., pp. 281-300.

[45] Ibid., p. 293. Note that Nietzsche, too, observes the close relation between paying attention in the present, and the capacity for recollection and forgetfulness, as well as the connection between passion and awareness. See Friedrich Nietzsche, "On the Uses and Disadvantages of History for Life," in *Untimely Meditations*, translated by R.J. Hollingdale (Cambridge: Cambridge University Press, 1983), pp. 88-95.

[46] Kierkegaard regards German Romantic irony as completely disconnected from actuality in this way, and wrote *Either/Or* partly as a satire on German Romanticism. Cf. Kierkegaard, *The Concept of Irony*, pp. 304-305.

[47] Kierkegaard, *Either/Or*, p. 38.

[48] G.W.F. Hegel, *Science of Logic*, translated by A.V. Miller (New York: Humanities Press, 1969), p. 411.

[49] Kierkegaard, *The Concept of Anxiety*, pp. 132-133.

[50] Kierkegaard, *Either/Or Part II: Kierkegaard's Writings IV*, translated by Howard V. Hong & Edna H. Hong (Princeton, N.J.: Princeton University Press, 1987), pp. 166-167.

[51] Ibid., p. 167.

[52] Søren Kierkegaard, *Philosophical Fragments: Kierkegaard's Writings VII*, translated by Howard V. Hong & Edna H. Hong (Princeton, N.J.: Princeton University Press, 1985), pp. 14ff.

[53] Elizabeth Goodstein defines modern boredom as "the democratization of skepticism." Cf. Goodstein, *Experience without Qualities*, p. 10.

[54] Cf. Thoreau, who claimed that it is not possible to kill time without injuring eternity. Henry David Thoreau, *Walden* (New York: W.W. Norton, 1951), p. 22.

[55] Kierkegaard, *The Concept of Irony*, p. 285.

[56] Ibid., p. 261.

[57] Ibid., p. 198.

[58] Cf. Sarah Kofman, *Socrates: Fictions of a Philosopher*, translated by Catherine Porter (Ithaca, N.Y.: Cornell University Press, 1998), p. 86.

[59] Kierkegaard, *Either/Or Part I*, p. 285.

[60] Ibid., p. 291; and *The Concept of Anxiety*, p. 133.

[61] Søren Kierkegaard, *Works of Love: Kierkegaard's Writings XVI*, translated by Howard V. Hong & Edna H. Hong (Princeton, N.J.: Princeton University Press, 1995), p. 252.

[62] Cf. ibid., p. 225, where faith and hope are subsumed by love.

[63] Howard V. Hong & Edna H. Hong translate "Opbyggelige Taler" as "Upbuilding Discourses," to capture the meaning with more Anglo-Saxon immediacy than the Latin-

derived "Edifying Discourses." To have been consistent, they should have translated it as "Upbuilding Talks." Cf. Søren Kierkegaard, *Eighteen Upbuilding Discourses: Kierkegaard's Writings V*, translated by Howard V. Hong & Edna H. Hong (Princeton, N.J.: Princeton University Press, 1990).

[64] Søren Kierkegaard, *Søren Kierkegaards Papirer*, 2nd edition, edited by P.A. Heiberg, V. Kuhr, E. Torsting, Niels Thulstrup & N.J. Cappelørn (Copenhagen: Gyldendal, 1968-1978), IV C 96.

[65] Kierkegaard, *Works of Love*, p. 179.

[66] For a thorough investigation of the notion of Christian love in Kierkegaard's writings, cf. Jamie Ferreira, *Love's Grateful Striving: A Commentary on Kierkegaard's* Works of Love (Oxford: Oxford University Press, 2001).

[67] Kierkegaard, *The Sickness Unto Death*, p. 13.

[68] Kierkegaard, *The Concept of Anxiety*, pp. 315, 360.

[69] Kierkegaard, *Philosophical Fragments*, p. 237.

[70] Kierkegaard, *Søren Kierkegaards Papirer*, IX A 382 (1848).

[71] Kierkegaard, *The Sickness Unto Death*, pp. 13-14.

[72] Cf. Kierkegaard, *Søren Kierkegaard's Journals and Papers*, II A 31 (1837).

[73] Kierkegaard, *Works of Love*, p. 249.

[74] Cf. *"purity of heart is to will one thing,"* Søren Kierkegaard, *Upbuilding Discourses in Various Spirits: Kierkegaard's Writings XV*, translated by Howard V. Hong & Edna H. Hong (Princeton, N.J.: Princeton University Press, 1993), p. 120.

[75] Cf. Kierkegaard, *The Concept of Anxiety*, p. 90. Cf. *Galatians* 4:4.

[76] Cf. Plato, *Parmenides*, 137c-157b.

[77] Cf. Plato, *Meno*, 85d-86d, where Socrates elicits the proof of Pythagoras's theorem from an apparently ignorant slave boy, thereby demonstrating that the boy must already have had the knowledge from his precarnate existence as a soul.

[78] Kierkegaard, *The Concept of Anxiety*, p. 91.

[79] Kierkegaard, *Either/Or Part I*, pp. 142-143.

[80] Kierkegaard, *The Concept of Anxiety*, p. 93.

[81] Ibid., p. 151.

[82] On the differences between erotic love, self-regarding love and *agape* in Kierkegaard's work, cf. William McDonald, "Love in Kierkegaard's *Symposia*," *Minerva – an internet journal of philosophy* 7 (http://www.ul.ie/~philos/vol7/kierkegaard.html) (November 2003), pp. 60-93.

[83] Far from attaining joy, the reflective aesthete revels perversely in becoming "the unhappiest one" by virtue of his temporal dislocation, in which he hopes for that which can only be recollected, and recollects only that which can be hoped. Cf. Kierkegaard, *Either/Or Part I*, pp. 217-230.

[84] Kierkegaard, *Either/Or Part II*, p. 49.

[85] This understanding of spirit as concern for others' well-being is not confined to Christianity. The current Dalai Lama, for example, has said: "The unifying characteristic of the qualities I have described as 'spiritual' may be said to be some level of concern for others' well-being. In Tibetan, we speak of *shen pen kyi sem*, meaning 'the thought to be of help to others.' And when we think about them, we see that each of the qualities noted is defined by an implicit concern for others' well-being. Moreover, the one who is compassionate, loving, patient, tolerant, forgiving, and so on to some extent recognizes the potential impact of their actions on others and orders their conduct accordingly. Thus spiritual practice according to this description involves, on the one hand, acting out of concern for others' well-being. On the other hand, it entails transforming ourselves so that

we become more readily disposed to do so. To speak of spiritual practice in any terms other than these is meaningless." Cf. Dalai Lama XIV, *Ethics for the New Millenium* (New York: Riverhead Books, 1999), p. 23.

[86] In her critique of Heidegger's understanding of boredom as a perennial malady, rooted in the ontology of human temporality, Goodstein is implicitly critical of Kierkegaard for returning to an understanding of boredom as *acedia*, instead of regarding it from an historicist perspective as discursively constructed (cf. Goodstein, *Experience without Qualities*, pp. 410-411). Yet Kierkegaard has a more nuanced understanding of boredom. On the one hand he does regard it as socially and discursively constructed, insofar as it becomes an epidemic and insofar as new forms of it appear (e.g. what I have dubbed "demonic boredom" – where boredom becomes an affectation). But Kierkegaard wants to hold on to the insights that the theological concept of *acedia* held – that human beings continue to be afflicted with a malaise of the spirit, due to a misrelation to eternity (and therefore to temporality). Kierkegaard regards it as a mistake in modernity to reject the spiritual analysis offered by the concept of *acedia* in favour of a purely secular, psychological, social and discursive concept, since the antidote remains a spiritual one, despite changes in nomenclature. To forget the potential within *acedia* for transformative suffering, and to regard it merely as an outmoded discursive construction, is itself a symptom of the same spiritual malaise which is responsible for modern boredom.

[87] While Goodstein acknowledges that "Kierkegaard connected the lived crisis of meaning characteristic of modern existence with the material transformations of modernity," she reduces his position to the assertion that "ennui was the fate of subjectivity as such" (Goodstein, *Experience without Qualities*, p. 159). This is patently false, since Kierkegaard regarded boredom as an affliction which can be overcome by means of a change in subjectivity. That change is to be effected by cultivating spiritual practices, which direct one's attention outside of oneself, especially to God as the absolute other. Goodstein goes on to accuse Kierkegaard of having an "idealistic and apolitical [response] to the perceived meaninglessness of existence" (Goodstein, *Experience without Qualities*, p. 160). This, too, is quite misleading, since Kierkegaard engages vociferously in the politics of the Danish People's Church, especially in his pamphlet, *The Moment*. This engagement is aimed precisely at shaking up the church as a political institution, to re-engage it in matters of the spirit, and thereby to motivate it to address the malaise of the times, one primary expression of which was the epidemic of boredom. For more on Kierkegaard's politics, cf. George Connell and C. Stephen Evans (eds), *Foundations of Kierkegaard's Vision of Community: Religion, Ethics and Politics in Kierkegaard* (Humanities Press, 1992). Cf. also, George Pattison and Steven Shakespeare (eds), *Kierkegaard: the Self in Society* (New York: St. Martin's Press, 1998), and Martin J. Matustik, *Postnational Identity: Critical Theory and Existential Philosophy in Habermas, Kierkegaard and Havel* (New York & London: The Guilford Press, 1993).

WORKS CITED

Bigelow, Patrick. "The Ontology of Boredom." *Man & World* 16.3 (1983): 251-265.

Dalai Lama XIV. *Ethics for the New Millenium*. New York: Riverhead Books, 1999.

Doehlemann, Martin. *Langeweile? Deutung eines verbreiteten Phänomens.* Frankfurt am Main: Suhrkamp Verlag, 1991.

Dunning, Stephen. *Kierkegaard's Dialectic of Inwardness: A Structural Analysis of the Theory of Stages.* Princeton, N.J.: Princeton University Press, 1985.

Ferguson, Harvie. *Melancholy and the Critique of Modernity: Søren Kierkegaard's Religious Psychology.* London & New York: Routledge, 1995.

Ferreira, M. Jamie. *Love's Grateful Striving: A Commentary on Kierkegaard's* Works of Love. Oxford: Oxford University Press, 2001.

Foucault, Michel. *The Order of Things: An Archaeology of the Human Sciences.* London: Tavistock, 1970.

Goodstein, Elizabeth S. *Experience without Qualities: Boredom and Modernity.* Stanford: Stanford University Press, 2005.

Hegel, G.W.F. *Hegel's Science of Logic.* Trans. A.V. Miller. New York: Humanities Press, 1969.

———. *Phenomenology of Spirit.* Trans. A.V. Miller. Oxford: Oxford University Press, 1977.

Kierkegaard, Søren. *Søren Kierkegaards Papirer,* 2nd edition. Ed. P.A. Heiberg, et.al. Copenhagen: Gyldendal, 1968-1978.

———. *Søren Kierkegaard's Journals and Papers Vol. 1, A-E.* Ed. and trans. Howard V. Hong and Edna H. Hong with the assistance of Gregor Malantschuk. Bloomington: Indiana State University Press, 1967-1978.

———. *Johannes Climacus: Or, De Omnibus Dubitandum Est.* Trans. T.H. Croxall. Stanford: Stanford University Press, 1967.

———. *The Concept of Irony: Kierkegaard's Writings II.* Trans. Howard V. Hong and Edna H. Hong. Princeton, N.J.: Princeton University Press, 1989.

———. *Either/Or Part I: Kierkegaard's Writings III.* Trans. Howard V. Hong and Edna H. Hong. Princeton, N.J.: Princeton University Press, 1987.

———. *Either/Or Part II: Kierkegaard's Writings IV.* Trans. Howard V. Hong and Edna H. Hong. Princeton, N.J.: Princeton University Press, 1987.

——. *Eighteen Upbuilding Discourses: Kierkegaard's Writings V.* Trans. Howard V. Hong and Edna H. Hong. Princeton, N.J.: Princeton University Press, 1990.

——. *Philosophical Fragments: Kierkegaard's Writings VII.* Trans. Howard V. Hong and Edna H. Hong. Princeton, N.J.: Princeton University Press, 1985.

——. *The Concept of Anxiety: Kierkegaard's Writings VIII.* Trans. Reidar Thomte. Princeton, N.J.: Princeton University Press, 1987.

——. *Stages On Life's Way: Kierkegaard's Writings XI.* Trans. Howard V. Hong and Edna H. Hong. Princeton, N.J.: Princeton University Press, 1988.

——. *Two Ages: Kierkegaard's Writings XIV.* Trans. Howard V. Hong and Edna H. Hong. Princeton, N.J.: Princeton University Press, 1978.

——. *Upbuilding Discourses in Various Spirits: Kierkegaard's Writings XV.* Trans. Howard V. Hong and Edna H. Hong. Princeton, N.J.: Princeton University Press, 1993.

——. *Works of Love: Kierkegaard's Writings XVI.* Trans. Howard V. Hong and Edna H. Hong. Princeton, N.J.: Princeton University Press, 1995.

——. *The Sickness Unto Death: Kierkegaard's Writings XIX.* Trans. Howard V. Hong and Edna H. Hong. Princeton, N.J.: Princeton University Press, 1980.

Koch, Carl Henrik. *Kierkegaard og "Det interessante".* Copenhagen: C.A. Reitzels Forlag, 1992.

Kofman, Sarah. *Socrates: Fictions of a Philosopher.* Trans. Catherine Porter. Ithaca, N.Y.: Cornell University Press, 1998.

Lepenies, Wolf. *Melancholy and Society.* Trans. Jeremy Gaines and Doris Jones. Cambridge, MA: Harvard University Press, 1992.

Lübcke, Poul. "An Analytical Interpretation of Kierkegaard as Moral Philosopher." *Kierkegaardiana 15* (1991): 93-103.

McCarthy, Vincent A. *The Phenomenology of Moods in Kierkegaard.* The Hague: Martinus Nijhoff, 1978.

McDonald, William. "Retracing the Circular Ruins of Hegel's *Encyclopedia.*" *International Kierkegaard Commentary Volume 12: Concluding Unscientific Postscript to "Philosophical Fragments."*

Ed. Robert L. Perkins. Macon: Mercer University Press, 1997: 227-245.

——. "Love in Kierkegaard's *Symposia*." *Minerva – an internet journal of philosophy* 7 (November 2003): 60-93 <http://www.ul.ie/~philos/vol7/kierkegaard.html>.

Nietzsche, Friedrich. "On the Uses and Disadvantages of History for Life." *Untimely Meditations*. Trans. R.J. Hollingdale. Cambridge: Cambridge University Press, 1983: 57-124.

Pattison, George. *Religion and the Nineteenth-Century Crisis of Culture.* Cambridge: Cambridge University Press, 2002.

Plato. *Protagoras and Meno*. Trans. W.K.C. Guthrie. Harmondsworth: Penguin Books, 1956.

——. *Parmenides*. Trans. Albert Keith Whitaker. Newburyport, MA: Focus Publications, 1996.

Raposa, Michael L. *Boredom and the Religious Imagination*. Charlottesville: University Press of Virginia, 1999.

Roberts, Robert C. "What An Emotion Is: A Sketch." *The Philosophical Review* 97 (1988): 183-209.

Svendsen, Lars. *A Philosophy of Boredom*. Trans. John Irons. London: Reaktion Books, 2005.

Thoreau, Henry David. *Walden*. New York: W.W. Norton, 1951.

CHAPTER 4

Metaphysics and the Mood of Deep Boredom:
Heidegger's Phenomenology of Mood

Matthew Boss

Martin Heidegger's phenomenological analysis of boredom has as its primary concern, not the psychological or anthropological investigation of a mood as something "merely subjective," but the fundamental philosophical questions that are traditionally the province of metaphysics. Heidegger's analysis takes boredom not as a "subjective experience" whose possible causes might be a matter of interest to psychology, but as a phenomenon with an essentially temporal character. For boredom is a mood in which time becomes suddenly conspicuous. Heidegger distinguishes three different forms of boredom which make time manifest in different ways. The mood's relevance to the questions of metaphysics is in the kind of time revealed by "deep" boredom in distinction from the "clock-time" of everyday life. It is Heidegger's basic philosophical position that our understanding of being always has an inner connection to time through its relation to human temporality.

The name of the twentieth-century philosopher Martin Heidegger is sometimes associated with the attempt to carry out an ontological examination of the phenomenon of mood as part of the treatment of certain questions in metaphysics. Yet it is incongruous that because of the – on principle inaccurate – received classification of him as an *existentialist* philosopher we associate him in this context largely with an obsession with the phenomena of the mood of Angst. The analysis of Angst appears prominently, as well as in other places, in his major work of 1927 *Sein und Zeit* (*Being and Time*) (*SZ*, 184ff. et passim).[1] But Heidegger's longest, most exhaustive phenomenological analysis of a mood is in fact that of the mood of *boredom* (*Langeweile*). This is presented in his 1929-30 lecture-course held in Freiburg and takes up fully one hundred and sixty pages of the current edition of the text of the course, published as *Die Grundbegriffe der Metaphysik* (*The Fundamental Concepts of Metaphysics*), thus dwarfing the analysis of Angst in *Sein und Zeit*. That Heidegger thinks the phenomenon of boredom deserving of such detailed analysis at all, however, and that a lecture actually on the subject of metaphysics should be, as it appears, suddenly interrupted in this way by a lengthy diversion into the investigation of a mood, requires some explanation. Why should philosophy be concerned with the purely "subjective" quality of boredom? What has boredom to do with metaphysics? The place where we might look for an answer to this question is suggested by the following: of all Heidegger's writings the analysis of boredom gives us perhaps the best insight available into the objectives and methods of his attempt to overthrow the *precedence of logic* in philosophy. His advocacy of such a reappraisal of the place of logic is best known from the short inaugural lecture of 1929 "Was ist Metaphysik?" (*W*, 103-122). Here Heidegger argues that metaphysical questions should not be approached under the terms of the "rule" of logic, in other words the "presupposition that in this question 'logic' is the highest authority, that understanding is the means and thinking the way" (*W*, 107). He takes as an example metaphysical question the "question of 'the nothing'." In order to address this question he does not make use of the analytical apparatus of formal logic but instead has recourse to the "illogical," to a mood, namely the "irrational feeling" of Angst. For "Angst manifests the nothing" (*W*, 112).

It is characteristic of Heidegger's philosophy of this period as a whole to deny that logic is a "presupposition" of metaphysics and to seek to show that, on the contrary, "logic [...] is grounded in metaphysics" (*MAL*, 128). His disputing of the presumed priority of logic is of a piece with his basic conviction as to the proper methodological character of philosophy, which he expresses in *Sein und Zeit* with the assertion that "*ontology* [i.e., roughly speaking, metaphysics] *is possible only as phenomenology*" (*SZ*, 35).[2] The appropriate way into a metaphysical question should be sought in certain determinate moods, laid bare by the methods of phenomenology. For "philosophy always occurs in a fundamental mood" (*GM*, 10).[3] There is no suggestion that boredom and Angst exhaust the spectrum of possible moods which could be chosen for the task, although the choice of mood is by no means arbitrary.

The question of the nothing is not the only metaphysical question discussed by Heidegger. To pursue further the theme of the "logical" tradition, we can consider a traditional problem in ontology concerning a subject of inquiry first opened up for investigation by Aristotle: the problem of the *categories*. In the following we shall examine Heidegger's view of this philosophical problem and his disputing of its merely "logical" status. This will allow us to see the connection between certain themes in traditional metaphysics and Heidegger's apparently "idiosyncratic" phenomenological method.

1. The Problem of the Categories and their Relation to Time

For Aristotle the categories constitute one of the four fundamental ways in which "entity" – i.e. anything that *is* – can be said (*Met.* Δ, 1017 a). Since they have to do with entities in terms of their most general characteristics the categories are a theme of ontology. A category is an a priori conceptual determination of an entity purely insofar as it has *being*, in other words *is*. Accordingly, Heidegger understands the categories as a possible entity's basic "characteristics of being" (*Seinscharaktere*) or "determinations of being" (*Seinsbestimmungen*) (*SZ*, 44, 45), which indicates that they characterise it ontologically rather than ontically. An ontic characterisation, on the other hand, would refer to such qualities of the entity as those ascertainable by empirical natural science, for instance, which can be known only a posteriori, not a priori.

On Heidegger's view the first philosopher to succeed in freeing himself from the traditional preconception as to the place of the categories within metaphysics, which had been long established, and to make them into a problem, namely the problem of their a priori (transcendental) foundation, was Kant. The problem of the foundation and "legitimacy" of the categories forms the central task of the *Critique of Pure Reason*'s "Transcendental Analytic." On the one hand the categories are "pure concepts of the understanding" (*reine Verstandesbegriffe*), but on the other they must be a priori applicable to any possible object of empirical intuition. They are not ontic, but are "ontological predicates" (cf. *KPM*, 55ff.). The legitimacy of the categories cannot be established empirically in the manner of a concept drawn from experience but only through a transcendental demonstration that they constitute "a priori grounds of the possibility of experience."[4] The *Critique* addresses the problem of the categories with an a priori demonstration of this kind in which Kant gives the categories their required "deduction" and "schematism."[5] In this way he provides an answer to what Heidegger would consider an important metaphysical question.

The question of the origin of the categories is metaphysical in the sense that it is ontological, concerning the *being* of entities (*das Sein des Seienden*). The subject of ontology is being (*Sein*), the investigation of which is what Heidegger sees as the fundamental task (*Fundamentalaufgabe*) of philosophy (*SZ*, 11). It is Heidegger's project to bring about a renewal of this fundamental task by returning to what (he asserts) lies at the basis of all questions of ontology: the "sense of being" (*Sinn von Sein*) in general. Where the sense of being has not been adequately investigated and clarified in advance "*all ontology [...] remains at bottom blind and a perversion of its most proper intention*" (*SZ*, 11). This preparatory investigation, carried out by Heidegger, reveals the following: the sense of being is *time*. This means that time is the universal and for us inescapable horizon of any understanding of being at all (*SZ*, 1 and *SZ*, 17). This general thesis guides the entire progress of the ontological investigations of *Sein und Zeit* towards their "preliminary goal" (*SZ*, 1) of preparing for a possible answer to the question of being (*Seinsfrage*). To say that time is the horizon of all understanding of being is to imply that the full elaboration and resolution of any ontological problem requires that we take account of something non-logical in the sense of the "sensual," the non-intellectual. For time is essentially something belonging to human sensibility, as Kant emphasises.[6] This "sensual" horizon is the ultimate horizon of all ontological inquiry. *"Time is the primary horizon of transcendental science, ontology*; or, for short, the *transcendental horizon"* (*GP*, 460). It follows that "the question of the essence of time [...] is the *origin of all questions of metaphysics"* (*GM*, 253). Their common relationship with time is what unifies all the seemingly disparate questions of metaphysics. Heidegger lays stress on the fact that this unifying, common source is in no way an "empty, logically formal possibility" (GM, 254), as it would be were it an abstract principle, but rather the precise opposite of this.[7] Time is not an abstraction but a concrete matter for philosophical investigation.

What is the evidence that all questions of metaphysics and the attempt at their resolution fall within the perspective of the horizon of time? Heidegger supports his general thesis by drawing attention to the terms in which the traditional ontological questions of Western philosophy have been answered. The ancient Greek philosophers, for instance, found themselves presented with the pressing ontological problem of the "nature" of being in the genuine sense. This led to what Plato describes as a veritable "struggle of the giants over being"[8]: the dispute over the ontological priority of the physical-material being of entities in nature and the ideal being of the forms. In the phenomenological terminology such a distinction of kinds of being is referred to as that of the various ontological *regions* (*Regionen*).[9] The sense in which a given entity can be said to *be* reflects a different specific meaning of the word "being" according to the region that it occupies. We say that the number five *is* in a very different sense from that in which an antelope is. Now in any distinction of this kind Heidegger sees the fundamental function of time at work. For the "struggle of the giants" is fought over the disputed priority of *temporal* being – the material – and *extra-temporal* being – the ideal, championed in the struggle by the "friends of the ideas." Whether positively (temporal being) or negatively (extra-temporal being), time is used to define both regions ontologically. Heidegger's thesis is that time defines all regions of being in general at the most fundamental level. He takes this to show that already at the beginnings of Greek ontology and throughout all subsequent philosophy "time is *one* 'index' for the division and demarcation of regions of being in general" (*PGZ*, 8). Ontology as such, it may be inferred, is *"temporal science [temporale Wissenschaft]"* (*GP*, 460).

An equivalent development becomes apparent in the case of the problem of the categories when we consider the solution given by Kant. This is particularly interesting in view of philosophy's preference for treating this problem as a "logical" one on the grounds that the categories are to be classed among the logical structures of judgement. Even Kant accepts and gives particular emphasis to the essential relationship between the categories and the act of judgement.[10] Yet Heidegger thinks it was Kant – alone among the philosophers of the Western metaphysical tradition – who came to recognise the fundamentally temporal and in this sense "extra-logical" origin of the categories. "The first and only one who in his investigations moved some distance of the way in the direction of the dimension of temporality, or let himself be compelled there by force of the phenomena themselves, is *Kant*" (*SZ*, 23). This interpretation is developed fully in Heidegger's second major work, *Kant und das Problem der Metaphysik* (1929). On his argument, Kant's deduction and schematism of the categories, in which their foundation as ontological predicates is carried out, are both based in time. This is confirmed by the text of the *Critique of Pure Reason* itself at least in the case of the schematism, in which Kant says explicitly: "The schemata [of the categories] are thus nothing other than *time-determinations* a priori according to rules."[11] Each category is ontologically founded in a pure transcendental time-determination. Hence the category-problem raises a metaphysical question whose resolution takes place within the horizon of time in its ontologically universal sense. In attributing this function to time Heidegger does not mean that philosophers have been conscious of their use of time as a general criterion. Indeed, he accuses Kant of evading the furthermost consequences of his discoveries (cf. *KPM*, 160ff.). Yet in spite of a lingering prejudice in favour of logic, "Kant must have had some inkling of this collapse of the rule of logic in metaphysics" (*KPM*, 244). The "temporal" character of this metaphysical question could not remain totally hidden.

2. The Task of an Ontological Phenomenology of Time

The Heideggerian renewal of the fundamental task of philosophy requires that it be rigorously demonstrated that time is the horizon of all ontological inquiry. Thus a phenomenological ontology that wants to free itself of all "free-floating constructions [...] [and] only seemingly established concepts" (*SZ*, 28) has to find a way to make time phenomenologically "visible." It needs to obtain a phenomenon of time. Even though time has long been used as an "ontological, or rather ontic criterion for the naïve discrimination of the various regions of entities" (*SZ*, 18), it has not been explicitly understood in a way consistent with its having this function. On Heidegger's view there is a prevailing "natural" or *vulgar* understanding of time (*vulgäres Zeitverständnis*) from which a natural *concept* of time is formed and establishes itself. This concept not only does not help but actively hinders the philosophically suitable conception of time as the horizon of all understanding of being. Philosophy's "spontaneous" recourse to time as criterion for the discrimination of the ontological regions implicitly takes it in an ontic sense: as if it itself had being, that is as if it were an entity of some kind. Time is seen as a given, i.e. *extant* temporal succession or – expressed in Kant's terms – as a pure one-dimensional manifold.[12] "Time is understood as a succession, as the 'flow' of the 'nows', as 'the course of time'" (*SZ*, 422). On Heidegger's diagnosis of the state of affairs, this understanding of time embodies a prevailing tendency towards the general neglect of the question of the sense of being and the resulting "blindness" of ontology.

One way that Heidegger proposes in which this tendency can be reversed and a properly clarified metaphysical interpretation of time guided by the phenomena made possible is through an analysis of the mood of boredom (*Langeweile*). When we find ourselves in this mood time appears to us in a new light and becomes strangely conspicuous. Certain phenomena of time start to show themselves. In boredom we say that time "drags," and we become acutely aware of it as something we want to make "go by faster." A conceptually rigorous analysis of boredom, however, first has to give an answer to the preliminary question: what is a mood? It is a preconception that Heidegger wants to reject to think of mood (*Stimmung*) as a "merely subjective" occurrence which affixes something like an "emotive colouring" to objects (to entities in the world). In this process of "colouring" the objects remain unaffected in themselves, which indicates that the mood is nothing "objective," merely something "subjective." This conception assumes a pre-existing subject-object relation, within the framework of which the mood "obviously" has to be attributed to the one or the other side of the relationship – and in fact comes to be attributed to the "subject." Heidegger, however, analyses mood as part of the ontological analysis in *Sein und Zeit* of the entity that we ourselves are, identified by the term of art *being-there* (*Dasein*)[13] (*SZ*, 41). One of the important intended consequences of the analysis is the overcoming of this traditional opposition of subject and object.[14]

3. Mood as an Ontological Characteristic

Because Heidegger wants to understand mood ontologically as part of his phenomenological ontological analysis, a preliminary clarification of his use of this concept is necessary. The following very brief summary gives only the basic outlines of Heidegger's ontological conception of mood.

Heidegger's term for the *ontological* character of mood, of which particular determinate moods present ontic instances, is *Befindlichkeit*, which we shall translate as *disposition* (*SZ*, 134).[15] This denotes "an original kind of being of being-there […] in which it is disclosed to itself *before* all knowing and willing and *beyond* their scope for disclosure" (*SZ*, 136). Mood is a mode of being in which we "find ourselves"[16] – indeed, mood is something that "overcomes us" (*SZ*, 136) – and in which we are disclosed to ourselves in a certain way. Our current mood is a phenomenon that involves a definite kind of self-disclosure and, at the same time, the revealing of the world of entities as a whole. It lets us see it in its "wholeness." Everyday experience confirms readily enough that when one is overcome with boredom *everything* "is boring," including oneself. And the mood of *fear*, for instance, brings with it its own disclosure of self and world; it reveals ourselves as afraid and things in the world as threatening or potentially so. "*Mood has always already disclosed being in the world as a whole*" (*SZ*, 137). Disposition is essential to our being-there as such and is thus so to speak a "category" of existence – what Heidegger calls an "existential" (*Existenzial*). It is "an *equioriginal disclosure* of world, being-there-with [*Mitdasein*] and existence of an existential fundamental kind" (*SZ*, 137).

What is characteristic of the way in which mood discloses the world is that it does not in the first instance make entities apparent one at a time, as it were, in their particularity, in consequence of which the "world" would come into view as a totality out of their subsequent "combination." Rather, mood primarily makes us aware first of all of the *whole* (*das Ganze*) to which entities belong. This is disclosed in a manner that is "beyond the scope" of any relation of disinterested knowing. Thus although the world of entities as a whole may well be contemplated cosmologically or theologically, for instance, it is not first and foremost a *known* totality in the sense of something grasped cognitively with a view to such a thing as its scientific investigation. "In fact *ontologically* we must on principle cede the primary discovery of the world to 'mere mood'" (*SZ*, 138). Hence disposition constitutes our "world-openness" (*SZ*, 137), allowing us to "find ourselves" within a space that gives to entities the possibility of showing themselves. A mood's disclosive character is just what Heidegger finds to be missing in the traditional classification of the phenomenon as something subjective and hence not "objective," as a mere qualitative modification of a subjective experience. Indeed, in reference to boredom it is easily seen that we directly qualify various things (the "objects") as "boring" (*langweilig*) as if the mood belonged to *them*. The characterisation "boring" is one "*belonging to the object* [*objektzugehörig*] and at the same time *related to the subject* [*subjektbezogen*]" (*GM*, 126). By this Heidegger wants to indicate, stated more correctly, that the phenomenon of mood makes apparent the inappropriateness of the general distinction between subject and object.

A given mood always has a certain "affect-character" which belongs to the way in which it discloses, and without which we would not consider it to be a mood at all. Heidegger describes the mood of fear, for instance, as a kind of bewildered dispiritedness (*verwirrte Gedrücktheit*) which is constituted ontologically by self-forgetting (*SZ*, 341ff.). Fear is a kind of revealing whose affective character is such that it confuses, and to a degree obscures what it at the same time reveals. Clearly the affect-character of boredom differs greatly from that of fear; it is essential that the investigation of boredom be carried out concretely, guided by the phenomena themselves.

4. The Analysis of Boredom: The Structure of Boredom

The investigation of the phenomenon of boredom proceeds in stages. As a kind of clue for the phenomenological analysis to follow, Heidegger begins with the specific mode of manifestation of the *boring entity*, the thing that we have before us when we are bored which conspicuously fails to hold our interest (*das Langweilige*, literally "that which is boring") (*GM*, 123ff.).

We call something "boring" when it somehow "holds us up" (*hält uns hin*), delays us or keeps us waiting but at the same time leaves us empty (*lässt leer*): a boring, badly written book, for instance, whose boringness is in its failure to "fill up" the time we spend reading it. This boring entity holds us up but leaves us empty. These two structural elements of *being held up* (*Hingehaltenheit*) and *being left empty* (*Leergelassenheit*) are constitutive of boredom in the way in which we experience it and provide the framework for Heidegger's subsequent phenomenological analysis (*GM*, 130). As the analysis proceeds Heidegger comes to identify more than one form of boredom, each of which requires separate investigation. It may turn out that that which holds us up and leaves us empty in a deeper sense is not identical with the "boring" entity to which we at first attribute these characteristics. Hence one of the objectives of the investigation is to determine the *specific* kind of being-held-up and being-left-empty found in each form according to the particular phenomenal character of the actual experience in question. Two different forms of boredom need not turn out to show precisely the same sort of emptiness, but may differ from one another in this respect.

5. The Analysis of Boredom. The First Form: "Something bores me"

The first concrete instance Heidegger examines is the admittedly "trivial phenomenon" (*GM*, 138) of boredom in a quite ordinary, indeed very trivial situation: being forced to wait for the next train at a station. "We are sitting, for example, in a tasteless railway station on some forgotten local line. The next train will not come for four hours" (*GM*, 140). We find ourselves overcome with boredom. In an attempt to suppress this unpleasant mood we are wont to resort to certain habitual activities. We look around unceasingly, though without success, for some pastime (*Zeit-vertreib*) or other, some way of *passing the time* or of "driving away" this superfluous time (*die Zeit zu vertreiben*) while we wait. We have begun to perceive time as dragging, moving too slowly; and we repeatedly catch ourselves in the act of looking at our watch, as if to measure how little time has passed since we last looked. This act is a symptom, as it were, of the extraordinary conspicuousness that the dragging course of time acquires in the mood of boredom.

The specific being-held-up of this first form of boredom, then, lies in our being struck with a kind of paralysis by "dragging" or "hesitating" time (*die lähmende Betroffenheit von der zögernden Zeit*) (*GM*, 148). We are not held up, strictly speaking, by any one entity in our surroundings, but by the dragging of the time (*GM*, 151ff.) which we ascertain by our almost involuntary, repeated glances at the watch. It is not so much the train which fails to arrive that holds us up, even though it is certainly the immediate *cause* of this; rather, in this *phenomenon* of boredom we feel ourselves to be held up by the "flow" of time itself, which has now taken on this persistent "hesitating" character. Time presses on us, or perhaps even oppresses us. And in being so held up we are also left empty by the things that belong to the current situation (*GM*, 155). These things are the entities that compose the "boring" environment in which we find ourselves at a complete loss. They are available and yet "offer us nothing" at the present time, no possible escape. The specific being-left-empty of this form of boredom is in these entities. They leave us empty because we cannot occupy ourselves with them in any way as a pastime, and they, too, are thus "boring." Hence the phenomenological analysis thus far has made evident the definite way in which entities come to be disclosed *as a whole* by the mood of boredom, which as a concrete instance of disposition has the character of revealing the world as such. Boredom brings with it a definite manifestation of entities as a whole and, together with them, of time. At this point in the analysis, however, the two essential elements of being held up and being left empty have been treated independently, but cannot yet be grasped as a unity (*GM*, 161ff.).

6. The Analysis of Boredom. The Second Form: "I bore myself"

Heidegger attempts to take the investigation further by looking for a form of boredom that is more original and in a certain sense *deeper* than the merely "superficial" form examined at the present stage of the analysis. This suggests the desirability of finding a "relatively extreme" case (*GM*, 165), one that stands so far as is possible in opposition to that of the first form of boredom and in which, therefore, the mood of boredom in the everyday sense seems to be altogether absent, at least at first glance. Heidegger takes the example of an invitation to a dinner-party. We are to imagine that we have allowed ourselves time for this occasion, having put work to one side for the evening; we let ourselves be "absorbed," so to speak, in the pleasant train of events. Heidegger describes the various details – good food, interesting company, engaging conversation – and makes it clear that the party itself, considered in terms of everything that goes to make up the situation, is not at all boring. In other words, this cannot be a case of the *first* form of boredom. "There is absolutely nothing to be found during the evening that might have been boring, neither the conversation nor the people, nor the setting" (*GM*, 165). And yet afterwards, reflecting on the evening and its events, we are nevertheless somehow compelled to admit to ourselves: "Yet I really was bored [*ich habe mich [...] gelangweilt*] this evening, at this party" (*GM*, 165).

There is a boredom which shows itself here in its *second* form and is deeper than that of the first because it does not lie on the surface; and there are no longer any things belonging to the situation that manifest themselves to us as "boring" and leave us empty. But can there be a boredom where no boring things are present? Heidegger sees a valuable hint at an answer to this question in the way in which the phenomenon is described by ordinary language (which for Heidegger means: in the German language). Whereas of the first form of boredom one might say *"etwas hat mich gelangweilt"* (something bored me), the appropriate way of expressing the second form is to use the *reflexive* construction: *"ich habe mich gelangweilt"* (literally: I bored *myself*). In this case the source of the boredom is not found in any determinate entity in our surroundings which we could point out. In this form of boredom, Heidegger identifies, in distinction from some determinate *boring thing* (*ein bestimmtes Langweiliges*), something indeterminate that *makes* us *bored* (*ein unbestimmtes Langweilendes*) (*GM*, 173). It is we who strictly speaking bore ourselves, and thus the corresponding emptiness of this boredom is an emptiness that "forms itself" (*bildet sich*), arising not externally but from out of our own being-there (*Dasein*) (*GM*, 180). It follows that the specific being-left-empty of this deeper boredom is not in the things that belong to the determinate situation; rather, what leaves us empty is the casualness (*Lässigkeit*) itself with which we let ourselves take part and "go along with" the proceedings (*GM*, 177). Having suspended any "serious" activities "for the time being," we have deprived ourselves of the possibility of genuinely "using up" the time and so filling this emptiness. Time no longer presses on or oppresses us (*GM*, 181). So far from becoming conspicuous in its interminable dragging, at the dinner-party the passing of time is not noticed or even noticeable, and we in fact stop experiencing time *as* passing. Rather than "flowing" in a manner which exhibits continual "dragging" or "hesitation," time shows itself without flowing at all, that is it *stands still* (*steht*) (*GM*, 183ff.). Time manifests itself in a kind of motionless present or as a standing, persisting "now" (*ein stehendes Jetzt*). The specific being-held-up of this form of boredom is in this standing "now." While being forced to wait at the station we found ourselves to be held up by the "hesitating" *course* of time. Now, in contrast, what holds us up is a time that does not "progress" at all, but stands still. Both forms of boredom bring with them a direct revealing of time, but in ways which are phenomenally distinct. In the standing "now" which we experience in this mood, past and future have undergone a modification in such a way that they dissolve into the pure present and cease to manifest themselves *as* past and future. "We, who are wholly the present for that which occurs, are cut off from our past [*Gewesenheit*] and future" (*GM*, 187).[17]

Boredom is constituted in both its forms by being held up and being left empty, and we have seen from the phenomenological analysis that the first and second forms exhibit these structures in different concrete ways (cf. *GM*, 196ff.). In the first form we are held up by the dragging course of time; in the second form, by the standing "now." We are left empty in the first form of boredom by the things which are available but "offer us nothing"; and in the second form by our own casualness, which has stopped even wanting to be "filled up" by anything. These differences should not be surprising in view of the fact that only the first form of boredom is immediately familiar to us as boredom, while the second occurs in a situation (an invitation to a party) which we at first do not even suspect of being boring. Indeed, the second form of the mood is apt to be "suppressed" by the first form, argues Heidegger, so that it goes undetected as the deeper kind of boredom that it is (*GM*, 234).

7. Excursus: The Concept of Time and the Constitution of Now-time

With the analysis of the phenomenon of boredom we appear to have reached the desired manifestation of time, and thus succeeded in making time "visible." Time should then be amenable to a philosophically rigorous conceptual analysis based in the phenomena themselves rather than arbitrary "free-floating constructions." However, the two aspects under which time has appeared have something essential in common which indicates that they are still too superficial. Time has shown itself either as a "flow" (or "stream") which was "in motion," though in a hesitating way, or as a "now" which held itself "motionless" in an enduring present. In the one or the other case time has appeared as that about which the question of its possible "moving" or "flowing" *can arise* in principle, without which it would make no sense to say that time were or were not "moving." To be sure, to say that time "flows" is not literally to attribute a motion to time – something possible only within time itself, and not a property *of* this time – how ever unavoidable we may feel this metaphor to be and to how ever great a degree it may conform to our experience of time. "Since it is not itself movement, [time] must somehow have something to do with movement," says Heidegger, paraphrasing Aristotle (*BZ*, 109; the reference is to *Phys.* Δ, 219 a). The time that is capable of being experienced as "flowing" is essentially "concerned with" movement, and so seems to acquire something of the character of movement itself. It is grasped in terms of the prevailing "natural" concept of time arising from out of the vulgar understanding of time – the concept which Heidegger regards Western metaphysics as having generally accepted without question or attempt at a fundamental critique. It is necessary, then, to consider exactly what this concept of time is. The following summary cannot present the details of Heidegger's extensive phenomenological discussion, but only give the essential outlines of this conception of time. In the summary we begin by considering only the time that "flows," not the time that stands still, since it is principally the former that the natural concept of time refers to.

It was Aristotle who first "brought the vulgar understanding of time unambiguously to a concept" (*GP*, 329). Observing the existence of a necessary connection between time and movement, Aristotle defines time as "a number of motion with respect to the 'before' and 'after'."[18] On this definition time is that which *measures* a motion. Every motion in general has a duration, which time measures. Hence time, in whose "flow" all movement takes place, is in a certain sense a "number," although clearly not in the sense in which we say that two or three (for instance) are numbers. We can call time a number in the sense that it is "that which we count"[19] when we measure the duration of a motion. All motion is thus *in* time. The "time" that is "a number of motion" is that within which natural events and historical occurrences, in general all processes of change or alteration, whether human or cosmic, take place. All entities that we find around us in the world, of which we are always somehow aware – either explicitly, such as when we turn our scientific attention to them, or in the original disposition of a mood – are in time. Aristotle's extraordinary definition of time appears, at the first glance, to be very far removed from the traditional, "natural" understanding of time as a continuous "flow" or temporal progression of time-points; but this is something Heidegger attributes to the superior clarity of Aristotle's analysis of time over those of his successors. The definition makes clear not only the specific character of the relation between "natural" time and movement, but also of the relation *we* have to it, that is in our *experience* of time.[20]

What is essential to the constitution of this time is that it is counted or in principle countable, which means that it must always be somehow accessible to us with the assistance of some kind of clock (time-measuring tool). The natural concept of time is the concept of a *clock*-time. A clock in general is any kind of physical arrangement – in other words an entity available to us in some way – that allows us to register the passage of time (*BZ*, 110), to count or "tell the time." Even where we have no specially prepared clock available, we always have at our disposal the "natural clock" provided by the sun in the sky (*SZ*, 413ff.). Our acquaintance with clock-time in the act of measuring time as it passes is thus no exceptional or only rarely encountered experience, but one which makes "perceptible" a time conforming to our common or "vulgar" understanding of time. But what kind of act is it to tell the time? It is essential to the act of telling or counting time by means of a clock that it always counts the time *now*. The counting of time is a "dating" of an arbitrarily selected moment with the "reading" that the clock gives *now* (at the respective time at which we use it). In each case this is done relative to the accuracy of the particular clock we are using – a quarter past two, six forty-eight, midday on Tuesday. But the time that the clock makes accessible is only ever *present*, not past or future time. "No clock ever shows the future or has ever shown the past" (*BZ*, 121). It always shows the time *now*. The basic act of time-measurement is the arbitrary fixing of a *now-point* (*Jetztpunkt*) in time, or for short a Now (*ein Jetzt*), an act in which time consequently comes to be perceived *as a whole* according to the paradigm of the now-point. Time as a whole is nothing but a series of successive "nows." Heidegger calls the so experienced time world-time (*Weltzeit*)[21] or now-time (*Jetzt-Zeit*) (*SZ*, 421). "This time which is made 'generally' accessible through clocks is thus so to speak discovered like an available manifold of 'nows' [*eine vorhandene Jetztmannigfaltigkeit*], although our time-measurement is not directed to time as such thematically" (*SZ*, 417). In this way time comes to be understood by the philosophical tradition after Aristotle as the "course" or "succession" of time, i.e. of the successive "nows," and this succession is conceived as infinite, irreversible and composed of homogeneous now-points in a continuous series (cf. *BZ*, 121).

In order to understand the intention of Heidegger's criticism of this natural concept of time in its metaphysical significance we must see past the apparent paradox it seems to contain. On the one hand, this concept of time, in its strict orientation towards the "now," fails to do justice to the other two dimensions of "three-dimensional" time, the dimensions of the past and the future. The natural concept of time "sees" only the present time counted by the clock, leaving the past and future out of the account. Time as a whole is simply now-time. On the other hand, to interpret the concept in such a fashion as Heidegger does appears questionable on two grounds. Firstly, it is clear that the "now" is itself only possible in virtue of the unrestricted horizon of three-dimensional time, or else it would not be possible to distinguish it *as* now, that is to distinguish it *from* the past and the future. To describe the "now" as *present* time is implicitly *also* to bring all three temporal dimensions into view in some manner, and cannot *entirely* exclude them. Secondly, the now-*manifold* or the temporal succession of now-points is of its essence infinite, admitting of no beginning or end; no first or last "now" is conceivable (cf. *SZ*, 424). Hence there seems to be, after all, no part of time remaining which this understanding of time could conceivably have "left out." What happens to be in the past or in the future at the moment is also part of the now-series in its totality. Is Heidegger's argument that the concept of time accepted by the philosophical tradition is reducible to now-time not, therefore, ultimately paradoxical? Not at all. To be sure, the natural concept of time *presupposes* three-dimensional time, without which the "now" would have no meaning; but this presupposition is one that is not then reflected in the resulting concept or in the generally prevailing, vulgar understanding of time. "The vulgar concept of time owes its provenance to a levelling down of original time" (*SZ*, 405). The "now" has its origin in three-dimensional time, of which, however, it is itself only the subsequent, inadequate and essentially truncated expression. And although the now-sequence is conceived as infinite in both directions, this is not a conception that corresponds to all three of time's dimensions in the genuine sense, since it takes the past and the future as mere modifications of the present, not as distinct dimensions in their own right. The past is understood as merely an "expired now," so to speak, one that *was* now but has "gone by," and the future as what *will be* now but is still "to come" (*SZ*, 423). The past is a "now" whose actuality is *retained* after some fashion, as a memory, for instance, and the future an *expected* "now," one we are waiting for.[22] "Then time is already construed as the present; the past is interpreted as the no-longer-present and the future as the indeterminate not-yet-present" (*BZ*, 121). Consequently the natural concept of time presupposes the full three-dimensional structure of original time, but then in fact neglects the past and the future, which it reduces to a modified present, and so fails to give adequate conceptual expression to time in the proper sense.

8. The Time Revealed in the First and Second Forms of Boredom

The two forms of boredom considered by the phenomenological analysis have succeeded only in revealing time as now-time. The second form of boredom is an experience of time as the standing "now" in which the past and the future fail to manifest themselves as such. The progress of the "stream" of time has been interrupted, and we find ourselves being held up by this "motionless" present. The first form of boredom, on the other hand, reveals time in a manner closer to our everyday experience of time, as a "flow" which has become conspicuous by its dragging or hesitating quality. Precisely because it is seen as such a "flow" or "succession," this phenomenon is of time in the sense of now-time, measurable with a clock. When overcome by boredom of this form we are constantly counting the passage of this "oppressive" time, hoping that it will start to go by faster. Thus in spite of the distinct phenomenal characters of the two forms of boredom, each has the function of revealing a time which manifests itself in one way or another in terms of the "now." But then the time which the phenomenological analysis of boredom has rendered "visible" thus far is that of the vulgar understanding, and is not adequate to the answering of metaphysical questions with their common basis in the question of the sense of being in general.

Heidegger holds that the now-time of the vulgar concept rests upon a phenomenally impoverished basis. It arises from a "levelling down" (*Nivellierung*) of original, three-dimensional time (*SZ*, 329). We have seen that now-time has in a certain sense only one dimension; the past and future are made "unnecessary" in their own right by the infinite extension of the "now" into an endless manifold. This finds expression in the *homogeneity* of the "nows" of which this infinite succession of "flowing" time is composed. The "nows" are universally measurable by the clock, and each "now" is like any other (they are homogeneous). The past, the present and the future, however, can never be like one another. But why does this "impoverishment" make the vulgar concept of time inadequate to the task of the resolution of questions in metaphysics? This concept arises from our experience of the use of a clock in the act of counting time. The "dating" of a moment in the vulgar time-series with a "reading" given by the clock, as takes place in this act, attaches a determinate time (the reading) to a worldly occurrence, which we also experience. The experience of clock-time is essentially one with the experience of an occurrence or event – a *motion* in the most general sense – of which the time that we count is the "number." But the event so experienced is an *entity*; as an event it must *be*, that is take place within the nexus of causes and effects. Hence the now-series itself with which these *extant* events are measured comes to acquire in its own manner the characteristic of being: the "now" *is* – after an admittedly somewhat obscure fashion. "The '*nows*' are thus in a certain sense *also available* [*mitvorhanden*, i.e. extant]: that is, we encounter entities *and also* the 'now'" (*SZ*, 423). Time becomes, in other words, something ontic (an entity of an unusual kind) rather than an ontological characteristic in terms of which being itself could be investigated and determined metaphysically.[23] But on Heidegger's argument as to the universal ontological significance of time in any metaphysical problem, it is precisely the essence of time in the genuine sense that this conception has missed.

9. The Analysis of Boredom. The Third Form: "It is boring for one"

Since there is an underlying connection between the structure of the two forms of boredom so far considered and time, the question arises whether there is in fact a still deeper form of boredom which reveals the essence of time more profoundly than the others (*GM*, 201ff.). There is indeed such a third form of boredom, argues Heidegger, which he refers to as deep or profound boredom (*tiefe Langeweile*), in other words a boredom which is the deepest of all, deep boredom per se. It follows from Heidegger's assertion to the effect that the first, common form has the tendency to "suppress" the deeper phenomena of boredom that this deep form, which is profounder than both the first and the second forms, must arise in a context in which the boredom is neither obvious nor familiar. There is no determinate *situation* that gives rise to this deep boredom, which Heidegger describes in the following way: "Deep boredom bores us at such a time as when we say or, better, when we silently know that *it is boring for one* [*es ist einem langweilig*]" (*GM*, 202). Whereas in the first form we find ourselves bored by the determinate things in our situation and in the second we "bore ourselves," in the third form of boredom both a determinate boring thing (*ein Langweiliges*) and an indeterminate something that makes us bored (*ein Langweilendes*) are wholly lacking. We are powerless to speak of our boredom other than by saying simply: "it is boring for one." The "it" of this peculiar expression "it is boring" is the essentially indeterminate "it" which also occurs in such a usage as "it is raining" (*es regnet*) and of which it makes no sense at all to ask *what* "it" is (*GM*, 203). And the "one" for whom it is boring is no longer properly to be referred to with the personal pronoun *we*. It is not, strictly speaking, boring *for us*, since this "one," which is wholly removed from any given, fixed situation of boringness, is no longer *I* or *you* but a wholly undifferentiated "no one" (*GM*, 203).

Because of the thoroughgoing indeterminacy that accompanies this mood, it is not possible on Heidegger's view to give an *example* in the proper sense of an occasion of deep boredom, dissociated as it is from any necessary connection with a possible concrete situation. Instead Heidegger suggests, as a "wholly non-committal provocation" to bring to mind the specific experience of deep boredom, the following: "'It is boring for one' when one walks through the streets of a large city on a Sunday afternoon" (*GM*, 204). What does he regard as striking about this experience, or an equivalent experience occurring on some other "non-committal," non-binding occasion? It is that the experience has the peculiar quality of reducing not only the entire situation and all things – all entities in the midst of which we find ourselves – but also *ourselves* to a total "indifference" (*Gleichgültigkeit*) (*GM*, 207ff.). This perfect indifference is the emptiness that belongs to this form of boredom, an emptiness encompassing *all* entities as a whole (*das Seiende im Ganzen*) (*GM*, 208). Accordingly, the specific being-left-empty of deep boredom is the utter helplessness (*Ausgeliefertheit*) of our being-there (*Dasein*) before entities which fail us as a whole (*GM*, 210). We are helpless before them because they offer us nothing whatever that we could "do" with them; utterly useless, they "leave us in the lurch."

In distinction from the state of affairs which obtained in the first form of boredom, in which entities (the things around us) left us empty in a given determinate situation by failing to provide us with a possible occupation for passing the time during some fixed period – e.g. when waiting for a train – in deep boredom, in contrast, the failure is absolute. It is not bound to any determinate situation. Rather, entities fail us *as a whole* in all their possibilities, which have now become pointless, a matter of indifference. In failing us as a whole they manifest themselves *as* so failing and *as* this "whole." Deep boredom is, then, a mood that exhibits in a relatively pure form the character of disposition of revealing – to varying degrees in each case – the world within which entities as a whole can appear. This "as-a-whole" of things in general, which is generally hidden behind the *particular* things with which we occupy ourselves, now, when we are suddenly bereft of all possible occupation, comes into the foreground. "Only when we are not specifically occupied with the things and with ourselves, and precisely then, are we overcome by this 'as a whole' [*dieses »im Ganzen«*], e.g. in genuine boredom. This is still distant when it is merely this book or this play, that occupation or this leisure activity that bores us. It breaks out when 'it is boring for one'. [...] This boredom manifests entities as a whole" (*W*, 110). Normally, when we are engaged with particular things in our environment and not in any way afflicted by boredom, we make use of the things in furthering one or other of our own "practical" possibilities. We put our own possibilities into effect by using various things (entities), e.g. in the use of a pen to write a letter.[24] In deep boredom, however, we first become genuinely aware of our possibilities in an extraordinary way because they now, in our helplessness before entities, "lie fallow." We find ourselves "referred" to the possibilities explicitly in view of their being now *refused* us; they are possibilities which we "cannot have," as the boredom is too overpowering. Heidegger interprets this "reference" to our fallow possibilities (*Verweisung auf die brachliegenden Möglichkeiten*) as the specific being-held-up of the third form of boredom (*GM*, 212). In this form of boredom the structural elements of being-held-up and being-left-empty are united in the phenomenon of the "as-a-whole" which reveals all entities in their indifference.

10. The Third Form of Boredom in its Structural Relation to Temporality

Each of the first two forms of boredom brought with it a definite way of revealing time, either the "standing" or the "flowing now," but it is hard to see any relation to time whatsoever in the third form, which seems, rather, to be altogether timeless (*GM*, 212). In it we are not made bored by a compulsion to wait for an expected event as in the first form, nor is it that we have "allowed ourselves time," as in the second, for some (in retrospect boring) social occasion or other – a time that we experience as standing still (cf. *GM*, 217). Rather, in the third form of boredom time has "expanded" in a remarkable way with the result that the "now" – whether "flowing" or "standing" – no longer manifests itself as such. Time as a whole has become a yawning, empty expanse. But this indicates that time certainly does reveal itself, although in such a manner that the "now" no longer has the kind of priority that as it were forces the past and the future into the mere periphery of the temporal phenomenon. The deep form of boredom, and only this form, is a mood that brings us directly before the phenomenon of time in the *original* sense. In this mood all entities fail us as a *whole*, which means that they have left us in the lurch with respect to all past, present *and* future possibilities. Hence the mood manifests time in all three of its dimensions equally, that is it manifests the all-encompassing *three-dimensional horizon* of time. It manifests time as the past, the present and the future. "Evidently entities as a whole are possible only insofar as entities are embraced by the simultaneously single and threefold horizon of time" (*GM*, 218). Three-dimensional time is the horizon of the total emptiness of deep boredom – a horizon which, in this boredom, becomes "visible" to us directly.

The apparent "timelessness" of deep boredom, as Heidegger argues, is due to the fact that original time is in a certain sense "beyond" the possible "flowing" or "standing" of mundane time, which we come across in the other forms of boredom (*GM*, 221). This indicates that even to raise the question of its possible "movement" is meaningless and that it cannot be understood in terms of the vulgar concept of time. In the experience of deep boredom we find that any reference to the clock has no sense. Time is not a succession but a horizon encompassing all entities, and is thus the horizon of all understanding of being. "*Temporality* [i.e. original time] assumes the function of making possible the understanding of being and hence of *making possible the thematic interpretation of being* [...], i.e. of making ontology possible" (*GP*, 323). Thus for Heidegger the metaphysical significance of boredom is that it gives us direct access of an extraordinary kind to the original phenomenon of time (temporality) rather than the more ordinary "levelled down" sort. *Sein und Zeit*, motivated by the same metaphysical problems, contains its own investigation and conceptual clarification of temporality in which the principal phenomenon is that of death experienced in the mood of Angst (cf. especially *SZ*, 265ff.). Of course, the analysis of boredom is not intended to be independent of this investigation or to replace it; on the contrary, if anything it presupposes the concepts that are first brought to light in *Sein und Zeit*.[25] Rather than proceeding independently, the analysis of boredom represents *another* "way" towards the elaboration of the question of being, just as *Sein und Zeit* itself is described as merely "*one* way" (*SZ*, 436). To be sure, the project of giving a rigorous demonstration of the interconnection between the question of being and temporality is one which Heidegger never completes in the form originally planned for the second half of *Sein und Zeit*, which remained unpublished.[26] Further treatment of Heidegger's concept of temporality and its relation to the "thematic interpretation of being," however, lies outside the scope of the present discussion.

11. The Phenomenology of Boredom as Phenomenological Ontology

In the above we have argued that Heidegger's phenomenological analysis of boredom aims at the manifestation of something he sees as fundamental to Western philosophy, and on which all questions of metaphysics turn. By analysing the "subjective" occurrence of the onset of particular moods we are able to obtain the phenomenon – as opposed to the "speculative," merely conceptually-based construction – of something "non-rational" without which metaphysical inquiry itself would not be possible, but which tends to remain hidden. This is the phenomenon of time. Time in the sense of temporality is largely "invisible" behind the more everyday phenomena of now-time, just as deep boredom comes to be suppressed by "common" boredom of the first form. Temporality is not the product of an abstract process of logical deduction, but something concrete which the phenomenologist undertakes to see and to describe. But Heidegger's attempt at such an analysis does not imply any reprehensible "subjectification" of the metaphysical investigation of "entities as entities" (ontology),[27] nor does it take place on an extraneous, extra-metaphysical excursion into psychology or anthropology.[28] Metaphysical questions, such as those dealing with the category-problem, are rooted in time, with which we, as the entities having the ability to ask such a thing as a metaphysical question, necessarily stand in a direct relationship. Not only do we stand in a relation to time, but also time, for its part, to us, emphasises Heidegger: "For its part, time stands in a relation of boredom to *us*. Hence this is the fundamental mood [*Grundstimmung*] of our philosophizing" (*GM*, 121).

The traditional approach to such an ontological problem as that of the categories, given the assumption that logic is the universal presupposition of metaphysics, would be to comprehend the essence of the categories under the "logical" concept of the assertion or the judgement. From this point of view – so frequently criticised by Heidegger – the category-problem becomes a logical problem pure and simple. And this approach is in keeping with the traditional conception of the basic character of *truth*, which holds that truth in general is the province of logic and that "the 'location' of truth is the assertion [*Aussage*] (the judgement [*Urteil*])" (*SZ*, 214). But Heidegger distinguishes from this the properly phenomenological conception of truth. This attempts to reach a more fundamental definition of the essence of truth, according to which an assertion can only *be true* on the basis that it *reveals* (*entdeckt*), that is that it lets us see the entity – the "subject" of the assertion in the traditional sense – as it is (see *SZ*, 218). This revealing is itself "the truth" in a more direct sense. This original truth is grounded in the disclosure of our being-there (*SZ*, 226).

Hence an attempt guided by the phenomenological method to discover the truth behind a metaphysical question recognises that this truth is dependent upon the truth (in the phenomenological sense) of time. It depends upon the *revealing* of time (its "truth" as phenomenon), in which the question itself, as a metaphysical question, has its origin. The analysis of boredom in its first two forms and the discussion of clock-time, however, showed that the direct manifestation of time in the original sense is for the most part prevented by the derivative but more familiar presentation of now-time. The manifestation of temporality, which is usually hidden from us, must first be won. Heidegger's inquiry into boredom is therefore neither anthropology nor "cultural critique," for instance, but the pursuit of this *ontological* task by means of a revealing experience of deep boredom. He understands this deep form of boredom as something "drifting back and forth in the abysses of our being-there like a silent fog" (*W*, 110), but not always revealed as such, instead constantly covered up by the first and second, superficial forms of this mood. Only an exacting analysis of the phenomenon of boredom can determine what it is that deep boredom reveals. Thus Heidegger's analysis of boredom has to be understood as the attempt to strike a path towards a non-traditional solution to a series of traditional philosophical problems, and therefore to demonstrate what is first asserted with special emphasis in *Sein und Zeit*: that it is "*only as phenomenology*" that ontology is possible (*SZ*, 35).

NOTES

[1] In the following all citations from works by Heidegger, which in some cases have multiple editions and dates of publication, for ease of identification give the initial letters of the work's German title, as is done here. All such abbreviations used refer to the following editions: *Der Begriff der Zeit* (Frankfurt/Main: Vittorio Klostermann, 2004) [*BZ*]; *Die Grundbegriffe der Metaphysik: Welt – Endlichkeit – Einsamkeit*, 1983. 3rd ed. (Frankfurt/Main: Vittorio Klostermann, 2004) [*GM*]; *Die Grundprobleme der Phänomenologie*, 1975. 3rd ed. (Frankfurt/Main: Vittorio Klostermann, 1997) [*GP*]; *Kant und das Problem der Metaphysik*, 1929. 6th ed. (Frankfurt/Main: Vittorio Klostermann, 1998) [*KPM*]; *Metaphysische Anfangsgründe der Logik im Ausgang von Leibniz*, 1928. 2nd ed. (Frankfurt/Main: Vittorio Klostermann, 1990) [*MAL*]; *Sein und Zeit*, 1927. 18th ed. (Tübingen: Max Niemeyer, 2001) [*SZ*; *Was ist das – die Philosophie?* 1956. 11th ed. (Stuttgart: Klett-Cotta, 2003) [*WP*]; *Wegmarken*, 1976. 3rd ed. (Frankfurt/Main: Vittorio Klostermann, 2004) [*W*]. All translations from the German are my own.

[2] Emphasis original. In all further quotations all italic text, if any, is so in the original.

[3] The importance of mood to Heidegger's philosophy as a general principle is noticed, for one, by his biographer Rüdiger Safranski: "He [Heidegger] criticises the philosophy that pretends to begin with thoughts. In reality, says Heidegger, it begins with a *mood*, with wonder, Angst, care, curiosity, jubilation," Rüdiger Safranski, *Ein Meister aus Deutschland: Heidegger und seine Zeit*, 1994. 3rd ed. (Frankfurt/Main: Fischer Taschenbuch Verlag, 2003), p. 15.

[4] Immanuel Kant, *Kritik der reinen Vernunft*, 1781/1787 (Hamburg: Felix Meiner, 2003), A 95.

[5] On "deduction" cf. B 129ff. = A 95ff.; on "schematism" cf. B 176ff. = A 137ff.

[6] Time is "a pure form of sensible intuition" (*eine reine Form der sinnlichen Anschauung*), Kant, *Kritik der reinen Vernunft*, B 47 = A 31.

[7] In a similar vein Heidegger in *Sein und Zeit* denies that the "question of being" has to do with "the most general of generalities" and suggests that it is in fact "*at once the most fundamental [die prinzipiellste] and the most concrete question*" (*SZ*, 9).

[8] Plato, *The Sophist*, 246 a; cf. *SZ*, 2.

[9] Edmund Husserl, *Ideen zu einer reinen Phänomenologie und phänomenologischen Philosophie*, 1913. 6th ed. (Tübingen: Max Niemeyer, 2002), p. 19.

[10] Kant, *Kritik der reinen Vernunft*, B 95ff. = A 70ff. et passim.

[11] Ibid., B 184 = A 145.

[12] Ibid., B 102 = A 77 et passim.

[13] It should be noted that in the following this term (*Dasein*) will always be translated *being-there* rather than being left untranslated as often occurs in the literature.

[14] On Heidegger's break with subject-philosophy, cf. in particular Friedrich-Wilhelm von Herrmann, *Subjekt und Dasein: Grundbegriffe von „Sein und Zeit"*, 1974. 3rd ed. (Frankfurt/Main: Vittorio Klostermann, 2004). The basic argument that Heidegger's analysis of being-there is misunderstood if seen as a mere "further progression" in the tradition of subject-philosophy is stated succinctly on pp. 9ff.

[15] On the justifiability of this translation, cf. *Was ist das – die Philosophie?*, in which Heidegger suggests the French *dis-position* (with deliberate hyphenation) as a philosophically appropriate translation for the German *Stimmung* (mood) (*WP*, 26).

[16] Cf. particularly Boris Ferreira, *Stimmung bei Heidegger: Das Phänomen der Stimmung im Kontext von Heideggers Existenzialanalyse des Daseins* (Dordrecht: Kluwer, 2002). Ferreira points out the appropriateness in this context of the semantic overlap that exists between *sich befinden* (approximately: to feel) and *sich finden* (to find oneself), of which Heidegger was of course aware (pp. 132ff.).

[17] Here Heidegger uses the idiosyncratic term *Gewesenheit*, which roughly denotes the past (*Vergangenheit*) but would more literally be translated "having been" or "beenness." His reasons for avoiding the usual word *Vergangenheit* cannot be adequately discussed here (cf. especially *SZ*, 325ff.).

[18] Aristotle, *Physics*, 219 b; cf. *SZ*, 421.

[19] Ibid., 219 b.

[20] It is in this sense that Heidegger describes Aristotle's definition of time as an "*access-definition* or *-characterisation*" (*GP*, 362), meaning a definition of time in terms of our mode of access to it, that is in terms of the way in which we experience it.

[21] For the purposes of rendering as clear as possible and in basic terms the *results* of Heidegger's analysis, the present discussion contains a slight oversimplification which deserves notice. Now-time of itself *already* implies a levelling down (*Nivellierung*) of the full structure of world-time, and *therefore* also of temporality (*Zeitlichkeit*) (cf. *SZ*, 422ff.). Hence although the simple *identification* of world-time and now-time is not strictly valid,

nonetheless the two essentially belong together as both arising from temporality's *inauthentic* "temporal self-generation" (*Zeitigung*) (cf. *SZ*, 329 et passim).

[22] The comportment that allows us to encounter something like a "now" is described as an "expectant-retaining making-present" (*ein gewärtigend-behaltendes Gegenwärtigen*). Heidegger uses this strange expression to denote, roughly speaking, the unity of the act of expecting a present "to come," retaining a present "gone by" and directly "perceiving" the current present (cf. *SZ*, 406ff., especially 408).

[23] In this context Heidegger remarks that Aristotle's treatise on time found in the *Physics* begins with the question whether and how time *is*, i.e. in what sense time is to be regarded as an entity (cf. *GP*, 330ff.).

[24] In the context of the analysis in *Sein und Zeit* of entities belonging to the environment (*Umwelt*) Heidegger lays emphasis on the fact that these entities only "have possibilities" of their own – such as that of the pen, which offers the possibility of writing – in virtue of *our* possibilities. We "see" possibilities in these tools because of *our* possible uses for them (cf. in particular *SZ*, 144ff.).

[25] Thus Heidegger mentions that in the context of the lecture he can do no more than "merely to intimate" (*lediglich anzudeuten*) the time-character of boredom (*GM*, 217); to give a full conceptual clarification would obviously require an extensive prior discussion of temporality.

[26] On the fate of the promised "second half" of *Sein und Zeit* cf. Friedrich-Wilhelm von Herrmann, *Heideggers „Grundprobleme der Phänomenologie": Zur „Zweiten Hälfte" von „Sein und Zeit"* (Frankfurt/Main: Vittorio Klostermann, 1991), especially pp. 17ff. As is hinted at by the title of this work, Heidegger does present some of the relevant material in his lecture-series *Die Grundprobleme der Phänomenologie* (*GP*), which he delivered shortly after the publication of *Sein und Zeit*.

[27] To guard against a similar misapprehension Heidegger mentions that the "ontico-ontological priority" (*ontisch-ontologischer Vorrang*) of being-there (*Dasein*) in ontological inquiry "evidently has nothing in common with a bad subjectification of the universe of entities" (*SZ*, 14).

[28] To be sure, in *Kant und das Problem der Metaphysik* Heidegger advocates what he calls a *philosophical* anthropology: a metaphysical undertaking, properly understood, and therefore one which has nothing to do with the "somatic, biological or psychological" investigation of the human being (*KPM*, 208ff.). By "philosophical anthropology" Heidegger in fact means an inquiry akin to the analysis of being-there carried out in *Sein und Zeit* – an analysis whose methodology he distinguishes from such disciplines as psychology, sociology and ethnography (*SZ*, 51).

WORKS CITED

Aristotle. *Physics*. Hamburg: Felix Meiner, 1987.

———. *Metaphysics*. Hamburg: Felix Meiner, 1989.

Ferreira, Boris. *Stimmung bei Heidegger: Das Phänomen der Stimmung im Kontext von Heideggers Existenzialanalyse des Daseins*. Dordrecht: Kluwer, 2002.

Heidegger, Martin. *Der Begriff der Zeit: Vortrag vor der Marburger Theologenschaft Juli 1924.* 1989. English-German ed. published as: *The Concept of Time.* Oxford: Blackwell, 1992. [*BZ*]

———. *Die Grundbegriffe der Metaphysik: Welt – Endlichkeit – Einsamkeit.* 1983. Frankfurt a. M.: Vittorio Klostermann, 2004. [*GM*]

———. *Die Grundprobleme der Phänomenologie.* 1975. 3rd ed. Frankfurt a. M.: Vittorio Klostermann, 1997. [*GP*]

———. *Kant und das Problem der Metaphysik.* 1929. 6th ed. Frankfurt a. M.: Vittorio Klostermann, 1998. [*KPM*]

———. *Metaphysische Anfangsgründe der Logik im Ausgang von Leibniz.* 1928. 2nd ed. Frankfurt a. M.: Vittorio Klostermann, 1990. [*MAL*]

———. *Sein und Zeit.* 1927. 18th ed. Tübingen: Max Niemeyer, 2001. [*SZ*]

———. *Was ist das – die Philosophie?* 1956. 11th ed. Stuttgart: Klett-Cotta, 2003. [*WP*]

———. *Wegmarken.* 1976. Frankfurt a. M.: Vittorio Klostermann, 2004. [*W*]

Herrmann, Friedrich-Wilhelm von, *Heideggers „Grundprobleme der Phänomenologie": Zur „Zweiten Hälfte" von „Sein und Zeit".* Frankfurt a. M.: Vittorio Klostermann, 1991.

———. *Subjekt und Dasein: Grundbegriffe von „Sein und Zeit".* 1974. 3rd ed. Frankfurt a. M.: Vittorio Klostermann, 2004.

Husserl, Edmund. *Ideen zu einer reinen Phänomenologie und phänomenologischen Philosophie.* 1913. 6th ed. Tübingen, Max Niemeyer, 2002.

Kant, Immanuel. *Kritik der reinen Vernunft.* 1781/1787. Hamburg: Felix Meiner, 2003.

Plato. *The Sophist.* Stuttgart: Philipp Reclam, 1990.

Safranski, Rüdiger. *Ein Meister aus Deutschland: Heidegger und seine Zeit,* 1994. 3rd ed. Frankfurt a. M.: Fischer Taschenbuch Verlag, 2003.

CHAPTER 5

Beckett's Boredom

James Phillips

Beckett is sometimes conspicuously tedious. The conspicuousness warns against interpreting the boredom of the audience or reader as a response to a shortcoming in the author's artistic ability. Beckett is not alone in twentieth-century art in questioning, even embracing that which the good taste of previous eras judged negatively. Philosophically, however, Beckett's new relationship to boredom can be profitably compared to Heidegger's account of boredom as a revelation from which the subject is shut off. In this light, the boredom in Beckett's work can be seen not as a judgement on the world, but as the world's judgement on the subject. Adorno is similarly not insensitive to the insignificance of the boring because for him spirit is self-questioning and not the contradictory reification of a spirit distinct from the boring. Heidegger's and Adorno's philosophical analyses help to situate the ways in which Beckett's work involves a redefinition of art's revelation and its relationship to metaphysics.

Now and again in his writings Beckett proceeds by way of permutations or reflections on permutations. In *Molloy* there are the pages devoted to the problem of the optimal rotation of sixteen sucking stones among the pockets of the narrator's greatcoat. *Film* includes a scene in which a cat and a dog are by turns ushered from the room and unwittingly readmitted. And the dramaticule *Quad* consists of instructions for the repetitious, interweaving movements of four similarly dressed figures. But this permutational aspect of Beckett's work is at its most naked and relentless in the novel *Watt*. Without the meditative perplexity of *Molloy*, without the slapstick of *Film*, and without the formulaic conciseness of at least the script of *Quad*, nothing curtails or relieves the monotony of its mechanical variations. One of the many series is set up in the following way: "With regard to the so important matter of Mr Knott's physical appearance, Watt had unfortunately little or nothing to say. For one day Mr Knott would be tall, fat, pale and dark, and the next thin, small, flushed and fair, and the next sturdy, middlesized, yellow and ginger ..."[1] Having given the twelve descriptive terms of which the series is composed, Beckett continues the sentence for the further 78 groupings that make up the total number of permutations. Let us say that the effect of such a passage is boredom. As nothing needs to be decided on this point, the statement does not suffer from being left in the condition of an hypothesis. What is at stake here is not an attempt to determine the psychological norm in the reception of a given text, but rather the question of what place boredom might occupy in a philosophy of art.

Beckett courts the boring. This is the most conspicuous perversity of his art. The passage in *Watt* on Mr Knott's physical appearance drives towards a "Too much" that is anything but the declaration of the Kantian sublime. In its disavowal of the sublime, the passage could not be less romantic. The driving aspiration of romantic art is alien to it. Instead of overtaxing our power of comprehension, it undertaxes it. In the *Critique of the Power of Judgment* Kant speaks of the sublime as the moment in which the imagination finds itself confronted with something that exceeds its capacity for comprehension. Before various manifestations of Nature the spectator's aesthetic (i.e., perceptual) comprehension is confounded and the faculty of Reason steps in to make sense of the magnitude and force of what is beheld. It is the Ideas of Reason that furnish us with a horizon within which the excessive power and size of a storm at sea or a waterfall, for whose correct estimation the imagination can discover within itself no aesthetic measure (the sense organs are unable to hold together an image of the whole of that with which they are presented), continues to be comprehended, albeit not in the same way. That which defeats our sensuous comprehension does not defeat our rational comprehension. The world, as the sum-total of all representations, can never be sensuously present: it is not a fact that we run up against, but an Idea of Reason. It is that in us which encompasses even those phenomena whose excessive magnitude and force scrambles the system of measures by which we negotiate everyday life, by which we organise the spaces we inhabit, relating them to the aesthetic measure that is the lived experience of our human bodies.

Before the boring there is also a breaking point, but this breaking point is accompanied by a declaration, not of "Too much," but of "Too little." In its guileless sycophancy towards comprehensibility, in its ready acquiescence to its own exhaustive formularisation, the boring feeds the conceit of the Kantian faculty of the understanding and overfeeds it. The boring stands before us in the complete destitution of its self-evidence. We recognise it as what it is, without uncertainty or vacillation. Holding the key to it, the concept under which it is to be subsumed in recognising it as what it is, we proceed to a supplementary recognition – the recognition of the object as boring. The understanding runs through its epistemic procedures in working up perceptions to a recognition, and if it does not stop there, but goes on to a further recognition of the object it faces as boring, it then truly comes to a standstill, and before the finished business of the boring it begins to shudder in its inactivity and the pain of this inactivity. While the unmysteriousness of the boring at first corroborates the procedures of the understanding, this unmysteriousness soon becomes an affront. The pain of the boring is proof of the understanding's guilty conscience, of what Adorno calls the "disenchantment of the concept." The understanding seeks the extinction of mystery and is nonetheless troubled by unmysteriousness. An art of the boring, which is a romantic art at least insofar as it adopts a critical stance towards conceptuality, works upon this contradiction in the faculty of understanding.

An art of the boring, by lexical necessity, cannot pre-date romanticism: the word "bore" does not appear in English prior to the middle of the eighteenth century. Earlier one may have fidgeted, felt listless or succumbed to accidie, but one could not have admitted to boredom. The word articulates a species of withdrawal from the environment in which one finds oneself, a shrinking back that is nonetheless distinct from abhorrence. Comparable to the gradual vitiation of affect in the meaning of the words "dreadful," "awful," "terrible," etc., "boredom" marks the historical boredom with abhorrence (orthographically the Spanish "*aburrir*" still maintains closer ties with the Latin "*abhorrere*," although it has undergone the same semantic shift). It is a secular as well as involuntary asceticism. It is a secular asceticism because it is a withdrawal from the world in order to pass judgment on it without, nonetheless, another world against which it might be judged. And it is an involuntary asceticism because it is not the subject that formulates this judgment: the subject, instead, has this judgment handed down to it and can only appeal against it (by trying to cook up reasons for an interest in the world). To characterise boredom as a modern phenomenon because it is an expression of the autonomous secular subject is therefore one-sided. Of course, in boredom the world as a whole is held up before the subject and found wanting: Greek wonder and Christian humility turn into affectations in the face of the irredeemable tawdriness of everything that is. But boredom is an affliction of the secular subject and as an affliction it is at best an equivocal proof of the latter's self-assertion and independence.

For Heidegger, in his 1929-30 lecture course *The Fundamental Concepts of Metaphysics*, what properly asserts itself in boredom is time. With this contention, Heidegger's account adheres to the German word for boredom, "*Langeweile*," whose two components "*lang*" ("long") and "*Weile*" ("while") already settle the question of the relevance of time. With the English "boredom" and its contested etymology – the French "*bourrer*" ("to cram") has been entertained only tentatively as the source – less has been decided in advance. Beside the German "*Langeweile*" with the perspicuousness of its roots, "boredom" is an inscrutable interloper. In one respect, this places a theoretical account in English at a disadvantage, because the word does not open up to an encompassing semantic network: "boredom" is itself ascetic with regard to the language in which it features. Bearing this asceticism and uncanniness in mind does not entail being on one's guard against Heidegger's exposition of the temporal nature of boredom, since what

Heidegger names as time and discerns in the experience of boredom is similarly uncanny and inscrutable – it is not time as we generally understand it.

A motive for discussing Heidegger's lecture course in conjunction with Beckett[2] is to raise the question whether Beckett is an end or a beginning, whether the activist boredom of his works pursues minimalism to strip back the world until it is its own definitive condemnation or marks the very opening up of the world.[3] This is a question for which Heidegger clears the way by refusing the prevailing negative evaluations of boredom. Boredom, for Heidegger, offers a chance to interrogate the conception of the world on which boredom passes judgment and of whose limitations boredom first makes us aware. In its revelatory excess boredom resembles wonder: the egoistic thrill of wonder, missing from boredom, is a specific, and here comparatively inessential difference.[4] As in the analysis of anxiety in *Being and Time*, Heidegger in his exposition of boredom shows a *poète-maudit* complicity with the distasteful and the distressing, yet since it is not at the dictate of an inverted aesthetic sensibility, Heidegger does not stop in nineteenth-century Paris but follows a secret passageway from there to ancient Greece. In boredom wonder returns without being recognised as wonder, without admitting us; instead, it passes sentence on the conception of the world with which we have become embroiled. Boredom is the dissatisfaction not so much we feel with the world as wonder feels with positivism – the modernity of boredom is dependent on the modernity of positivism.[5]

This is to leap ahead to a summary of Heidegger's account that furthermore interprets it in the light of certain critical strands in his thinking as a whole. In the lecture course from 1929-30, Heidegger explains his philosophical engagement with boredom and the general aversion for boredom with reference to the larger theme of attunement:

> Boredom in the ordinary sense is disturbing, unpleasant, and unbearable. For the ordinary understanding all such things are also of little value, they are unworthy and to be condemned. Becoming bored is a sign of shallowness and superficiality. Whoever sets a proper task for his or her life and gives it content does not need to fear boredom and is secure in the face of it. Yet it is hard to tell which is the greater in this morality – its hypocritical self-assuredness or its banality. However none of this – the fact that ordinary understanding makes such judgments about boredom – is accidental, but has its reasons. One decisive reason for misunderstanding boredom is the failure to appreciate the essence of attunement in general.[6]

Boredom, as it is generally understood, is a "sign of shallowness and superficiality." Heidegger here wishes to record the verdict on boredom in the early decades of the twentieth century, a verdict which presumably it is uncontentious to claim is still upheld. Boredom has lost its nineteenth-century cultural cachet.[7] It no longer testifies to the oversized soul of a Byron or a French dandy, having become simply childish petulance. The fault attributed to boredom is the prematurity of its judgment on life. It does not take life with the requisite seriousness, when taking life seriously means plunging into it and thus precisely not withdrawing from it in boredom. The moralising of this disapprobation of boredom has its roots, for Heidegger, in a "failure to appreciate the essence of attunement in general." Boredom is an attunement before it is, if ever correctly, a judgment on the world on the part of an ego. Boredom is one way in which the world of human existence is attuned, one way in which it opens itself up and shows itself. As an attunement, as a mood, boredom is not simply a subjective and emotional patina on an objective, independently existing state of affairs. It is this reduction of attunement to pathology that Heidegger seeks to contest.

In this task of an acknowledgement of moods, Nietzsche is an obvious, if not the only precursor. Nietzsche and Heidegger both contribute to a polemic against the conception of modern science as the dispassionate, moodless observation of what is. In *The Genealogy of Morals* Nietzsche traces the modern critical attitude back to the Christian mortification of the flesh, making light of all critiques of Christianity, his own included ("Don't come to me with science when I ask for the natural antagonist of the ascetic ideal"[8]). The world is believed to show itself to modern science as it is, because Christianity has led us to believe in the possibility of holding ourselves in check, of preventing our desires from interfering with our perceptions. For Nietzsche, this abnegation is fraudulent, since at the basis of the commitment to the idea of objectivity is the will to power. Nietzsche's doctrine of the will to power does not convert into the thesis that everything is subjective (to oppose subjectivity to objectivity would be to little effect, in any case, given their definitional interdependence), since the will to power is not a faculty under the command of the subject. The phenomenon of boredom with oneself and the world, to which Nietzsche is not blind (as witnessed by the soothsayer's diagnosis in Part Two of *Thus Spake Zarathustra*), is thus a legitimate obstacle to identifying the ubiquity of the will to power with the self-assertion of the subject.

Yet with respect to the way in which it is generally viewed nowadays, boredom is sheer self-indulgence. It is the peevish vanity in which a subject asserts itself and pretends to the authority to pass judgment on the world as a whole. Boredom is an interpersonal stratagem of the subjective will to power that is transparent to everyone. But in this assessment no space is given to the unpleasantness of boredom, the boredom of loneliness, and to the fact that the subject suffers from it and would rather not assert its autonomy at all than assert it in this way. Boredom may be an occasion for the subject's judgment on the world, yet it is also a power to which the subject falls victim. Boredom is an expression of the subject's autonomy that first creates this autonomy and, moreover, creates it as an affliction.

Heidegger reconfigures the debate surrounding boredom. Whereas for the bored boredom tells us something about the world (its triteness) and whereas for the prevailing, negative understanding boredom tells us something about the bored (their superciliousness), for Heidegger boredom tells us something about the larger conception of the world that is the horizon of sense within which the bored still remain when they withdraw from the conception of the world with which they are bored.[9] And inasmuch as boredom tells us something about a more fundamental conception of the world, it is not a "sign of shallowness and superficiality." Heidegger calls boredom an attunement (*Stimmung*) not because he wants to maintain the notion of a subject in distinction from the world with which it enters into various attunements. It is not a question of independently existing parties. Attunement, instead, indicates the variety of moods (*Stimmungen*) in which the world of human existence discloses itself. There is always a mood (objectivity is itself a mood) and it arises neither from the side of the subject nor from the side of its environment, but rather from their essential solidarity, from the unity of Being-in-the-world. Boredom is the mood in which Heidegger's more encompassing conception of the world asserts itself, passing sentence on the smaller so-called objective world and yet exacting the penalty from the autonomous subject bored with this world.

Boredom breaks the spell of our engagements because it disrupts the understanding of temporality in which act follows upon act, in which time is something we *have*, a quantity we know how to manage and to apportion. In boredom there is too much time. It throws the clocks out of kilter. Boredom abducts us to another understanding of temporality, within which we lose the bearings otherwise assured by the movements of clocks and the passage of the sun. Temporally we become idiots since we cannot explain to others the different rhythm of time into which we have been transported. And as we are unable to explain it, they become impatient with us. Our boredom bores them – it is a self-indulgent idiosyncrasy. But as an experience of time, boredom, for Heidegger, is irreducible to a hermetically sealed subject. The hermetically sealed subject, which is the starting point of dogmatic scepticism's incomprehensible thought experiment, can have no experience of time (and hence no experience at all and no existence) because it disavows the *possibility* that something might happen *to* it. The breach that boredom opens is not between "universal" time and subjective caprice, but between the recognised codes of positivism (the stable, "objective" world) and originary, existential temporality (the time we are): "*Boredom springs from the temporality of Dasein.* Boredom [...] arises from a quite determinate way and manner in which our own temporality temporalizes itself."[10] The temporality specific to an individual existence is the temporality in which an existence is an exposure to the world: it is meaningless to talk of a specific temporality other than in terms of the specific exposure to the possibility that something might happen to existence. Boredom privatises, not by withdrawing the subject from the world but by individuating the exposure of an existence to its world.

Can the temporal aspect, however, of boredom be interpreted differently? Is what is oppressive in boredom's dilation of time the conviction, rather, that nothing *can* now happen *to* us? This conviction, which in bravery is uplifting, is debilitating in boredom. The experience of time, which rests on an exposure to the world, on the openness to possibility by which time overreaches the present, becomes in boredom proof of an invulnerability to the world. But again, the pain of boredom, the fact that it is an affliction, means that it is an equivocal proof of the subject's autonomy. Even though the subject may in boredom feel convinced that nothing will happen to it, this conviction of invulnerability is grounded in the experience of its vulnerability with regard to time: boredom is a possibility that befalls it. And as Malone says, "Nothing is more real than nothing."[11]

In the history of twentieth-century theatre, Beckett is the proper name of the boredom in which naturalism (broadly understood by the aspiration to represent everyday reality faithfully) expired in the shadow of cinema. His plays are the honesty of this death. Where the cinema is able to convince at once of the veracity of its world, the naturalistic stage had to rely on an ever longer line of credit with its audience, on an increasingly begrudged suspension of disbelief, until the point at which, provincial productions and self-conscious revivals aside, there were no longer any investors, no longer any takers for the game. Overdrawn and friendless, the naturalistic stage had become a power of tedium. Objects on stage lost their naturalness and acquired, in its place, a ponderous and frequently fatal meaningfulness. Incapable of matching the realism of cinema, the naturalistic stage could offer only promissory notes and mere symbols of reality in the form of the props and costumes all too desperately intended to call up an entire environment. The audience sees through the fragments and their artifice and is bored. Brecht's earlier response to the breakdown in the collusion in the construction of reality was the attempt to appropriate this breakdown, configuring it as a propaedeutic alienation effect in a pedagogic programme. Beckett, by contrast, chooses not to try to fight off boredom with sententiousness. Indeed, he gives it its head.[12] The stage does not pull itself out of its vacancy to create, together with the audience, actors and props, a world. Giving up its mythopoetic function, Beckett's stage ceases to be the rallying point of a community. It is the scene of the failure of communal storytelling. Does this failure have to be taken as a metaphor of the failure of community as such? Or is there instead a radically different conception of

community in the boredom of Beckett's theatre, namely, a community that is
not bound together by myth?

Beckett's theatre stands back from an engagement with a constructed
world – where the naturalistic theatre bored, Beckett's theatre is itself bored.
In its disengagement Beckett's theatre is bored, rather than reflective. Its
characters are clowns, rather than thinkers. Krapp might even be called a
thinker who has turned into a clown. *Krapp's Last Tape* begins with some
slapstick with a banana peel: whereas a clown performing for children can
get by with old business because it is new at least to the audience, by and
large the audience of *Krapp's Last Tape* is left to wonder why it is being
served up such stale fare (it cannot be expected to laugh).[13] The disruptive
function of the clown, whether in relation to the grave proceedings of a
Shakespearean tragedy or the perilous feats of skill in a circus, cannot come
into play where there is nothing to disrupt. Beckett gives the stage over to
clowns and thereby prevents it from turning into the romantic theatre of
reflection (with which Beckett's theatre notwithstanding shares a sense of
worldlessness and an awareness of play).[14] The audience in a theatre,
listening and watching with an energy for attentiveness syphoned off from
the capacity for action suspended by the adoption of the spectatorial attitude,
and conscious of its disengagement from the events played out on the stage,
is predisposed to reflection … and to boredom. While the theatre cannot hope
to compete, by means of ingenious sets and unaffected acting, with the
veracity of the worlds that the cinema shows, a bad night at the theatre can
rouse monsters of boredom to which the spectator of even the worst film is
never prey. With a film our disengagement from the events it shows is a fact:
what we see is a reproduction of something over and done with.[15]
Disengagement is thus not asked of us by the conventions of cinema-going.
With a play our disengagement from the events it shows is an act, more
precisely, an act against action: we are asked to accept, on one level, that the
actors on stage are in another time and place from us, i.e., that different
conventions of behaviour apply to them and that we should not disturb them.
And because we are made a party to the performance, because the
performance is for our benefit and we are expected to applaud it, when the
performance is boring, the boredom is all the fiercer for the shame and anger
of complicity. In the power to awaken boredom the ancient art of theatre does
not give ground to the new medium of cinema.

Beckett is open to boredom. This is something whose possibilities and
ramifications he does not leave to an inadequate cast to explore. It is a topic
over which he himself wishes to look the reader in the eye. In his work, as is
clear from the sighs of "What tedium" with which Malone, for example,
breaks off his stories, boredom is not the preserve of the reader. His writing
reaches out to claim as its own the boredom by which a reader's
estrangement from a work expresses itself. The reader is left without an

unambiguous means of escape (and an escape, to be truly an escape, cannot be ambiguous) since the rejection of the work, by means of which the reader asserts a distance and independence from it, has been pre-empted. The etiquette between creator and consumer is flouted. At the moment when the reader is to pass judgment on the work of art, the author intervenes and supplants the judge, a *deus ex machina* that confounds the terms of the sentence.

But to interpret Beckett's treatment of boredom as a stratagem for encircling the reader is arguably to miss a chance to interrogate the understanding of art propagated by what Heidegger discusses as the metaphysics of subjectity. If this opportunity is not taken up, the phenomenon of boredom risks being converted here into the will of the author, whereby boredom's genuine provocation – the horror of its vacuity – is disregarded in favour of everyday intelligibility. The meaninglessness of boredom quickly becomes meaningful: it becomes evidence of the artist's mastery over intractable material. Boredom at last allows itself to be "spiritualised," which is to say domesticated under the stamp of *homo faber*.

Is it the philistine who is bored by Beckett? Or does philistinism display itself in the very reluctance to be bored? The always tenuous distinction between philistinism and bourgeois art-worship here collapses. The transubstantiation of Beckett's work into symbols, cultural criticism and observations on the "human condition" is arguably a reaction against the raw "fact" of boredom.[16] Beckett, once he has been construed as the author who steals a march on the disaffected reader, is paired up with the reader who sees through everything to its "real" meaning. For an interpretative practice that lives in dread of the sheer phenomenality of boredom, of the thought that the object under scrutiny is nothing more than what it appears to be, this pair of figures serves to articulate the view of the work of art as but a cipher of spirit ("everything must be meaningful"). The philistinism of this dread lies in its disregard for whatever in the work of art is not spirit and which, in its difference from spirit, has always been constitutive of the problematic metaphysical identity of art. In looking too quickly for the "meaning" of Beckett's art, in wanting to be done too quickly with that which is not already spirit in his works, such philistinism assumes that for metaphysics the identities of art and metaphysics are questions that have been answered, that needed to be answered and were. But philosophy does not begin in wonder as in a predicament of indecision from which it has to extricate itself in order to be philosophy.

To heed the provocation of boredom is to rethink the irreducibility that metaphysics has always attributed to art and against which metaphysics has defined itself. The provocation of boredom is the very poverty of its provocation. It does not openly raise a challenge to metaphysics and incite its appropriation. That which is boring has nothing to say. It is meaningless while nonetheless concealing its meaninglessness as an issue for metaphysics. It is boring by virtue of its transparency and the ease with which its meaning is grasped. That which is boring bores because it comes too late: it reiterates with excruciating clarity what has long been familiar. The provocation of boredom is not the primeval meaninglessness that confronts spirit and in defiance of which, in dialectical contamination with which spirit first consolidates its own meaningfulness. The provocation of boredom is the meaninglessness immanent to spirit as its own historical exhaustion. The meanings on which spirit has turned its back cease to be meaningful without acquiring any of the agonistic lustre of absolute meaninglessness. They are the detritus of spirit in its passage through history. Their meaninglessness is not the dialectical truth of the meaning of spirit. It is not the a-signifying at the heart of the definition of the signifying, but rather the merely insignificant.

The meagreness of boredom is its uncanniness. Boredom is both within and without spirit. Its meaninglessness cannot be pinned down. It is irreducible to spirit but not in the sense that its difference from spirit can be supposedly isolated and recognised as such (the distinctness of any such difference belies the claim that it has departed from spirit's sphere of the establishment of distinctions). Hegel, in the Preface to his *Philosophy of Right*, intimates that boredom is the proper business of spirit: "As the thought of the world, [philosophy] appears only at a time when actuality has gone through its formative process and attained its completed state. [...] When philosophy paints its grey on grey, a shape of life has grown old, and it cannot be rejuvenated, but only recognized, by the grey in grey of philosophy."[17] What should be heard in this passage is not a note of resignation. Philosophy may seem here to resign its activism and to arrogate for itself only the task of stating things as they are: philosophy surrenders to positivism. Is the task of philosophy, in truth, not so much the task of stating things as they are as the tediousness of this task? The grey in grey would then denote, rather than the senility of metaphysics, the indiscernibility and indecision that is its chance and condition of possibility.

In Beckett the question of boredom becomes entangled with the question of art. Certainly boredom characterised the reception of earlier works as a possibility, but with Beckett boredom notably ceases to be simply a reaction to deficiencies in the work of which the author alone is ignorant. Boredom no longer distinguishes the work that has failed. This is not to say that Beckett's writing is a success: the boredom of Beckett's art suspends the distinction between artistic success and failure. The objective criteria by which a work is judged a success or failure have themselves become boring. Differentiating between that which is boring and that which is not, taste includes itself in the former category.

The boredom of a particular work of art cannot be a property of the work in question. The positivistic understanding of art according to which art is a distinct set of entities with recognisable properties can only ever toy with the notion of art's irreducibility to metaphysics: the irreducibility is something that it has itself set up (and thereby vitiated). Likewise, to situate this irreducibility in meaninglessness as such is to arrange for immediate dialectical recovery of this irreducibility by means of its blank opposition to meaning. Arguably the irreducibility of art to metaphysics is best interpreted as the irreducibility of boredom to spirit. If the metaphysical importance of the problem of art is art's irreducibility to metaphysics, irreducibility needs to be reformulated so that reflection on the problem of art might enable metaphysics to address the true foundations of its own identity.

The boredom of a work of art marks it in the ambiguity of its irreducibility to metaphysics. Of course boredom is not the privilege of those entities conventionally designated as works of art: metaphysical texts have likewise aroused feelings of boredom. But then that which has distinguished art, historically, in the judgment of metaphysics has also never been alien to metaphysics itself. Where sensuousness was proposed as the mark of the work of art, it was never with the implication that metaphysical texts are without a footing in the phenomenal world, since their legibility and transmission depend on it. The tedious and the sensuous are comparable in having been left behind by spirit. The tedious, however, haunts spirit even more intimately than the sensuous haunts it. The repetition in which boredom has its element overlaps the repetition in which spirit sets up the universality of the concept in contradistinction to the sensuous particular. The question of boredom involves the question of spirit. Boredom, as the double and hence unrecognisable other of spirit, is the difference that spirit contains within itself. It is the "essence" of art's constitutive difference from metaphysics. Boredom is not to be torn away from the work of art and attributed to the individual who passes judgment on its faults or explained away, as in the case of Beckett, with reference to an authorial sleight of hand and the deceptiveness of appearances. Metaphysics, as it seeks to grasp the essence of all things, must seek to grasp the essence of art. It must seek to grasp that against which it has defined itself as the irreducibility of its unrecognisable other. The problem of the understanding of art is not extrinsic to metaphysics but rather its innermost problem. Metaphysics cannot rest content with metaphysical definitions of art even as it cannot cease misapprehending the essence of art.

In the judgment of metaphysics, art is a broken promise. Denying for himself the title of the inventor of the quarrel between philosophy and poetry, Plato has Socrates call for the banishment of mimetic poets from the ideal city because they do not give what they seem to give.[18] Specific to their art is a refusal to be simply what it is and nothing else. The incorrigible badness of art, whether it is through mimesis or boredom that it rebuffs the pretensions of metaphysics to illuminate all that is, is its irreducibility to metaphysics. The paradox of metaphysics is that it constitutes itself in the distance at which it keeps from what in art is not itself and yet makes light of this distance in its claim to grasp the essence of all that is. Metaphysics is not served, but merely indulged by literary criticism that simply closes the distance between it and the work of art. The badness of the work of art, since it holds in itself the key to an understanding of the defining limits of metaphysics, stands in need of an elaboration rather than an apology.

Does Adorno, for example, defend, which is to say dispel through re-spiritualisation, the boredom of Beckett's art? Yes and no. To be sure, Adorno speaks of the pre-eminent spiritualisation of Beckett's work, but spirit for Adorno is not the spirit of a vulgar Platonism or Hegelianism. Adorno's sympathy with the disagreeableness of Beckett's art is not different in nature, as can be shown, from Heidegger's reappraisal of metaphysics in the light of boredom. In *Aesthetic Theory*, which he planned to dedicate to Beckett and which was published posthumously in 1970, Adorno writes: "Spiritualization provided art anew with what had been excluded from it by artistic practice since Greek antiquity: the sensuously unpleasing, the repulsive; Baudelaire virtually made this development art's program."[19] For Adorno, Beckett inherits Baudelaire's agenda and consummates it through his inscription of the unpleasing not only in the content of the work but also in its very form. The spiritualisation of art is revealed less in the formal mastery by which unpleasing material is worked over for a possible judgement of artistic beauty than in the capacity of art to dispense with such reprocessing. Here spirit is not simply domination of nature. It does not seek to bring the boring back under its heel by reinvesting it with meaning, since whatever vigour metaphysics would thereby impart to the boring would be at the price of an opportunity to restore its own vigour through an interrogation of its definition in the face of the irreducibility of the boring. Spirit, in order to be the self-questioning it claims to be, must refrain from an artistic appropriation for the conceptual, of that which for a vulgar Platonism is non-spiritual. Adorno ascribes to spiritualisation the inclusion of the unseemly in nineteenth-century art. But through such spiritualisation art only belatedly catches up with metaphysics and matches its inclusiveness: already in the *Parmenides* (130c-e) the young Socrates is chided for believing that thought must hold itself aloof from the brute nature of dirt and hair.[20] Adorno notes the spiritualisation in Beckett's work, but this spiritualisation does not translate the distraction of boredom into the collectedness in which spirit is said to come to itself. For Adorno, the spirit of art cannot come to itself because it is always beside itself: "What appears in artworks and is neither to be separated from their appearance nor to be held simply identical with it – the nonfactual in their facticity – is their spirit."[21] Spirit is the difference immanent to the work itself: "Spirit cannot be fixated in immediate identity with its appearance. But neither does spirit constitute a level above or below appearance; such a supposition would be no less of a reification."[22] Spirit, for Adorno, given that it is that which differs from the thingly, cannot contract into a determinate position: it must be distracted. Spirit, like boredom, must be both within and without spirit in its conventional definition as the collectedness of conceptual thinking.

If reification is contrary to the nature of spirit and if spirit is reified as soon as it is localisable, how is Adorno able to single Beckett's work out for praise of its spiritualisation? Is Adorno's praise not implicitly a criticism, an objection to its reification? Adorno explicitly and immediately dilutes the encomium: "Only radically spiritualized art is still possible, all other art is childish; inexorably, however, the childish seems to contaminate the whole existence of art."[23] Drawing a distinction between spiritualised art and childish art and thus sounding uncomfortably like a newspaper art critic, Adorno catches himself and submits the distinction to dialectical contamination. The childishness of Beckett's work is not merely its surface for Adorno. It pervades it and by putting spirit into question, it rediscovers spirit in the indefiniteness of that to which it falls to define what is. The childishness is not an isolated lapse of good sense that can be shown to be justified by a reading of the whole.

That which as spirit Adorno praises in Beckett is spirit as the fundamental self-questioning of metaphysics. It is not the spirit that holds itself aloof as much as possible from the sensuousness of art and courts conceptuality. Hence it is arguable that Adorno does not shirk the challenge of the boredom of Beckett's work. He does not overlook the phenomenon of boredom for the sake of its supposed truth, the non-boring essence of boredom that is the work's adequacy to the age. He does not put up with the tedium of Beckett's art, as though in obedience to Freud's reality principle, with an eye to the subsequent pleasure of theory. What Adorno perhaps means by the timeliness of Beckett's work is the provocation of boredom to which metaphysics in its constitutive self-critique has now brought itself to heed. Both Adorno and Plato delight in the badness of art, but where for Plato the badness of art seems to play its role in an apology of metaphysics (as though any apology would not effectively be a disservice), for Adorno the badness of art is a charge levelled at the complacency of the reified, self-identical spirit of metaphysics. Adorno's fascination with Beckett is with an artist who does not ape metaphysics, who unlike Schiller and Sartre does not merely sweep the path in advance of the concept. In his essay on *Endgame* Adorno writes: "What philosophy Beckett provides, he himself reduces to cultural trash, like the innumerable allusions and cultural tidbits he employs."[24] Beckett's work does not yield an idea. It has no message. In the face of spirit's procedures of abstraction and interpretation it simply bores. The task of metaphysics is to think this boredom, to succumb to it without ceasing to be thought. Admittedly, the odds for this are not very good.

NOTES

[1] Samuel Beckett, *Watt* (New York: Grove Press, 1970), p. 209.

[2] Lance St. John Butler's *Samuel Beckett and the Meaning of Being* (New York: St. Martins' Press, 1984) devotes a sizeable, albeit hapless section to a discussion of Beckett in relation to Heidegger (pp. 7-73).

[3] Alain Badiou sets out what he considers the method and purpose of Beckett's ascesis: like Descartes and Husserl, Beckett strips back in order to make a return. The return, however, is not to science, but rather to the beauty of the world. Cf. Badiou, *On Beckett*, eds. Alberto Toscano and Nina Power (Manchester: Clinamen Press, 2003), p. 77: "At the end of the methodical ascesis, the following happens, which is entirely comparable to the emergence of the Great Bear at the end of Mallarmé's *Coup de dés*." Badiou then quotes a passage from Beckett's *Worstward Ho*. There is the beauty to which admittance is granted the subject (the beauty that appears) and there is, in boredom, the beauty to which admittance is refused the subject (the beauty that withholds itself and sucks dry of life whatever appears). It is the latter beauty that this essay hopes to address.

[4] It is debatable whether the egoistic thrill with which wonder is nowadays generally associated has anything at all to do with the *thauma* of the ancient Greeks. The comparison of boredom and wonder need not then be seen as yet another attempt to escape the clutches of boredom for something more "rewarding." In his essay, "Being Bored: Heidegger on Patience and Melancholy" in the *British Journal for the History of Philosophy* 12/2 (2004), pp. 277-95, Espen Hammer does seem to make such an attempt by comparing boredom with patience. The motivation given for this comparison is a defence of Heidegger against Levinas. If we convert boredom into the patience of the Jews with respect to the Messiah (instead of into the wonder of the ancient Greeks), then, according to Hammer, Levinas's criticisms of the disavowal of the ethical in *Being and Time* lose their edge: "The attunement of 'It is Boring for One' is better described as a form of patience (anticipating, perhaps, the *Gelassenheit* of the later writings), of an awaiting without anything specific being awaited, in short an openness which, in the moment of vision, can be transformed into an explicit acknowledgment of responsibility" (p. 291). Yet Heidegger's account of boredom in 1929-30 does not have to be called in to defend *Being and Time*, because Levinas, at least as Hammer reconstructs his position, misreads the earlier text: "Levinas seeks to reverse Heidegger's relation between death and time. For Levinas, death is not the condition of possibility of temporality; rather, it is time, as phenomenologically attested to in the experience of hope, the patient turning toward the neighbor, which allows the Other to affect me and thus place me in a relationship of irreplaceable and undeniable responsibility." (p. 279) This is easily reconciled with Heidegger. See §50 of *Being and Time*, trans. John Macquarrie and Edward Robinson (London: SCM Press, 1962), p. 296: "As regards its ontological possibility, dying is grounded in care." The sentence is italicised in Heidegger's text. Levinas is thus actually in agreement with Heidegger when he makes our relations to others a more fundamental basis of temporality than death. It is not because we die that we care, but rather because we care that we die. Death is the essential possibility of existence; it is the future event that will befall existence and in befalling existence prove the latter's radical exposure to the world. But although death is the demonstration of this exposure (its *ratio cognoscendi*), it is not its ground (*ratio essendi*). As death for Heidegger, contrary to Levinas's caricature, is not the essential interruption of a worldless self, it is not through the fissure it creates that our

correspondingly merely incidental and trivial cares for others spill through in panicky advance of the end of life.

[5] For a different account of the modernity of boredom, see Elijah Millgram, "On Being Bored Out of Your Mind" in *Proceedings of the Aristotelian Society* 104 (2004), pp. 163-84. Drawing on John Stuart Mill's *On Liberty*, Millgram discerns in boredom a regulative function of modern liberal democracy. Boredom lays final ends open to contestation and thus does the work that Mill attributes to free speech in preventing received opinions from turning dogmatic. It is because we can become bored with our final ends that our final ends do not become a constrictive, lifeless shell, i.e., mind-deadeningly boring. The possibility of boredom, as a subjective response, is our safeguard against the objective installation of boredom, as unthinking dogmatism. Boredom, according to Millgram, gives us the space in which to review our final ends and to alter them. This suggests that boredom, for Millgram, never reaches the point where the world as a whole is found boring and no final end merits adoption. Indeed, Millgram writes: "People without final ends are so unusual that I'm not sure I would know what to make of someone who didn't have any" (p. 165). Boredom, so long as it is a response to specific final ends rather than final ends as such, can be justly compared to the recurrent minor crises that liberal democracy has made its element and that are thus immanent to it. In its extreme form, however, boredom is not just an expression of modernity, but a judgment on it.

[6] Martin Heidegger, *The Fundamental Concepts of Metaphysics: World, Finitude, Solitude*, trans. William McNeill and Nicholas Walker (Bloomington: Indiana University Press, 1995), pp. 158-59.

[7] Kracauer, in his essay of 1924, strikes a nostalgic note, which because it is unconvincing is all the more in keeping with the *pose* of boredom affected by the nineteenth-century aesthete. See his "Boredom" in *The Mass Ornament: Weimar Essays*, ed. and trans. Thomas Y. Levin (Cambridge, MA: Harvard University Press, 1995), p. 334: "Boredom becomes the only proper occupation, since it provides a guarantee that one is, so to speak, still in control of one's existence. If one were never bored, one would presumably not really be present at all."

[8] Friedrich Nietzsche, *On the Genealogy of Morals*, trans. Walter Kaufmann (New York: Vintage Books, 1989), p. 153.

[9] This larger conception of the world is one of the fronts that phenomenology establishes in its campaign against positivism. As this conception is clearly articulated in *Being and Time*, it is not simply a case of bad luck that in 1983, the year in which *The Fundamental Concepts of Metaphysics* first appeared in German as volume 29-30 of Heidegger's *Gesamtausgabe*, Patrick Bigelow published an essay constructing a "Heideggerian" account of boredom that clashes with Heidegger's most extended treatment of the relations between boredom and world. In "The Ontology of Boredom: A Philosophical Essay" in *Man and World* 16/3 (1983), Bigelow writes: "The worlding of the world [...] is thrown away" (p. 262) and "boredom is the defiant denunciation of time" (p. 263). Arguably, the definitions here of "world" and "time" are taken from positivism and/or pragmatism, rather than Heidegger. With far less philological excuse, Lars Svendsen, in his *A Philosophy of Boredom*, trans. John Irons (London: Reaktion Books, 2005), claims: "In boredom there is a loss of world" (p. 128). He then proceeds to criticise Heidegger for ignoring the world. One reason for Heidegger's expansion of the concept of world is so that the subject need not flatter itself for the condescension of its engagement with a "puny," loseable world: the pompous alternation between condescension and loss in the subject's relations to this small-sized conception of the world is symptomatic of the nihilism with which Heidegger charges the modern metaphysics of the subject.

[10] Heidegger, *The Fundamental Concepts of Metaphysics*, p. 127.

[11] Beckett, *Trilogy* (London: Calder, 1994), p. 193.

[12] Cf. Bamber Gascoigne's review of *Play*, entitled "How far can Beckett go?" in *The Observer Weekend Review*, 12 April 1964, p. 24: "Even as early as *Waiting for Godot* Beckett was apparently shying away from his power to reach an audience. Peter Hall's production in London revealed the play as very human and very funny, though at the same time duly macabre; it made one laugh, shudder, think; it was exhilarating. But Beckett, I gather, disliked it and preferred the Paris version – an ordeal which I found literally painful to sit through, since Lucky shook with a violent palsy for his entire time on the stage. The effect was irritating rather than disturbing."

[13] The body of the play, with its extraction from loneliness of a company of discontinuous selves, with its exchanges between a tape-recording of a younger Krapp and an older, corporeally present Krapp is of course by no means hoary stage business, even if one admits a precedent four years earlier in the 1954 musical by Richard Adler and Jerry Ross, *The Pajama Game*, where John Raitt sings the duet "Hey There" with a dictation machine.

[14] Cf. the "metaphysical" reading of the clown's disruptive function in Günther Anders, *Die Antiquiertheit des Menschen* (Munich: C. H. Beck, 1956), pp. 217-18.

[15] In another sense, by closing out its audiences through offering them a reproduction of something over and done with, cinema acquires a documentary value that permeates its every aspect, and thus a further means of engaging audiences. The Maysles Brothers' *Grey Gardens* (1976) is a filmic *Endgame* with its depiction of the recluses Edith Bouvier Beale and her daughter Edie, revealing their mutual interdependence, the proneness of the one and the departure plans of the other, and the squalor into which they had descended. But it is also a document of a world that is lost. Pastness is able to redeem unremarkable details by rendering them illustrative of an epoch.

[16] Vivian Mercier is one such interpreter unwilling to stay the course. Cf. his discussion of *Waiting for Godot* in *Beckett/Beckett* (New York: Oxford University Press, 1977), p. 172: "Let us consider what problems confront a dramatist who wishes to write a play about waiting – a play [in] which virtually nothing is to happen and yet the audience are to be cajoled into themselves waiting to the bitter-sweet end. Obviously those who wait on stage must wait for something that they and the audience consider extremely important. We are explicitly told that when Godot arrives, so Vladimir and Estragon believe, they will be 'saved.' An audience possessing even a tenuous acquaintance with Christianity need no further hint: an analogy, they deduce, is being drawn with Christ's Second Coming. They do not have to identify Godot with God; they do, however, need to see the analogy if the play is not to seem hopelessly trivial. ... In other words, a play like *Waiting for Godot* could hardly 'work' artistically if it did not invoke the Judaeo-Christian Messianic tradition and its political derivatives." Nonetheless it may well be that coming across as hopelessly trivial is a lesser danger for the play than its inscription in the Judaeo-Christian Messianic tradition. *Waiting for Godot* is unlike Beckett's other works because its approach to the question of boredom is through waiting and disappointment. It is less overt in its collusion with boredom – and this collusion is one of Beckett's signatures – because, in however debatable a way, it adheres to the prospect that something will happen.

[17] G. W. F. Hegel, *Elements of the Philosophy of Right*, trans. H. B. Nisbet (Cambridge: Cambridge University Press, 1991), p. 23.

[18] Cf. Plato, *The Republic*, 607 b, where it is called an old quarrel (*palaia diaphora*).

[19] Theodor Wiesengrund Adorno, *Aesthetic Theory*, trans. Robert Hullot-Kentor (Minneapolis: University of Minnesota Press, 1997), p. 92.

[20] Plato, *Parmenides*, 130 c-e.

[21] Adorno, *Aesthetic Theory*, p. 86.

[22] Ibid., p. 87.

[23] Ibid., p. 92.

[24] Adorno, "Trying to Understand *Endgame*" in *Notes to Literature*, trans. Shierry Weber Nicholsen (New York: Columbia University Press, 1991), vol. 1, p. 241.

WORKS CITED

Adorno, Theodor Wiesengrund. *Aesthetic Theory*. Trans. Robert Hullot-Kentor. Minneapolis: University of Minnesota Press, 1997.

——. "Trying to Understand *Endgame*." *Notes to Literature*. Vol. 1. Trans. Shierry Weber Nicholsen. New York: Columbia University Press, 1991. 240-75.

Anders, Günther. *Die Antiquiertheit des Menschen*. Munich: C. H. Beck, 1956.

Badiou, Alain. *On Beckett*. eds. Alberto Toscano and Nina Power. Manchester: Clinamen Press, 2003.

Beckett, Samuel. *Watt*. New York: Grove Press, 1970.

——. *Trilogy*. London: Calder, 1994.

Bigelow, Patrick. "The Ontology of Boredom: A Philosophical Essay." *Man and World* 16.3 (1983). 251-65.

Gascoigne, Bamber. "How far can Beckett go?" *The Observer Weekend Review*, 12 April 1964. 24.

Hammer, Espen. "Being Bored: Heidegger on Patience and Melancholy." *British Journal for the History of Philosophy* 12.2 (2004). 277-95.

Hegel, G. W. F. *Elements of the Philosophy of Right*. Trans. H. B. Nisbet. Cambridge: Cambridge University Press, 1991.

Heidegger, Martin. *Being and Time*. Trans. John Macquarrie and Edward Robinson. London: SCM Press, 1962.

——. *The Fundamental Concepts of Metaphysics: World, Finitude, Solitude*. trans. William McNeill and Nicholas Walzer. Bloomington: Indiana University Press, 1995.

Kracauer, Siegfrid. "Boredom." *The Mass Ornament: Weimar Essays*. Ed. and trans. Thomas Y. Levin. Cambridge, MA: Harvard University Press, 1995. 331-34.

Mercier, Vivian. *Beckett/Beckett*. New York: Oxford University Press, 1977.

Millgram, Elijah. "On Being Bored Out of Your Mind." *Proceedings of the Aristotelian Society* 104 (2004). 163-84.

Nietzsche, Friedrich. *On the Genealogy of Morals.* Trans. Walter Kaufmann. New York: Vintage Books, 1989.

Plato. *The Republic.* Translated by Paul Shorey. Loeb Classical Library. Vol. 237. Cambridge, Massachusetts: Harvard U. Press. 1994.

———. *Parmenides.* Translated by H. N. Fowler. Loeb Classical Library. Vol. 167. Cambridge, Massachusetts: Harvard U. Press. 1977.

St. John Butler, Lance. *Samuel Beckett and the Meaning of Being.* New York: St. Martins' Press, 1984.

Svendsen, Lars. *A Philosophy of Boredom.* trans. John Irons. London: Reaktion Books, 2005.

CHAPTER 6

The Atrophy of Experience:
Walter Benjamin and Boredom

Carlo Salzani

The essay relates Walter Benjamin's analysis of boredom, especially in convolute "D" of the *Arcades Project* ("Boredom, Eternal Return"), to his critique of experience and thus to a number of central concepts in his work, like *ennui*, *spleen* and *melancholy*. In the notes for the *Arcades Project* and the Baudelaire book, boredom can be related to *Erlebnis*: it is the "malady" that accompanies the disintegration of the traditional forms of experience, which Benjamin called the "atrophy of experience." However, thanks to its connection to allegory, boredom also plays a fundamental role in Benjamin's revolutionary project: the melancholy gaze of the allegorist reduces the historical event to ruin, showing its *facies hippocratica*, its "death mask," thus exposing the naked truth of the demise of experience. This is the dialectical potential of allegory and thus of spleen.

Benjamin devoted a whole section of the *Arcades Project* – Convolute "D" – to the problem of Boredom. He thus recognized that boredom is a fundamental component of modern life and of its phantasmagoria and planned to include its analysis in his work on the prehistory of modernity. However, this chapter of his work was never written and a systematic and coherent approach to boredom is thus absent from his corpus. Rather, in his work the analysis and uses of boredom are extremely inconsistent. In his writings of the 1920s and 1930s Benjamin utilized a number of terms almost as synonyms – *Langeweile*, *ennui*, *taedium vitae* – often in connection to Baudelairean *spleen* and melancholy, often also contradictorily. He also used the term *acedia*, albeit very rarely and not in relation to boredom. As the recent literature on boredom explains, these terms are all connected, though took different connotations in the evolution of the concept: if the roots are in medieval *acedia* – almost equated with *melancholia* in the Renaissance – *ennui*, *Langeweile* and *boredom* took a very specific connotation after the industrial revolution and are therefore strictly connected to modernity.[1] These terms have been used in different ways and with different connotations in different contexts, and cannot be said simply to coincide. They certainly present national, cultural, social and historical particularities that cannot be reduced to a unity. However, their relation can be taken as constitutive of a "discourse," what Elizabeth Goodstein calls the "discourse on boredom."[2]

This discourse is related by Goodstein to the modern concept of experience: she thus defines modern boredom, with a Musilian wink, as "experience without qualities."

Though Benjamin never gave a clear definition of boredom, and did not explicitly relate it to his analysis of experience, in his work the connection is evident. This essay will attempt to construe an analysis of Benjamin's boredom through his concept of experience. It will thus highlight the distinction between pre-modern and modern boredom, and then connect the few notes on boredom to be found in Benjamin's writings to his analysis of modernity. The goal is not to find a monolithic and coherent definition of boredom, but rather to explore a discourse.

1. Erfahrung and Erlebnis

"Why is storytelling on the decline?," Benjamin asks in a short piece published in the *Frankfurter Zeitung* in November 1932 and titled "The Handkerchief." "This is a question I often asked myself when I sat with other guests around a table for an entire evening feeling bored." The answer is, he argues, that "people who are not bored cannot tell stories. *But there is no longer any place for boredom in our lives*" [*Die Langeweile aber hat in unserem Tun keine Stelle mehr*]. Boredom is here associated with those pre-modern activities – "weave and spin, tinker and scrape" – which were "covertly and inwardly bound up with it" and are progressively disappearing from modern life. The decline of storytelling depends on the fact that the traditional rhythms of pre-modern life, with their relaxed and ancestral repetition, and which were accompanied by stories, are dying out. "If stories are to thrive," he concludes, "there must be work, order, and subordination" (*GS* 4.2:741/*SW* 2:658, emphasis added).[3]

The same point is made in "The Storyteller" (1936): "storytelling," Benjamin writes, "is always the art of repeating stories, and this art is lost when the stories are no longer retained." Stories are retained when they are integrated in the listener's own experience, which will lead him or her to repeat them one day. The process of assimilation requires "a state of relaxation" [*Entspannung*]: "boredom is the apogee of mental relaxation," he states; "boredom is the dream bird that hatches the egg of experience" [*Erfahrung*] and this state is becoming "rarer and rarer." The activities intimately associated with this kind of boredom – "weaving and spinning"[4] – are already extinct in the city and are progressively disappearing from the traditional community. This means that, without boredom, "the gift for listening is lost and the community of listeners disappears."[5] "Wisdom," the "intelligence coming from afar" transmitted through storytelling, is dying out in modern life: the new form of communication is "information," which supplies "a handle for what is nearest" in space and time, and "lays claim to prompt verifiability" (*GS* 2.2:446-7, 442-4/*SW* 3:149, 146-7). The boredom associated to the repetitive rhythms of the traditional world plays no role in this new experience: the state of mind of the newspaper reader is certainly not "mental relaxation," but rather "impatience" [*Ungeduld*] (*GS* 2.2:628/*SW* 2:741).

The operative term in this passage from "The Storyteller" is *experience*. The essay in construed on the contraposition between modern and pre-modern experience, which is a key topic in Benjamin's work, though a problematic one. From his early writings for the student journal *Der Anfang* through to the *Arcades Project*, Benjamin developed a critique of experience which underlies his critique of modernity. However, this critique is locked into the antinomy between the yearning for a lost authenticity and the celebration of new revolutionary possibilities. In "The Storyteller" (1936), the Berlin *memoires* and the writings on Kafka, Proust and Baudelaire (especially "On Some Motifs in Baudelaire," 1939), Benjamin mourns the demise of the old concept of experience; in essays such as "Surrealism" (1929), "The Destructive Character" (1931), "Experience and Poverty" (1933) and the Artwork essay (1936), he celebrates instead the dawn of a new era. The question of boredom is interlocked with that of experience, which will thus constitute the *fil rouge* of the present analysis. In broad lines, the issue can be defined as follow: in pre-modern times, experience presented a connectedness and durability which implied a relation to memory and community. The term used by Benjamin to designate this experience is *Erfahrung*, which etymologically refers to the verb *fahren*, to travel, and is thus something learned from life and travels over an extended period of time and that can be narrated. Modern experience, for which Benjamin uses the term *Erlebnis*, is instead broken, immediate, limited and disconnected from memory and community. Etymologically *Erlebnis* refers to the verb *leben*, to live, and hints thus as something "lived," sometimes with temporal and spatial limitations – "a single, noteworthy experience," explain the translators of the Harvard edition (SW 2:267n).[6] The argument of "The Storyteller" relies on this contraposition: the frenzy of modern existence has disrupted the millenarian rhythms of life and their monotonous (but relaxed) repetition, thus eliminating the conditions of possibility for storytelling. By relating here boredom to *Erfahrung*, Benjamin is establishing a temporality of experience based on repetition and continuity. This connection is called "habit."

The discussion of "habit" is fundamental both for the definition of experience and the question of boredom. It can be introduced by the analysis of "play." In "Toys and Play" (1928), Benjamin relates children play to the "basic rhythms" [*ursprünglichen Rhythmen*] of life, the rhythms "in which we first gain possession of ourselves" and which are based on the "law of repetition" [*Gesetze der Wiederholung*]. By repeating the same experience over and over again, the child learns how to "master frightening fundamental experiences": where the adult turns to storytelling as a way to relieve "his heart from its terrors" and to double happiness, "a child creates the entire event anew and starts again right from the beginning." The essence of play is thus the "transformation of a shattering experience into habit" and as such is the "mother of every habit" [*Wehmutter jeder Gewohnheit*] (*GS* 3.1:131/*SW* 2:120).[7] Repetition in habit creates a web of connections which relates the child and the adult to their environment and to history. Therefore, Benjamin can write in the *Arcades Project* that "habits [*Gewohnheiten*] are the armature of connected experiences [*Erfahrungen*]. This armature is assailed by individual experiences [*Erlebnissen*]" (m4,5). This does not mean that there are no longer habits once *Erlebnis* has substituted *Erfahrung*: "even the distracted person can form habits," Benjamin writes in the Artwork essay; "what is more, the ability to master certain tasks in a state of distraction first proves that their performance has become habitual" (*GS* 7.1:381/*SW* 3:120).[8] However, these new habits fail to build up an armature, a structure that connects experience to memory and community. Consequently, they fail to provide that mental relaxation which he defines in "The Storyteller" as boredom.

By arguing that "there is no longer any place for boredom in our lives," Benjamin is investing boredom with the positive aura of *Erfahrung*. However, this operation contrasts with the place he gives to boredom in his analysis of the prehistory of modernity, especially in the *Arcades Project*. The same ambiguity also connotes his uses of "habit" and "repetition." The question of boredom needs thus to be explored through a redefinition of the vocabulary of modernity.

2. The Time of the Machine

1839 *"La France s'ennuit"*
Lamartine (D4a,3)

"The Storyteller" was published in *Orient und Occident* in October 1936. In the same years, Benjamin was writing that "boredom began to be experienced in epidemic proportions during the 1840s" (D3a,4). In the notes for the *Arcades Project* and the Baudelaire book, boredom is not related to *Erfahrung*, but rather to *Erlebnis*: it is the "malady" [*Leiden*] (D3a,4) that accompanies the disintegration of the traditional forms of experience.[9] Its temporality, as well as its relation to repetition and habit, must thus be redefined.

Benjamin's generation was strongly influenced by the analysis of metropolitan life made by Georg Simmel. "The psychological basis of the metropolitan type of individuality," he wrote in "The Metropolis and Mental Life," "consists in the *intensification of nervous stimulation* which results from the swift and uninterrupted change of outer and inner stimuli."[10] The metropolis creates a psychological condition structured by the superabundance of sounds and images, the discontinuity in their reception and the unexpectedness of sudden impressions. The metropolitan man must develop a protection against the psychological threats that this situation generates. Simmel calls this protection the "blasé attitude":

> [It] results first from the rapidly changing and closely compressed contrasting stimulations of the nerves. [...] A life in boundless pursuit of pleasure makes one blasé because it agitates the nerves to their strongest reactivity for such a long time that they finally cease to react at all. In the same way, through the rapidity and contradictoriness of their changes, more harmless impressions force such violent responses, tearing the nerves so brutally hither and thither that their last reserves of strength are spent; and if one remains in the same milieu they have no time to gather new strength. An incapacity thus emerges to react to new sensations with the appropriate energy. This constitutes the blasé attitude.[11]

As a consequence, the meaning and differing values of things are "experienced as insubstantial": to the blasé person everything appears "in an evenly flat and grey tone."[12] This greyness is the colour of boredom, the unbearable uniformity that Benjamin will find in rain, fog, dust. The same defensive strategy is identified by Freud. He wrote in "Beyond the Pleasure Principle":

> *Protection against* stimuli is an almost more important function for the living organism than *reception of* stimuli. The protective shield is supplied with its own store of energy and must above all endeavour to preserve the special modes of transformation of energy operating in it against the effects threatened by the enormous energies at work in the external world – effects which tend towards a levelling out of them and hence towards destruction.[13]

Benjamin quotes this passage in "On Some Motifs in Baudelaire" as a way of describing *Erlebnis* and its effects, especially *shock*. Shock is in fact the threat of the "enormous energies at work in the external world" and is what mainly characterizes *Erlebnis*; Freud describes it as a "breach in the shield against stimuli."[14] This overstimulation and the consequent defensive strategy of the conscience produce what Benjamin calls the "atrophy of experience" [*Verkümmerung der Erfahrung*] (*GS* 1.2:611/*SW* 4:316-17). It is this atrophy that destroyed that kind of boredom as mental relaxation which was a product of the pre-modern rhythms of life, but at the same time also produced a new form of boredom.[15]

Overstimulation is only one among many factors which contribute to this new boredom. Repetition is another. Repetition, which in the child's play helps mastering fundamental experiences and construing the armature of

Erfahrung, becomes in the new rhythms of city life the repetition of the machine. A repetition that still construes habits, but not as the *wieder-tun* of the child's play, a "doing again" which is active creation [*schaffen*] (*GS* 3:131-2/*SW* 2:120). Rather, these new habits are a *Wieder-kehr*, a passively suffered *return* of the same as a numbing anaesthetic. These new habits are subject to the temporality of the machine. In "Central Park," Benjamin notes that "boredom in the production process arises as the process accelerates (through machinery) (*GS* 1.2:679/*SW* 4:181). In the *Arcades Project* he quotes Engels' *Die Lage der arbeitenden Klasse in England*:

> The miserable routine of endless drudgery and toil in which the same mechanical process is repeated over and over again is like the labour of Sisyphus. The burden of labour, like the rock, always keeps falling back on the worn-out labourer. (D2a,4)[16]

Unlike in "The Storyteller," here Benjamin recognises that it is precisely the destruction of the traditional rhythms of life and the frantic, shock-producing acceleration of the production process that cause boredom. It is the meaningless and empty repetition of shocking *Erlebnisse* that numbs the senses into a miserable state of insupportable monotony. The "futility, emptiness" and "inability to complete something," he writes in "On Some Motifs in Baudelaire," characterise "the activity of a wage slave in a factory": "the hand movement of the worker at the machine has no connection with the preceding gesture for the very reason that it repeats that gesture exactly." The "shock experience" [*Chockerlebnis*] of the worker at his machine is devoid of any substance, is isolated and disconnected, and as such it is miserable routine and endless drudgery (*GS* 1.2:632-33/*SW* 4:329-30).[17]

The boredom at the machine is paralleled by the boredom of the bourgeois: "Factory labour," Benjamin argues, is the "economic infrastructure of the ideological boredom of the upper classes" (D2a,4). The mechanical repetition found in labour constitutes the "absolute qualitative invariance" which "generates exchange values" and as such it is the "greyish background against which the gaudy colours of sensation [*Sensation*] stand out" (J92,4). The temporality of the machine constitutes the temporality of modernity, in labour as much as in leisure, and the "gaudy colours" of the upper classes' leisure hours are simply a (futile) attempt to escape the drudgery through *Sensation*. Leisure provides merely an illusion of escape from the monotony of machine time. Moreover, leisure time is informed by the mechanical repetition of machine time, which thus constitutes its "qualitative invariance": leisure time and machine time are qualitatively identical.[18] *Sensation* constitutes appropriately the *raison d'être* of a specific kind of escapist literature, the detective and mystery story, which is precisely a product of the modern atrophy of experience: it provides the leisure classes with a narrative that transforms the city into a place of danger, adventure and heroic deeds, thereby phantasmagorically hiding the dullness of *Erlebnis* and the boredom of urban existence.[19]

A book published in 1903 by Emile Tardieu, *L'Ennui*, tries to justify, and thus epitomizes, this phantasmagoria. It is therefore for Benjamin "a sort of breviary for the twentieth century" (D2,8). Tardieu argues that "life is purposeless and groundless and that all striving after happiness and equanimity is futile" (D2,8): all human activity is shown in the book to be a "vain attempt to escape from boredom," but, at the same time, "everything that was, is, and will be appears as the inexhaustible nourishment of that feeling." Far from investigating and explaining the reasons of modern boredom, Tardieu gives free rein to "his own spiritually barren, petty-bourgeois discontent" (D1,5) (K°,21).[20] Romanticism is possibly to blame for this hypostatization of *ennui*, though Benjamin does not elaborate on this point.[21] What he finds in Tardieu's book, however, is the expression of the profound melancholy that characterizes bourgeois life. The coziness [*Gemütlichkeit*] of the bourgeois *intérieur*, he writes in "Moscow," is paid with melancholy [*Melancholie*] (*GS* 4.1:328/*SW* 2:30). In spite of the intoxicating effects it has on the self-satisfied burgher, comparable to the effects of hashish, at the centre of the *intérieur* tower "nothingness," the "petty" and the "banal," and the contentment it gives is "satanic" nihilism (I2,6). This nihilism is the major conveyor of melancholy and boredom and incarcerates its inhabitants – the self-deceived bourgeois, but most of all the child – in the embrace of nothingness. The child is a central figure in the analysis of experience, and becomes thus fundamental in the analysis of boredom. In the bourgeois apartment the child is a "prisoner" (*GS* 4.1:287/*SW* 3:404): though it is also a figure of redemption, as it will be shown in the last section, its fundamental experience in the *intérieur* and in the city are loneliness and boredom. The *promesse de bonheur* that the modern metropolis puts forward, the excitement and adventure it promises, is broken at the end of the day: "the city promised me something new each day and by evening it was left wanting" (*GS* 4:291/*SW* 3:378, translation modified).[22] This melancholy has transformed the dream of the collective: "The dream has grown grey," Benjamin writes in "Dream Kitsch." "The grey coating of dust on things is its best part. Dreams are now a shortcut to banality." Kitsch, as "the side worn through by habit and patched with cheap maxims" (*GS* 2.2:620/*SW* 2:3), is its mark.

Modern life as *Erlebnis*, be it in the factory, among the city crowd or in the bourgeois *intérieur*, cannot escape boredom.

3. The Eternal Return of the Same

Erlebnis provokes a transformation in the sense of time, and thus in the temporality of modernity. This constitutes its fundamental connection with boredom. As the etymology of the German term *Lange-weile* implies, in boredom time slows down, "stagnates": "When yawning," Benjamin writes in "Central Park," "the human being himself opens like an abyss. He makes himself resemble the time stagnating around him" [*Er macht sich der langen Weile ähnlich, die ihn umgibt*] (*GS* 1.2:682/*SW* 4:184). This stagnation is what causes the melancholy of the modern subject, epitomized by Baudelaire's *spleen*. In spleen, Benjamin writes in "On Some Motifs on Baudelaire," "time is *reified* [*verdinglicht*]: the minutes cover a man like snowflakes. This time is historyless [*geschichtlos*], like that of the *mémoire involontaire*. But in spleen the perception of time is supernaturally keen. Every second finds consciousness ready to intercept its shock." In the single and disconnected shocks of *Erlebnis*, the individual "loses his capacity for experiencing" and thus "feels as though he has been dropped from the calendar. The big-city dweller knows this feeling on Sundays" (*GS* 1.2:642-3/*SW* 4:335-6). The eternal Sunday of *Erlebnis* excludes history, tradition, memory, and thus also any sense of *future*[23]: it entails a lack of memory and simultaneously a lack of consequences [*Folgenlosigkeit*] (O12a,1). What is lost is thus the historical "force field" [*Kraftfeld*] which characterizes *Erfahrung* (m1a,4).[24] Outside the force field of history, time is merely repetition, the dull and meaningless recurrence of shock-moments without any connection, scope or aim. It is the eternal return of the same.[25] This is the necessary connection that Benjamin establishes in Convolute "D" between boredom and eternal return.[26]

The melancholy temporality of eternal recurrence is paradoxically given by the "new": "Monotony feeds on the new," Benjamin quotes from Jean Vaudal (D5,6).[27] Eternal recurrence and the new constitute the dialectic of commodity production: the novelty of products constitutes the stimulus to demand, but at the same time mass production is "the eternal return of the same" [*Immerwiedergleiche*] (J56a,10). "What is 'always the same thing' [*immer wieder dasselbe*]," reads an early note, "is not the event but the newness of the event, the *shock* with which it eventuates" (Q°,23, emphasis added). Shock is the mark of *Erlebnis*: an experience disconnected from memory and history, *Erlebnis* is always new, but at the same time is always the same shock, and this shock of the new is fed by the "fata-morgana" logic of commodity production (D2a,8). The frenzy of novelty is *Schein*, deceptive semblance, and spells the fact that "there is nothing really new" (D5a,5). This *Schein*, Benjamin proposes in the 1935 exposé, is the key element to interpret modernity: "This semblance of the new is reflected, like one mirror in another, in the semblance of the ever recurrent. [...] Just as in the seventeenth century it is allegory that becomes the canon of dialectical images, in the nineteenth century it is novelty" (*GS* 5.1:55-6/*SW* 3:40-1).

"Fashion is the eternal recurrence of the new" [*die ewige Wiederkehr des Neuen*] (*GS* 1.2:677/*SW* 4:179) and is thus a key topic in the analysis of modernity. The first epigraph for the Convolute dedicated to fashion, Convolute "B," is a line from Leopardi's "Dialogue between Fashion and Death": "Fashion: Madam Death! Madame Death!.." The first entry is significantly a commentary on this epigraph, which relates fashion and boredom: "And boredom is the grating [*Gitterwerk*] before which the courtesan teases death. [Ennui]" (B1,1) (Fº,11). The deceptive teasing of death through the cult of novelty constitutes also the "tempo of news reporting" (B2,4) and is the powerful drug that intoxicates the dreaming collective.[28] The new, Benjamin quotes from Paul Valéry, is "one of those poisonous stimulants" to which the modern subject becomes addicted "until they are fatal. [...] It is a curious habit – growing thus attached to that perishable part of things in which precisely their novelty consists" (S10,6). But the only radical novelty – "and always the same one" – in a time dominated by the eternal recurrence of *Erlebnis*, is precisely death (*GS* 1.2:668/*SW* 4:171). The second epigraph for Convolute "B" is a quotation from Balzac: "*Rien ne meurt, tout se transforme.*" This epigraph unfolds for Benjamin "*the temporality of hell*": modernity in news reporting and fashion mocks death, but in so doing it flees history (B2,4).

The modern is "the new in the context of what has always already been there [*immer schon Dagewesen*]. The always new, always identical" (S1,4). As such, modernity is "the time of hell." The famous quotation from the *Arcades Project* reads:

> The punishments of hell are always the newest thing going in this domain. What is at issue is not that "the same thing happens over and over," and even less would it be a question here of eternal return. It is rather that precisely in that which is newest the face of the world never alters, that this newest remains, in every respect, the same. – This constitutes the eternity of hell. To determine the totality of traits by which the "modern" is defined would be to represent hell. (S1,5)[29]

In the time of hell, the new is always "the eternally selfsame" (S2a,3), and this constitutes the notion of history as "catastrophe": when the historical event, through the idea of eternal recurrence, is transformed into a "mass-produced article," then the notion of historical progress is reduced to obtuse repetition. "That things are 'status quo' *is* the catastrophe" (*GS* 1.2:663, 683/*SW* 4:166, 184). The temporality of hell as eternal recurrence constitutes the mythic character of modernity: if "the essence of mythic happenings is recurrence" (*GS* 1.3:1234/*SW* 4:404),[30] then "'eternal return' is the *fundamental* form of the *urgeschichtlischen*, mythic consciousness. (Mythic because it does not reflect.)" (D10,3). Eternal recurrence constrains life within a magic circle and thus confines life and history to the auratic (D10a,1), to the experience of spleen Benjamin finds in the works of Blanqui and Baudelaire.[31] This constitutes also a critique of Nietzsche: the myth of progress cannot simply be replaced by an equally mythical notion of eternal recurrence, which constitutes the hellish repetition of the new in commodity society.

Erlebnis as the temporality of hell is epitomised by the figure of the gambler. Games of chace represent an escape route for the modern individual, constrained by the increased pressure of administrative norms and by the burden of having to wait (D10a,2).[32] In "Central Park" Benjamin notes: "Games of chance, flânerie, collecting – activities pitted against spleen" (*GS* 1.2:668/*SW* 4:171). However, this momentary alleviation of boredom is deceptive: the temporality of gaming is in itself splenetic, gambling converts time "into a narcotic" (*GS* 5.1:57/*SW* 3:42), and thus this temporality is "infernal."[33] In "On some Motifs in Baudelaire," *Erlebnis* is epitomized both by the temporality of factory labour and by the temporality of gambling: both activities are futile, empty, and in themselves do not lead to any completion:

> The jolt in the movement of a machine is like the so-called *coup* in a game of chance. The hand movement of the worker at the machine has no connection with the preceding gesture for the very reason that it repeats that gesture exactly. Since each operation at the machine is just as screened off from the preceding operation as a *coup* in a game of chance is from the one that preceded it, the drudgery of the labourer is, in its own way, a counterpart to the drudgery of the gambler. Both types of work are equally devoid of substance. (*GS* 1.2:633/*SW* 4:330)

The gambler, like the factory worker, "cannot make much use of experience" (*GS* 1.2:634/*SW* 4:331); therefore, his or her activity perfectly epitomises "the lack of consequences that defines the character of *Erlebnis*" (O12a,1).[34] The same temporality characterises also the flâneur: his "ostentatious nonchalance [*Gelassenheit*]" is a protest against the production process which causes boredom (*GS* 1.2:679/*SW* 4:181). The arcades and the crowd are his refuge and provide him "with an unfailing remedy for the kind of boredom that easily arises under the baleful eye of a sated reactionary regime" (*GS* 1.2:539/*SW* 4:19); they provide the excitement and novelty that (illusorily) break the monotony of the machine time.[35] His resistance to the tempo of the production process is heroic: what Baudelaire called the "heroism of modern life" consists, Gilloch writes, "in the attempt, doomed to failure, to escape the ultimate terror of contemporary existence: namely, boredom."[36] However, this same heroism, played through pose and amusement, becomes itself tedious: "*Erfahrung*," Benjamin writes, "is the outcome of work; *Erlebnis* is the phantasmagoria of the idler" (m1a,3). The pursuit of excitement that is the goal of the flâneur is the pursuit of

Chockerlebnisse, of the shock which constitutes *Erlebnis*. This shock is though always the same: excitement from shock is thus a phantasmagorical illusion, because *Erlebnis* can only result in boredom. The modern hero, incapable of escaping boredom, becomes a "profoundly melancholic figure."[37]

The modern subject, isolated from community and detached from history, has one last resort: "there remains to the isolated subject in the grip of the *taedium vitae* one last thing – and that is empathy" [*Einfühlung*] (m4a,3). In order to while away time, the modern subject frantically seeks enjoyment, but the only enjoyment available in this society is the "empathy with commodities," the identification with all the pleasures which connote commodity society (cf. "The Paris of the Second Empire in Baudelaire," *GS* 1.2:561/*SW* 4:34). Melancholy thus threatens every form of leisure and idleness (m5,3), and the melancholic subject, oppressed by boredom, is drawn towards the commodity: "Boredom and: the commodity's wait to be sold" (O°,45). Empathy with the commodity is thus the end result of the atrophy of experience. This empathy becomes, in the construction of history, empathy and identification with the victor, and, significantly, *acedia* is the motor of splenetic historicism (cf. "On the Concept of History," *GS* 1.2:696/*SW* 4:391).[38]

4. Ennui, Spleen, Acedia

In Benjamin's "discourse on boredom," Baudelaire's work plays a fundamental role. The emptying out of experience in *Erlebnis* that characterizes modernity is expressed in his poetry as *spleen*. Spleen corresponds to "the utter void of time to which man is surrendered" (J69a,1) and pervades every representation in Baudelaire. It is the principal accent "the modern" takes in his poetry and is usually counterposed to ("it fractures") the *ideal* (*GS* 5.1:55/*SW* 3:40). Spleen simultaneously disrupts the sense of history and community that was characteristic of *Erfahrung*, and is a "hollowing out of the inner life" which is caused by "self-estrangement" [*Selbstentfremdung*] (J67a,4) (J67a,5). In Benjamin's reading of Baudelaire, spleen is ambiguously related to, and at times confused with, *ennui*: "One of the central motifs of this poetry," Benjamin quotes from François Porché, "is, in effect, boredom in the fog, ennui and indiscriminate haze (fog of the cities). In a word, it is spleen" (D1,4). Benjamin simply follows a fashion in the Baudelairean critique which treats spleen and ennui as synonyms: both are characterized by "dull, glib sadness" (D2,5), "weariness" [*Müdigkeit*] (J82,5) and "naked terror" [*nackten Schreckens*] (*GS* 1.2:658/*SW* 4:162).[39]

Spleen and ennui, with their connection to allegory, play a fundamental role in Benjamin's revolutionary project. In Baudelaire, "modernity is always citing primal history" (*GS* 5.1:55/*SW* 3:40). This is a central point. For Baudelaire, "modernity is nothing other than the 'newest antiquity'," and this because "spleen lays down centuries between the present moment and the one just lived" (J59a,4); "it is spleen that tirelessly generates 'antiquity'" (*GS* 1.2:661/*SW* 4:166). Baudelaire's spleen, like the Baroque melancholy, is "the feeling that corresponds to catastrophe in permanence" (J66a,4), it is an allegorical mode of vision that makes obsolete every event and situation. As the melancholy allegory constituted the armature of the seventeenth century, so Baudelaire's allegorical mode of vision represents the armature of modernity (J59a,4). Allegory reduces the historical event to ruin, it shows the *facies hippocratica*, the death mask of history as decay, with the corpse as its epitome: "From the perspective of spleen, the buried man is the 'transcendental subject' of historical consciousness" (*GS* 1.2:661/*SW* 4:165).[40]

This is the dialectical potential of allegory and thus of spleen: it destroys the *Schein*, the deceptive appearance of organic wholeness, and exposes the naked truth of the demise of experience. In its destructive "rage," in its "profound hatred,"[41] Baudelaire's spleen is "demonic" (*GS* 1.2:671/*SW* 4:174), but it is precisely this devilish violence that "exposes the isolated experience [*Erlebnis*] in all its nakedness. To his horror, the melancholy man sees the earth revert to a mere state of nature. No breath of prehistory surrounds it – no aura" (*GS* 1.2:643-4/*SW* 4:336). *Erlebnis* is shown as primal history, that is, as devoid of history, and so are the economic circumstances to which the notion of eternal return owes its topicality (*GS* 1.2:663/*SW* 4:166-7). The importance of the return of baroque allegory in Baudelaire is thus that, by melancholically petrifying and disrupting its object – history –, it unveils and exposes the *Schein* of modern experience. "Melancholy," Benjamin wrote in the *Trauerpiel* book, "betrays the world for the sake of knowledge. But in its tenacious self-absorption it embraces dead objects in its contemplation, in order to redeem them" (*GS*1.1:334/*OT* 157).[42] Likewise, Baudelairean spleen betrays the *Schein* of modern experience in order to redeem it from its atrophic decay.

Here the connection to the concept of "aura" must be developed. Benjamin writes that "Baudelaire's spleen is the suffering entailed by the decline of the aura" (J64,5), but also that "life within the magic circle of eternal return makes for an existence that never emerges from the auratic" (D10a,1). The contradiction here is due to the ambiguous use of the term "aura." Aura is defined in the Artwork essay as what produces the perception of "distance no matter how close [the object] is" (*GS* 7.1:355/*SW* 3:105). In the context of this essay, aura presents a negative connotation, since it perpetuates the authority of the tradition that hinders popular participation. To this connotation can be related the quotation from Convolute "D": the "magic circle of eternal return" can be read here as the perpetuation of the mythical authority of tradition, which thus is auratic. However, unlike in the Artwork essay, in "On Some Motifs in Baudelaire" aura has no negative connotation and is described as the association of memory and perception that cluster around an object. Here aura is the gaze that the inanimate or natural objects return to us, which builds a network of connections with the world around us, and thus corresponds to the positive connotation of *Erfahrung*. The modern decline of the aura is compared to the loss of the "ability to look," and in this sense we can read spleen as the suffering arising from the decline of *Erfahrung* (*GS* 1.2:644-8/*SW* 4:337-9).[43]

However, in Benjamin's reading of Baudelaire this suffering cannot be related to *acedia*, to a melancholic passiveness which ends up in resignation and political quietism.[44] "Spleen as a bulwark against pessimism" [*Spleen als Staudamm gegen den Pessimismus*], he writes in "Central Park" (*GS* 1.2:658/*SW* 4:162). Rather, in his revolutionary project, Baudelaire's spleen becomes a corollary of that "revolutionary nihilism" Benjamin identifies as the most interesting trait of Surrealism (*GS* 2.1:299/SW 2:210). The violent destruction of the *Schein* is the necessary step towards a revolutionary and constructive practice. This is no minor issue in Benjamin scholarship: the accounts and personal recollections of Theodor W. Adorno, Gershom Scholem and Hannah Arendt all depict Benjamin as a melancholic, an "*accidioso*," and all link his thought to his Saturnian disposition in a mode that tends to be dismissive, or at least patronising. These accounts were extremely influential for the posthumous reception of Benjamin's work and led to a trend in Benjamin scholarship culminating is Susan Sontag's essay "Under the Sign of Saturn."[45] All these readings, diverse and heterogeneous as they are, strongly rely on the stereotype of the intellectual as melancholic which has its origin in Aristotle and dominates the history of Western culture.[46] What is important for the present analysis, however, is not whether Benjamin had or not a melancholic nature; he certainly did. The problem is rather the connection that has been established between his melancholic nature and the politics of his work. That is, we should focus not on melancholy as a trait of his character, but as a concept in his work. To emphasise melancholy as the key determinant of Benjamin's thought means to misread the role of melancholy and allegory in his work and the meaning of his revolutionary project as a whole. Recent scholarship has helped to correct this misinterpretation, though the "aura" of the sorrowful, clumsy and unfortunate intellectual remains attached to any representation of Benjamin as a person. Max Pensky, among others, has shed light on the role and politics of melancholy and allegory in Benjamin's work.[47] It is also important to note that the melancholic intellectual was harshly attacked by Benjamin himself in the 1931 piece "Linke Melancholie," in which the *acedia* of German left intellectuals is reduced to "decayed bourgeois mimicry of the proletariat," devoid of any political signification, and thus in the end only "tortured stupidity" (*GS* 3:280-21/*SW* 2:424-5). Melancholy and spleen, with their connection to allegory, must be read as an opposition to this a-political despair. They are necessary steps in Benjamin's revolutionary project, but constitute merely its *pars destruens*, which must be complemented by a positive *pars construens*.

5. Convolute "D": Waiting and Awakening

Attendre c'est la vie
Victor Hugo (D10a,3)

This final section will attempt to outline the "constructive" potentiality that Benjamin found in boredom through a reading of Convolute "D."[48] Here the analysis of boredom departs from the "destructive" connection of *Erlebnis* with ennui and spleen/melancholy that characterizes the reading of Baudelaire. The emphasis is rather on a constructive aspect of boredom that opens up revolutionary possibilities. It is interesting to note that boredom is not precisely and clinically defined by Benjamin, but rather identified descriptively through images. The first is the weather: boredom is associated to images of dreary sky, fog and rain. The cosmic forces have a "narcotizing effect" on the modern individual (D1,3). Dust then is singled out as imposing a grey uniformity on the arcades and the bourgeois *intérieur*; the modern city is grey in de Chirico's paintings (D1a,7). As Andrew Benjamin notes, it is the grey *sameness* they impose on the world that makes rain, fog and dust boring[49]: "Rain makes everything more hidden, makes days not only grey but uniform" (D1a,9). The same entry makes though a fundamental statement: "Only someone who has grown up in the big city can appreciate its rainy weather, which altogether slyly sets one dreaming back to early childhood" (D1a,9). An early version of the same entry relates rainy weather and childhood to "dreams" (Bº,5).[50] This relation is important because introduces two fundamental notions Benjamin connects to boredom: threshold and waiting.

As a prisoner of the bourgeois apartment, the child is a victim of the boredom of modern urbanization. However, this figure is extremely important in Benjamin's project for two reasons: first, it represents a condition preceding the Fall into bourgeois modernity, still immune to the phantasmagoria of the city and of the commodity, and is thus related to pre-modern *Erfahrung*; secondly, it epitomises the state of *waiting*, which is for Benjamin the fundamental threshold into a revolution of experience. An important passage in *Berlin Childhood around 1900* reads:

> Among the caryatids and atlantes, the putti and pomonas, which in those
> days looked at me, I stood closest to those dust-shrouded specimens of the

race of threshold dwellers [*Schwellenkundigen*] - those who guard the entrance to life, or to a house. For they are versed in waiting [*sie verstanden sich aufs Warten*]. (*GS* 4.1:238/*SW* 3:354)

The child feels affinity with the race of threshold-dwellers because, like them, he lives in a state of waiting. The loggias and the "little rooms" of the bourgeois apartment which look out into the backyard, are "waiting-stations" [*Warteplätze*] where "time grew old" [*die Zeit veraltete*] (*GS* 4.1:295/*SW* 3:345, 346). Benjamin credits his "passion for waiting" [*Leidenschaft des Wartens*] (*GS* 6:482/*SW* 2:608), "something that others call my patience,"[51] to the fact that as a child he was often sick:

> The predilection for seeing everything I care about approach me from a distance, the way the hours approached my sickbed. Thus, when I am travelling, I lose the best part of my pleasure if I cannot wait a long time in the station for my train. And this likewise explains why giving presents has become a passion with me: as the giver, I foresee long in advance what surprises the recipient. In fact, my need to look forward to what is coming – all the while sustained by a period of waiting, as a sick person is supported by pillows at his back – ensured that, later on, women appeared more beautiful to me the longer and more consolingly I had to wait for them. (*GS* 4.1:269-70/*SW* 3:362-3)

A specific place in the Tiergarten epitomizes waiting: the otter's enclosure. The young Benjamin spent endless hours peering into the "black and impenetrable depths" of the enclosure, hoping to catch sight of the animal in the oval basin with a background of grotto-shaped rock formations. But the most he could get of the otter was an instantaneous and fleeting glimpse, after which the animal would disappear again. However, he enjoyed "long, sweet days there," made even longer and even sweeter "when a fine- or thick-toothed drizzle slowly combed the animal for hours and minutes." The rain would "whisper to me of my future, as one sings a lullaby beside the cradle." The otter's enclosure "bore traces of what was to come" [*trug ...die Züge des Kommenden*] and thus possessed the virtue of conferring the power to see into the future (*GS* 4.1:256-7/*SW* 3:365-6).

Sigrid Weigel calls the threshold the "prominent location of Benjamin's *Passagen* project," and gives it a "paradigmatic significance."[52] The figure of the threshold recurs many times in his work: the image of the putti and pomonas as *penates* and guardians of the urban rites of passage is found not only in *Berlin Childhood*, but also in the *Arcades Project* (I1a,4) (C2a,3) and "The Return of the Flâneur" (*GS* 3:197/*SW* 2:264-5). In the Berlin memoires, the prostitute is associated to the threshold dweller: she ushers the (male) citizen into adulthood, but also represents a crossing of class boundaries (*GS* 6:471-2/*SW* 2:600). The flâneur stands on the threshold – of the metropolis as of the middle class (*GS* 5.1:54/*SW* 3:39) – and the entrance of the arcades are thresholds, marked by an "expectant posture" reflecting the fact that, "altogether unknowingly, [...] a decision lies ahead" [*daß ...man vor einem Entschluß steht*] (C3,6). Defining the threshold [*Schwelle*], Benjamin points out that it must be distinguished from the boundary [*Grenze*]: a threshold is a "zone," and indeed a zone of "transition" [*eine Zone des Überganges*]. It is "transformation, passage, flight," "wave action" [*Wandel, Übergang, Fliehen, Fluten*], which Benjamin etymologically relates to the verb *schwellen*, to swell (O2a,1).[53] "Out of the field of experience proper to the threshold evolved the gateway that transforms whoever passes under its arch" (M°,26) (C2a,3). The atrophy of *Erfahrung* in modernity means that "we have grown very poor in threshold experiences": in modern life, rites of passage for birth and death, puberty, marriage etc. have almost disappeared, "these transitions are becoming ever more unrecognizable and impossible to experience"; falling asleep and, importantly, waking up, are perhaps the only such experience that remain to us (O2a,1).[54] Boredom is defined in Convolute "D" as "the threshold to great deeds" [*die Schwelle zu großen Taten*] (D2,7).

The same entry gives what is the closest to a definition of boredom in Benjamin's work: "We are bored when we don't know what we are waiting for [*Langeweile haben wir, wenn wir nicht wissen, worauf wir warten*]. That we do know, or think we know, is nearly always the expression of our superficiality or inattention" (D2,7).[55] Boredom is thus a waiting without an object. In a sense, Benjamin specifies, waiting is "the lined interior of boredom" [*die ausgefütterte Innenseite der Langenweile*] (D9a,4). Boredom and waiting constitute a "complex" which needs its own metaphysics ("a metaphysics of waiting is indispensable" [O°,26]). As Andrew Benjamin notes, awaiting thus transforms time.[56] The time of the *Erlebnis* is a "passing" [*vertreiben*] or a "killing" [*austreiben, abschlagen*, literally "expelling" and "knocking off"] of time. Such is the temporality of the gambler ("time spills from his every pore") and the flâneur ("To store time as a battery stores energy"). But the one who waits [*der Wartende*] "invites in" time, "takes in the time and renders it up in altered form – that of expectation [*Erwartung*]" (D3,4).[57] The man who waits – "a type opposed to the flâneur" (M°,15) – is not a victim to that intoxication of time, so similar to a hashish intoxication, which is the end result of *Erlebnis* and produces only doubt [*Zweifeln*] (M4a,1). This awaiting is a transformation – a threshold – of the experience of time: as Andrew Benjamin writes, "awaiting and expectation" produce a transformation of time "in which the future becomes a condition of the present, rather than the present being a series of empty moments awaiting a future."[58]

The temporality of the flâneur, as representative of the temporality of *Erlebnis*, is dream. An important entry reads:

> Boredom is a warm grey fabric lined on the inside with the most lustrous and colourful of silks. In this fabric we wrap ourselves when we dream. We

are at home then in the arabesques of its lining. But the sleeper looks bored and grey within his sheath. And when he later wakes and wants to tell of what he dreamed, he communicates by and large only this boredom. For who would be able at one stroke to turn the lining of time to the outside? (D2a,1)[59]

The arcades are the space where life flows "without accent, like the events in dreams," and flânerie constitutes "the rhythmics of this slumber," which mimics the pace of the tortoise (D2a,1). Boredom appears as an "ornament," "a mark of distinction" to the flâneur and the dandy, because it "is always the external surface of unconscious events" (D2a,2). The dandy makes a show of it, Benjamin ventures, because it constitutes an "index to participation in the sleep of the collective" (D3,7). This is the importance of Surrealism for Benjamin: in focusing its interest on the "dream kitsch," on the banality of the everyday and "the grey coating of dust on things" (*Dream Kitsch, GS* 2.2:620/*SW* 2:3), it unveiled the dreamy state of modern life, and embraced the dream: "Life seemed worth living only where the threshold between waking and sleeping was worn away" (*Surrealism, GS* 2.1:296/*SW* 2:208). It is precisely in the dream – or better, in this *threshold* between dream and wake – that Surrealism found "revolutionary energies" and transformed the outmoded and the destitution of this dream into "revolutionary nihilism" (*GS* 2.1:299/*SW* 2:210). However, the limit of the Surrealist project is that it chooses to persist "within the realm of dream," embracing the intoxication and mythology of modern life (N1,9). It therefore remains "inadequate" and "undialectical," disconnected from history and community (*GS* 2.1:307/*SW* 2:216). Benjamin's project, to the contrary, is concerned "to find the constellation of awakening" [*die Konstellation des Erwachens*], to dissolve the modern mythology "into the space of history" (N1,9).

Awakening is the key term of the *Arcades Project*. Convolute "K" defines it at "the dialectical – the Copernican – turn of remembrance" [*der kopernikanischen Wendung des Eingedenkens*] (K1,1). Significantly, this awakening is related to the figure of the child: the "child's side" is defined as the sleep stage of every epoch, "a side turned toward dreams." The Copernican revolution in historical perception consists in the awakening from the childish dream – the arcades, the nineteenth-century childish dream of progress and consumerist plenty – into a stage of historical wakefulness. The "teleological moment in the context of dreams" is "waiting," because "the dream waits secretly for the awakening"; so, too, the dreaming collective waits for the second when it cunningly wrest itself from the clutches of dream (K1a,2). "The first tremors of awakening serve to deepen sleep" (K1a,9) and this is the revolutionary potentiality of boredom. Awakening has a "dialectical structure" (hº,4): boredom can be read as the "Trojan horse" through which "the imminent awakening steals into the dream" (Nº,5). When

Benjamin thus asks "what is the dialectical antithesis to boredom?" (D2,7), the answer is awakening, is revolutionary action.[60]

Benjamin recognises that that kind of boredom connected to *Erlebnis*, to that atrophy of experience which arises from the reification and fragmentation of time and history into commodified, disconnected, always identical unities, is a specific and defining product of modernity. However, he finds in its dialectical structure a redemptive potentiality that makes of it an instrument of revolution: as spleen, it destroys the *Schein* of the phantasmagoria of progress and capitalism; as *Langeweile*, it prepares the awakening from this phantasmagoria and a re-founding of time and experience.

NOTES

[1] Academic interest in boredom has grown in the past thirty years or so. If Reinhard Kuhn was a sort of initiator (Reinhard Kuhn, *The Demon of Noontide: Ennui in Western Literature* [Princeton, NJ: Princeton University Press, 1976]), his work failed to identify the change that modernity imposed on the concept of boredom, and the terminological differences that characterise the historical and national developments. More recent works tend rather to emphasise these differences. Cf. for example Seán Desmond Healy, *Boredom, Self, and Culture* (London and Toronto: Associated UP, 1984); Orrin E. Klapp, *Overload and Boredom: Essays on the Quality of Life in the Information Society* (New York: Greenwood Press, 1986); Christopher Schwarz, *Langeweile Und Identiät: Eine Studie Zur Entstehung Und Krise Des Romantischen Selbsgefühls* (Heidelberg: Unviersitätsverlag C. Winter, 1993); Patricia Meyer Spacks, *Boredom: The Literary History of a State of Mind* (Chicago and London: The University of Chicago Press, 1995); Michael Raposa, *Boredom and the Religious Imagination* (Charlottesville and London: University of Virginia Press, 1999); Genrich Krasko, *This Unbearable Boredom of Being: A Crisis of Meaning in America* (iUniverse.com, 2004); Lars Svendsen, *A Philosophy of Boredom*, trans. John Irons (London: Reaktion, 2005); the most thorough philosophical investigation to date is Elisabeth S. Goodstein, *Experience without Qualities: Boredom and Modernity* (Stanford, CA: Stanford UP, 2005). The analysis of the differences between *taedium vitae*, *acedia*, *ennui*, *Langeweile*, *spleen*, and boredom goes beyond the scope of this essay; however, these differences will be briefly and partially explored in the course of the analysis.

[2] Goodstein, *Experience without Qualities*, p. 3n.

[3] All references to Benjamin's works are made parenthetically in the text. All references to *The Arcades Project*, ed. Rolf Tiedemann, trans. Howard Eiland and Kevin McLaughlin (Cambridge, MA: Belknap Press of Harvard University Press, 1999), are to the convolute number. When other materials included in this volume are quoted, the volume is cited as *AP*. For the other works, references are provided both to the German text of the *Gesammelte Schriften* (Collected Writings), ed. Rolf Tiedemann and Hermann Schweppenhäuser, 7 vols. in 15 (Frankfurt am Main: Suhrkamp, 1972–89), (hereafter cited as *GS*), and to the English translation of the *Selected Writings*, ed. Marcus Bullock and Michael W. Jennings, 4 vols. (Cambridge, MA: Belknap Press of Harvard University Press, 1996–2003) and *The Origin of the German Tragic Drama*, trans. John Osborne

(London: Verso, 1998), (hereafter cited as *SW* and *OT*, respectively). Where no English translation is available, I will use my own.

[4] Benjamin continues: "The more self-forgetful the listener is, the more deeply what he listens to is impressed upon his memory. When the rhythm of work has seized him, he listens to the tales in such a way that the gift of retelling them comes to him all by itself. This, then, is the nature of the web in which the gift of storytelling is cradled. This is how today it is unravelling on every side after being woven thousand of years ago in the ambience of the oldest forms of craftsmanship," *GS* 2.2:447/*SW* 3:149.

[5] Patricia Meyer Spacks misinterprets this passage: she reads Benjamin as one of the "enthusiasts of boredom," who "find the state desirable for the lack of desire and – at least in fantasy – of tension it embodies. [...] Such imagined boredom may imply a kind of suspended attention comparable to that of a listening psychoanalyst. It 'hatches the egg of experience' by allowing the semiconscious brooding that integrates and interprets past happenings. Avoiding distraction, it makes space for creativity. In Benjamin's view, it constitutes creativity's necessary precondition." What Meyer Spacks fails to notice is that Benjamin is here talking about a pre-modern experience and not that modern boredom, "the resentment-loaded endurance [...], the tedium of required activity, of compulsory contact, of repetitive demand" which "generate the tension we associate with boredom in the negative construction of the condition, leaving no room for creativity." Benjamin's treatment of modern boredom will be different. Cf. Meyer Spacks, *Boredom*, p. 261.

[6] The connotation of *Erfahrung* and *Erlebnis* is not constant in Benjamin's writings and varies with the years and the contexts: *Erlebnis* presents usually a negative connotation, with a vitalistic and irrationalist emphasis (in a polemic contraposition to the theories of Dilthey, Klages and Jung); *Erfahrung* in the early writings refers (with a negative connotation) to the Kantian and neo-Kantian science-based experience, but in the later works it designates a more authentic concept of experience (cf. "On Some Motifs in Baudelaire"). A thorough exposition of this concept can be found for example in Thomas Weber, "Erfahrung," *Benjamins Begriffe*, ed. Michael Opitz and Erdmut Wizisla (Frankfurt am Main: Suhrkamp, 2000), pp. 230-59.

[7] The passage continues: "Eating, sleeping, getting dressed, washing have to be instilled into the struggling little brat in a playful way, following the rhythm of nursery rhymes. Habit enters life as a game, and in habit, even in its most sclerotic forms, an element of play survives to the end. Habits are the forms of our first happiness and our first horror that have congealed and become deformed to the point of being unrecognizable" (*GS* 3.1:131/*SW* 2:120).

[8] The whole passage reads: "Tactile reception comes about not so much by way of attention as by way of habit. The latter largely determines even the optical reception of architecture, which spontaneously takes the form of casual noticing, rather than attentive observation. Under certain circumstances, this form of reception shaped by architecture acquires canonical value. *For the tasks which face the human apparatus of perception at historical turning points cannot be performed solely by optical means - that is, by way of contemplation. They are mastered gradually - taking their cue from tactile reception - through habit.* Even the distracted person can form habits. What is more, the ability to master certain tasks in a state of distraction first proves that their performance has become habitual" (*GS* 7.1:381/*SW* 3:120, emphasis in the original).

[9] "Lamartine is said to be the first to have given expression to the malady. It plays a role in a little story about the famous comic Deburau. A distinguished Paris neurologist was consulted one day by a patient whom he had not seen before. The patient complained of the typical illness of the times – weariness with life, deep depressions, boredom. 'There's

nothing wrong with you,' said the doctor after a thorough examination. 'Just try to relax – find something to entertain you. Go see Deburau some evening, and life will look different to you.' 'Ah, dear sir,' answered the patient, 'I am Deburau'" (D3a,4).

[10] Georg Simmel, "The Metropolis and Mental Life," trans. Kurt H. Wolff, *The Sociology of Georg Simmel*, Kurt H. Wolff ed. (New York: The Free Press, 1950), pp. 409-10, emphasis in the original.

[11] Simmel, "The Metropolis and Mental Life," p. 414.

[12] Ibid.

[13] Sigmund Freud, "Beyond the Pleasure Principle," *Standard Edition of the Complete Psychological Works*, James Strachery ed., vol. XVIII (London: The Hogart Press, 1955) p. 27, emphasis in the original.

[14] Ibid., p. 31.

[15] Benjamin write in *A Berlin Chronicle*: "...what kind of regimen cities keep over imagination, and why the city – where people make the most ruthless demands on one another, where appointments and telephone calls, sessions and visits, flirtations and the struggle for existence grant the individual not a single moment of contemplation – indemnifies itself in memory..." (*GS* 6:490/*SW* 2:614).

[16] Benjamin also quotes Schlegel's accusation in *Lucinde* against Prometheus who "seduced mankind into working" and, chained to the rock, is a figure for the man chained to the machine, and will have "plenty of opportunity to be bored [*wird noch Langeweile genug haben*], and will never be free of his chains" (J87a,1).

[17] Simmel also adds: "This discrepancy results essentially from the growing division of labour. For the division of labour demands from the individual an ever more one-sided accomplishment, and the greatest advance in a one-sided pursuit only too frequently means dearth to the personality of the individual. In any case, he can cope less and less with the overgrowth of objective culture. The individual is reduced to a negligible quantity, perhaps less in his consciousness than in his practice and in the totality of his obscure emotional states that are derived from this practice. The individual has become a mere cog in an enormous organization of things and powers which tear from his hands all progress, spirituality, and value in order to transform them from their subjective form into the form of a purely objective life," Simmel, "The Metropolis and Mental Life," p. 422.

[18] This remark of course constitutes the negative side of the mechanization of modern life not explored in the Artwork essay and is very close to Adorno's and Horkheimer's critique of the "Culture Industry" in *Dialectic of Enlightenment* (trans. John Cumming, London: Allen, 1973).

[19] Graeme Gilloch writes: "As an escape from the *ennui* of modern urban existence, the *tedium vitae* produced by the nothing-new of fashion and the faceless uniformity of the metropolitan crowd, the city was transformed by Poe, Dumas and Sue into a place of adventure. It was dressed up as a locus of unspoken dangers, menacing shadows, villainous figures stalking the city's streets and of evil lurking in every dimly lit alley-way," Graeme Gilloch, *Myth and Metropolis: Walter Benjamin and the City* (Cambridge: Polity Press, 1996), p. 148. For an analysis of the detective story as phantasmagoria of modern life, cf. Carlo Salzani, "The City as Crime Scene: Walter Benjamin and the Traces of the Detective," *New German Critique* 34.1 (Winter 2007), 165-87.

[20] Elizabeth Goodstein analyses in depth Tardieu's book. *L'Ennui*, she writes, "epitomizes the persistence of idealist assumptions within a disenchanted, scientific worldview." Strongly influenced by Schopenhauer, but also indebted to the scientific positivism of the time, it offers a taxonomy of the "innumerable" forms of ennui and sees it as the physiologically inevitable end result of the Enlightenment. It is "a paradigmatic example of

the fin-de-siècle discourse on boredom," which, "despite his avowed commitment to the rational, scientific analysis of the phenomenon, [...] circles back to a mythical vision of ennui as the thinking man's ailment," Goodstein, *Experience without Qualities*, pp. 163-68.
[21] In the *Arcades Project* Benjamin quotes from an article by Roger Caillois: "'Romanticism ends in a theory of boredom, the characteristically modern sentiment; that is, it ends in a theory of power, or at least of energy...Romanticism, in effect, marks the recognition by the individual of a bundle of instincts which society has a strong interest in repressing; but, for the most part, it manifests the abdication of the struggle...The Romantic writer...turns toward...a poetry of refuge and escape. The effort of Balzac and of Baudelaire is exactly the reverse of this and tends to integrate into life the postulates which the Romantics were resigned to working with only on the level of art...Their effort is thus linked to the myth according to which imagination plays an ever-increasing role in life.'" (D4a,2). Some recent literature on boredom tends to "blame" Romanticism for the modern "epidemic" of boredom: for Svendsen, for example, it is only with Romanticisms that "the demand arises for life to be interesting, with the general claim that the self must realize itself," but as the traditional sources of meaning withdraw, life becomes boring (Svendsen, *A Philosophy of Boredom*, p. 25ff). Cf. also Goodstein, *Experience without Qualities*, pp. 107-140.
[22] The child's melancholy is the melancholy of the city dweller, as Benjamin writes in "Marseille": "childhood is the divining rod of melancholy, and to know the mourning of such radiant, glorious cities one must have been a child in them" (*GS* 4.1:362/*SW* 2:234).
[23] Joe Moran writes: "the capacity to assimilate, recollect and communicate experience to others is replaced by the sense of life as a series of disconnected impressions with no common associations. The man who is denied the potential for *Erfahrung* is a hostage to boredom," Joe Moran, "Benjamin and Boredom," *Critical Quarterly* 45.1 (July 2003), p. 169.
[24] The whole passage reads: "In place of the force field that is lost to humanity with the devaluation of experience, a new field of force opens up in the form of planning. The mass of unknown uniformities is mobilized against the confirmed multiplicity of the traditional. To 'plan' is henceforth possible only on a large scale. No longer on an individual scale – and this means neither *for* the individual nor *by* the individual." (m1a,4)
[25] The deformation of time and place experienced by the hashish eater presents similarities with *Erlebnis*, which can thus also be classified as a state of intoxication. Compare these passages: "The objects are only mannequins; even the great moments of world history are merely costumes beneath which they exchange understanding looks with nothingness, the base, and the commonplace. They reply to the ambiguous wink from Nirvana"; "The first serious sign of damage is probably the inability to deal with future time. When you look into this more closely, you realize how astonishing it is that we can exercise control over the night, or even individual nights – that is to say, over our usual dreams. It is very hard to control the dreams (or the trance) resulting from hashish" (*Main Features of My Second Impression of Hashish*, GS 560-1, 563/*SW* 2: 85-6, 87). "Now the hashish eater's demands on time and space come into force. As is known, these are absolutely regal. Versailles, for one who has taken hashish, is not too large, or eternity too long. Against the background of these immense dimensions of inner experience, of absolute duration and immeasurable space, a wonderful, beatific humour dwells all the more fondly on the contingencies of time and space" (*Hashish in Marseille*, GS 4.1:410/*SW* 2:674). "Prostitution of space in hashish, where it serves all that has been (spleen)" (*Central Park GS* 1.2:661/*SW* 4:165).
[26] *Erlebnis* and eternal return transform radically the concept of habit: "The idea of eternal recurrence transforms the historical event itself into a mass-produced article. But this

conception also displays, in another respect – on its obverse side, one could say – a trace of the economic circumstances to which it owes its sudden topicality. This was manifest at the moment the security of the conditions of life was considerably diminished through an accelerated succession of crises. The idea of *eternal* recurrence derived its lustre from the fact that it was no longer possible, in all circumstances, to expect a recurrence of conditions across any interval of time shorter than that provided by eternity. The quotidian constellations very gradually began to be less quotidian. Very gradually their recurrence became a little less frequent, and there could arise, in consequence, the obscure presentiment that henceforth one must rest content with cosmic constellations. Habit, in short, made ready to surrender some of its prerogatives. Nietzsche says, "I love short-lived habits," and Baudelaire already, throughout his life, was incapable of developing regular habits. Habits are the armature of long experience [*Erfahrung*], whereas they are decomposed by individual experiences [*Erlebnisse*]" (J62a,2).

[27] This is the reason for the importance of Baudelaire poetry: "Baudelaire's poetry reveals the new in the ever-selfsame, and the ever-selfsame in the new" (*Central Park GS* 1.2:650/*SW* 4:175).

[28] "The dreaming collective knows no history," reads a very important entry in Convolute "S." "Events pass before it as always identical and always new. The sensation of the newest and most modern is, in fact, just as much a dream formation of events as 'the eternal return of the same.' The perception of space that corresponds to this perception of time is the interpenetrating and superposed transparency of the world of the flâneur. This feeling of space, this feeling of time, presided at the birth of modern feuilletonism [Dream Collective]" (S2,1).

[29] As Susan Buck-Morss notes, the notion of modernity as the time of hell provides a counterimage to the myths of progress – the Golden Age – which intoxicated the nineteenth century. A note to the 1935 exposé reads: "Hell—Golden Age. Keywords for Hell: Boredom, Gambling, Pauperism. A canon of this dialectic: Fashion. The Golden Age as catastrophe" (*GS* 5.2:1213). Cf. Susan Buck-Morss, *The Dialectics of Seeing: Walter Benjamin and the Arcades Project* (Cambridge, MA and London: The MIT Press, 1989), p. 96.

[30] "The essence of the mythical event is return. [...] (The hell of eternal damnation has perhaps impugned the ancient idea of eternal recurrence at its most formidable point, substituting an eternity of torments for the eternity of a cycle.)." (D10a,4)

[31] "The formula of *L'Eternité par les asters* – 'The new is always old, and the old is always new' – corresponds most rigorously to the experience of spleen registered by Baudelaire" (J76,2). "The consciousness of someone prone to spleen furnishes a miniature model of the world spirit to which the idea of eternal recurrence would have to be ascribed" (S8a,4).

[32] "Why do anxious people have an irresistible tendency toward games of chance? Perhaps because their policy is to bury their heads in the sand, or because they are able to endure the prospect of the future only if it is grotesquely disguised" (*In Parallel with My Actual Diary*, *GS* 6:191/*SW* 2:414).

[33] "The infernal time of gaming is something Baudelaire got to know less through the actual practice of gambling than through those seasons when he was prey to spleen" (J88a,3). "In the sixteenth section of Baudelaire's *Spleen de Paris*, 'L'Horloge', we come upon a conception of time which can be compared to that of the gambler" (O9,7).

[34] Moran thus comments this passage: "In reality, of course, this frantic search for instant gratification is still under the spell of the commodity, and the spinning of the roulette wheel, while charged with dramatic possibilities for the gambler, is actually as repetitive and predictable as the movements of the factory worker. [...] The leisure classes, though,

are unable or unwilling to understand that their idleness is the result of specific historical conditions," Moran, "Benjamin and Boredom," pp. 169-70.

[35] Benjamin quotes from Baudelaire's *L'Art romantique*: "In the essay on Guys, the crowd appears as the supreme remedy for boredom: 'Any man,' he said one day, in the course of one of those conversations which he illumines with burning glance and evocative gesture, 'any man…who can yet be *bored in the heart of the multitude* is a blockhead! A blockhead! And I despise him!'" (D5,3).

[36] Gilloch, *Myth and Metropolis*, p. 151.

[37] Ibid. The boredom of the flâneur and of the blasé individual presents a peculiar connotation: in English, the French term *ennui* is often retained in order to designate this particular kind of boredom. *Ennui* presents intellectual, artistic, aristocratic, almost glamorous characters, in contrast to the dull boredom of the worker and the low classes. *Ennui*, Meyer Spacks writes, "belongs to those with a sense of sublime potential, those who feel themselves superior to the environment"; she also blames Kuhn for limiting the focus of his book to ennui, rejecting "as beneath consideration the emotion of the bored housewife" (Meyer Spacks, *Boredom*, pp. 12, 27; Cf. also Goodstein, *Experience without Qualities*, pp. 33-68). An example of this intellectual ennui can be found in Siegfried Kracauer. To the "vulgar boredom of daily drudgery" which reduces the individual to be "merely one more object of boredom," Kracauer counterposes a sort of sophisticated *ennui*, whereby "boredom becomes the only proper occupation" which guarantees that the individual is "so to speak, still in control of one's own existence." Embracing this glamorous version of leisure boredom, the "legitimate boredom" of the intellectual, the individual eventually "becomes content to do nothing more than be with oneself" and can even experience "a kind of bliss that is almost unearthly." Siegfried Kracauer, "Boredom," trans. Thomas Y. Levin, *The Mass Ornament: Weimar Essays*, Thomas Y. Levin ed. (Cambridge, MA & London: Harvard UP, 1995), pp. 331-34.

[38] Michael Löwy explains: "The origin of the empathy that identifies with the triumphal procession of the dominators is to be found, according to Benjamin, in *acedia*, a Latin term which denotes indolence of the heart, melancholia. Why? What is the relationship between *acedia* and *Einfühlung*? Thesis VII does not explain this in any way, but we can find the key to the problem in *The Origin of German Tragic Drama* (1925): *acedia* is the melancholy sense of the omnipotence of fate which removes all value from human activities. It leads, consequently, to total submission to the existing order of things. As profound, melancholy meditation, it feels attracted by the solemn majesty of the triumphal procession of the powerful. The melancholic, par excellence, dominated by indolence of the heart – *acedia* – is the courtier. Betrayal is his element, because his submission to destiny always makes him join the victor's camp," Michael Löwy, *Fire Alarm: Reading Walter Benjamin's 'on the Concept of History'*, trans. Chris Turner (London and New York: Verso, 2005), pp. 47-8. Benjamin uses the term *acedia* very few times: apart from the famous thesis VII of "On the Concept of History," *acedia* is found in the *Trauerspiel* book to describe the melancholic prince (cf. *GS* 1.1:331-3/*OT* 155-6), and in the *Arcades Project* in a quotation from Baudelaire (cf. J35a,8). Benjamin thus connects *acedia* to melancholy and spleen, and not to his analysis of boredom. The literature on boredom concords in considering *acedia* the forerunner of modern boredom, but also highlights their fundamental differences: the former was a moral concept, mostly circumscribe to the cast of monks, whereas the latter is a psychological state, in modernity experienced by everyone. Kierkegaard, in his analysis of boredom, is often dismissed as mixing the two concepts and giving a pre-modern reading of a modern phenomenon (cf. Goodstein,

Experience without Qualities, p. 36). Benjamin transcribes few quotes from *Entweder-Oder* (J62a,3 to J63,6), but does not comment on them.

[39] In the same way that the French word *ennui* was retained in English in order to connote a particular kind of boredom, so the English word *spleen* was introduced into French and made famous by Baudelaire. *Spleen* refers to the predominance in the organism of black bile, the Greek *melan-kole*, which was believed to be the physiological cause of the melancholic character. As Goodstein writes, Baudelaire used "spleen" "to link historically distinct rhetorics of reflection on subjective experience – to represent the kaleidoscope in which ancient elements such as melancholy, *taedium vitae*, and acedia are refracted through modern, materialist interpretations of subjective malaise to form modern ennui" (Goodstein, *Experience without Qualities*, p. 235). Together with *ennui*, *taedium vitae*, *acedia* and melancholy, it belongs to the "discourse on boredom" which was taking shape in the nineteenth century, and provides thus the *trait d'union* between boredom and melancholy for the present analysis.

[40] "The hopeless decrepitude of the big city is felt particularly keenly in the first stanza of 'Spleen I'" (J69,3). "The awareness of time's empty passage and the *taedium vitae* are the two weights that keep the wheels of melancholy going" (J69,5).

[41] "The rage [*Zorn*] explodes in time to the ticking of the seconds that enslaves the melancholy man" (*GS* 1.2:642/*SW* 4:335). "On idleness: 'Imagine a perpetual idleness...with a profound hatred of that idleness.' ...letter to his mother of Sat. Dec. 4 1847" (J87,6).

[42] Benjamin recognized the difference between Baroque and Baudelairean allegory: "Melanchthon's phrase 'Melancholia illa heroica' provides the most perfect definition of Baudelaire's genius. But melancholy in the nineteenth century was different from what it had been in the seventeenth. The key figure in early allegory is the corpse. In late allegory, it is the 'souvenir' [*Andenken*]. The 'souvenir' is the schema of the commodity's transformation into an object for the collector. The *correspondances* are, objectively, the endlessly varied resonances between one souvenir and the others. 'J'ai plus de souvenirs que si j'avais mille ans,'" (*GS* 1.2:689/*SW* 4:190).

[43] For the question of aura cf. Marleen Stoessel, *Aura, Das Vergessene Menschiche: Zu Sprache Und Erfahrung Bei Walter Benjamin* (Munich: Carl Hanser, 1983); Josef Fürnkäs, "Aura," *Benjamins Begriffe*, ed. Michael Opitz and Erdmut Wizisla (Frankfurt am Main: Suhrkamp, 2000), pp. 95-146.

[44] Cf. note 38.

[45] Cf. Theodor W. Adorno, "A Portrait of Walter Benjamin," trans. Samuel and Shierry Weber, *Prisms* (London: Neville Spearman, 1967), pp. 227-42; Theodor W. Adorno, "Introduction to Benjamin's *Schriften*," trans. Shierry Weber Nicholsen, *Notes to Literature*, vol. Two (New York: Columbia UP, 1992) pp. 220-32; Gershom Scholem, "Walter Benjamin and His Angel," trans. Werner Dannhauser, *On Walter Benjamin: Critical Essays and Recollections*, ed. Gary Smith (Cambridge, MA, and London: The MIT Press, 1988) pp. 51-89; Hannah Arendt, "Walter Benjamin: 1892-1940," *Walter Benjamin, Illuminations*, Arendt, Hannah ed. (New York: Schoken Books, 1969), pp. 1-55; Susan Sontag, "Under the Sign of Saturn," *Under the Sign of Saturn* (New York: Farrar, Straus, Giroux, 1980), pp. 109-136. An unsympathetic analysis of their portraits of Benjamin can be found in Françoise Meltzer, "Acedia and Melancholia," *Walter Benjamin and the Demands of History*, ed. Michael P. Steinberg (Ithaca and London: Cornell University Press, 1996), pp. 141-63.

[46] Aristotle devoted an important section of the *Problemata Physica* (xxx, i) to the preponderance of black bile (*melan-kole*) in the melancholic nature, making it the mark of

"all great men." Neo-Platonism in the Renaissance echoed and amplified this account construing the stereotype of the melancholic intellectual (cf. Kuhn, *The Demon of Noontide*, 18-20; Goodstein, *Experience without Qualities* 37-9ff). In "Agesilaus Santander," Benjamin wrote that he was born "under the sign of Saturn – the planet of slow revolution, the star of hesitation and delay" (*GS* 6:521/*SW* 2:713), acknowledging thus his melancholic nature – and also adhering to the classical stereotype.

[47] Cf. Max Pensky, *Melancholy Dialectics: Walter Benjamin and the Play of Mourning* (Amherst: The University of Massachusetts Press, 1993).

[48] This reading of Convolute "D" and the revolutionary potentiality of boredom strongly rely on its analysis in Andrew Benjamin, "Boredom and Distraction: The Moods of Modernity," *Walter Benjamin and History*, ed. Andrew Benjamin (London and New York: Continuum, 2005), pp. 156-70.

[49] Ibid., p. 165.

[50] "Dreams vary according to where you are, what area and what street, but above all according to the time of the year and the weather. Rainy weather in the city, in its thoroughly treacherous sweetness and its power to draw one back to the days of early childhood, can be appreciated only by someone who has grown up in the big city. It naturally evens out the day, and with rainy weather one can do the same thing day in, day out – play cards, read, or engage in argument – whereas sunshine, by contrast, shades the hours and is furthermore less friendly to the dreamer." (B°,5)

[51] Sholem writes that: "Benjamin was the most patient human being I ever came to know, and the decisiveness and radicalism of his thinking stood in vehement contrast to his infinitely patient and only very slowly opening nature. And to deal with Benjamin one had to have the greatest patience oneself. Only very patient people could gain deeper contact with him," Scholem, "Walter Benjamin and His Angel," p. 73.

[52] Sigrid Weigel, *Body- and Image-Space: Re-Reading Walter Benjamin*, trans. Georgina Paul, Rachel McNicholl and Jeremy Gaines (London and New York: Routledge, 1996), p. 48.

[53] The English translators of the Harvard edition add a note to this passage: "*Schwelle*, cognate with the English word 'sill,' has the root sense of 'board,' 'structural support,' 'foundation beam.' According to current information, it is etymologically unrelated to *schwellen*," (*AP* 991).

[54] According to Andrew Benjamin, the threshold is important because, precisely due to its *ambivalence*, it becomes a possibility: "Ambivalence is marked by a potentiality within which interruption will have conditions of possibility that resist the hold of eternal return," Benjamin, "Boredom and Distraction," p. 163.

[55] Andrew Benjamin thus comments this passage: "Benjamin provides a way into this formulation of the problem of time – the temporality of moods – in terms of what he describes as the temporality of awaiting. What is the time of awaiting? Benjamin's response to this question necessitates that this awaiting be distinguished from an awaiting in which the image of the future determines both what is to occur as well as its having occurred. What cannot be expected – even though it is too often expected – is victory to come through continuity. This recalls the passage cited earlier in which Benjamin dismisses as a form of binary opposition boredom linked to not knowing what is awaited as one pole, and the superficiality or lack of attention inherent in the claim that we can give a form to that which is awaited as the other." And also: "Boredom is an awaiting without object. This cannot be countered by the presentation of images of the future. Boredom works as a threshold precisely because the move away from boredom is carried by it as a potentiality. The site of potentiality is the present. However, it is not a conception of the

present that is reducible to the moment thought within the passage of chronological time. Rather, the present moment is the event happening as the 'now of recognizability'," Ibid. pp. 166, 168.

[56] Ibid. p. 167.

[57] An early version of this entry called the one who waits "the synthetic type" [*der synthetische Typ*]: "takes in the energy 'time' and passes it on in altered form" (O°,78). A similar entry calls it "the impassive thinker" [*der Kontemplative*] (M4a,1).

[58] Benjamin, "Boredom and Distraction," p. 167.

[59] An early entry relates dream and dust: "Boredom and dust. Dream a garment one cannot turn. On the outside, the grey boredom (of sleep). Sleep state, hypnotic, of the dusty figures in the Musée Grévin. A sleeper is not a good subject for wax. Boredom [*Langeweile*] is always the external surface of unconscious events. Therefore, it could appear to the great dandies as a mark of distinction. For it is precisely [?] the dandy who despises new clothing: whatever he wants must appear slightly frayed. As opposed to the theory of dreams that would reveal to us 'psyches,' the world that comes to seem pointless. What about it?" (F°,8).

[60] Andrew Benjamin writes: "the dialectical antithesis to boredom is experimentation; experimentation both as a mood and as act. [...] Experimentation has to be thought in relation to its inherent fragility. Once again it is that very fragility that demands the affirmation of experimentation – an affirmation in the face of the inescapable possibility for its recuperation. That affirmation is the project of criticism. equally, it is the project of politics," Benjamin, "Boredom and Distraction," p. 170.

WORKS CITED

Adorno, Theodor W. "Introduction to Benjamin's *Schriften*." Trans. Shierry Weber Nicholsen. *Notes to Literature*. Vol. Two. New York: Columbia UP, 1992. 220-32.

——. "A Portrait of Walter Benjamin." Trans. Samuel and Shierry Weber. *Prisms*. London: Neville Spearman, 1967. 227-42.

Adorno, Theodor W. And Max Horkheimer. *Dialectic of Enlightenment*. Trans John Cumming. London: Allen, 1973.

Arendt, Hannah. "Walter Benjamin: 1892-1940." Walter Benjamin, *Illuminations*. Arendt, Hannah ed. New York: Schoken Books, 1969. 1-55.

Benjamin, Andrew. "Boredom and Distraction: The Moods of Modernity." *Walter Benjamin and History*. Ed. Andrew Benjamin. London and New York: Continuum, 2005. 156-70.

Benjamin, Walter. *The Arcades Project*. Ed. Rolf Tiedemann. Trans. Howard Eiland and Kevin McLaughlin. Cambridge, MA: Belknap Press of Harvard University Press, 1999.

——. *Selected Writings*. Ed. Marcus Bullock and Michael W. Jennings. Cambridge, MA: Belknap Press of Harvard University Press, 1996-2003.

——. *The Origin of the German Tragic Drama*. Trans. John Osborne. London: Verso, 1998.

——. *Gesammelte Schriften*. Ed. Rolf Tiedemann and Hermann Schweppenhäuser. Frankfurt am Main: Suhrkamp, 1972-89.

Buck-Morss, Susan. *The Dialectics of Seeing: Walter Benjamin and the Arcades Project*. Cambridge, MA and London: The MIT Press, 1989.

Freud, Sigmund. "Beyond the Pleasure Principle." *Standard Edition of the Complete Psychological Works*. James Strachery ed. Vol. XVIII. London: The Hogart Press, 1955. 7-64.

Fürnkäs, Josef. "Aura." *Benjamins Begriffe*. Ed. Michael Opitz and Erdmut Wizisla. Frankfurt am Main: Suhrkamp, 2000. 95-146.

Gilloch, Graeme. *Myth and Metropolis: Walter Benjamin and the City*. Cambridge: Polity Press, 1996.

Goodstein, Elisabeth S. *Experience without Qualities: Boredom and Modernity*. Stanford, CA: Stanford UP, 2005.

Healy, Seán Desmond. *Boredom, Self, and Culture*. London and Toronto: Associated UP, 1984.

Klapp, Orrin E. *Overload and Boredom: Essays on the Quality of Life in the Information Society*. New York: Greenwood Press, 1986.

Kracauer, Siegfried. "Boredom." Trans. Thomas Y. Levin. *The Mass Ornament: Weimar Essays*. Thomas Y. Levin ed. Cambridge, MA & London: Harvard UP, 1995. 331-4.

Krasko, Genrich L. *This Unbearable Boredom of Being: A Crisis of Meaning in America*. New York: iUniverse, 2004.

Kuhn, Reinhard. *The Demon of Noontide: Ennui in Western Literature*. Princeton, NJ: Princeton University Press, 1976.

Löwy, Michael. *Fire Alarm: Reading Walter Benjamin's 'on the Concept of History'*. Trans. Chris Turner. London and New York: Verso, 2005.

Meltzer, Françoise. "Acedia and Melancholia." *Walter Benjamin and the Demands of History*. Ed. Michael P. Steinberg. Ithaca and London: Cornell University Press, 1996. 141-63.

Meyer Spacks, Patricia. *Boredom: The Literary History of a State of Mind.* Chicago and London: The University of Chicago Press, 1995.

Moran, Joe. "Benjamin and Boredom." *Critical Quarterly* 45.1 (July 2003): 168-81.

Pensky, Max. *Melancholy Dialectics: Walter Benjamin and the Play of Mourning.* Amherst: The University of Massachusetts Press, 1993.

Raposa, Michael L. *Boredom and the Religious Imagination.* Charlottesville: UP of Virginia, 1999.

Salzani, Carlo. "The City as Crime Scene: Walter Benjamin and the Traces of the Detective." *New German Critique* 34.1, Winter 2007. 165-87.

Scholem, Gershom. "Walter Benjamin and His Angel." Trans. Werner Dannhauser. *On Walter Benjamin: Critical Essays and Recollections.* Ed. Gary Smith. Cambridge, MA, and London: The MIT Press, 1988. 51-89.

Schwarz, Christopher. *Langeweile Und Identiät: Eine Studie Zur Entstehung Und Krise Des Romantischen Selbsgefühls.* Heidelberg: Unviversitätsverlag C. Winter, 1993.

Simmel, Georg. "The Metropolis and Mental Life." Trans. Kurt H. Wolff. *The Sociology of Georg Simmel.* Kurt H. Wolff ed. New York: The Free Press, 1950. 409-24.

Sontag, Susan. "Under the Sign of Saturn." *Under the Sign of Saturn.* New York: Farrar, Straus, Giroux, 1980.

Stoessel, Marleen. *Aura, Das vergessene Menschliche: Zu Sprache und Erfahrung bei Walter Benjamin.* Munich: Carl Hanser, 1983.

Svendsen, Lars. *A Philosophy of Boredom.* Trans. John Irons. London: Reaktion, 2005.

Weber, Thomas. "Erfahrung." *Benjamins Begriffe.* Ed. Michael Opitz and Erdmut Wizisla. Frankfurt am Main: Suhrkamp, 2000. 230-59.

Weigel, Sigrid. *Body- and Image-Space: Re-Reading Walter Benjamin.* Trans. Georgina Paul, Rachel McNicholl and Jeremy Gaines. London and New York: Routledge, 1996.

CHAPTER 7

The Quick and the Flat:
Walter Benjamin, Werner Herzog

Rachel June Torbett

In "The Work of Art in the Age of its Technological Reproducibility," Benjamin emphasises the revolutionary potentiality of cinema: oppressive tradition is dismantled, and the spectator is freed from the shackles of "auratic" time and experience. However, there is an undeniable ambivalence in Benjamin's philosophy of time and experience, one that has been described as "the return of the auratic." Such ambiguity can be articulated through the cinema of Werner Herzog. Like Baudelaire's poetry, Herzog's images both destroy the aura, and evoke its return. As auratic artworks, Herzog's films side with the time of boredom, but they do so within an art form arrested by distraction. Timeliness makes a return to the cinema, but cinema does not return to tradition. Quite differently, time returns to Herzog's cinema ambiguously, and ferociously, in the rubble of tradition. Cinematic experience is neither entirely distracting, nor is it strictly boring either, imitating Baudelaire again, something "lived through" is given the "weight of experience."

Being bored has never been so distracting. So distracting, perhaps, that boredom can no longer be experienced by a modern audience. If this is so, then the modern experience of boredom is never without ambiguity. Unreliable in theory, the word is nevertheless frequently used, and "boredom" seems to be as relevant now as ever. In the context of cinema, it is often said that films are boring; and what's more, certain filmmakers even make boredom their project. From the avant-garde to the post modern, certain directors have attempted to "take away" from modern experience, rather than repeat or add to it. These films are slow rather than fast, and it becomes conceivable to sit in front of a single shot of the Empire State Building for 8 hours. But the subject of this essay is Werner Herzog, not Andy Warhol, and Herzog's films do not sit comfortably within the genre of "slow cinema," then again, his films do not sit comfortably in any genre at all. Nevertheless, his films still have a relationship to boredom, and not simply because people say that Herzog's films are boring. Many say that they are not boring at all. Boredom steps into Herzog's films as a matter of time, and with this time, the following essay will link Herzog to Walter Benjamin's theory of modern experience as distraction. Just as boredom is different from distraction, Herzog is an inappropriate exemplar of Benjamin's theory of cinema. Yet for all that Werner is Walter's adversary, there is also a more obscured camaraderie between them. For Herzog brings all the ambiguity to the state of boredom, which I propose, is also present within Benjamin's theory of distraction.

Herzog is the strange master of the boring image. He does not represent the world, so much as he plasticises it, making it flat, removed, and as boring as pornography. Realism is always dishonest to Herzog. He has published a short manifesto condemning cinema verité, and no matter how ironic or silly this "Minnesota Declaration" might appear, Herzog is quite serious about his distrust of the "accountant's truth."[1] Written in 15 minutes, the document was motivated by television and sleeplessness. Disgusted by the "boring" and "uninspired" documentaries on every channel, he switched the television off, but still unable to sleep, he switched it back on: "There was a porno film on and I had the feeling, yes, even though it's just a physical performance, it comes closer to what I call truth. It was more truthful than those documentaries."[2]

The rejection of verité is also a rejection of proximity. Like pornography, Herzog's documentaries are always performances, reality is made into image, not the other way around. His camera never captures things, so much as it is used to distance them. Thus, rather than using the camera to bring the spectator closer to the world, Herzog does the exact opposite. Frequently filming from the sky, at a vast distance, or in a tracking shot, the camera's perspective is not proximate or everyday. Withdrawn, the earth's landscapes become foreign, and distorted beyond what they are. The camera does not act as an intermediary, it is more like a god, soaring above, or rushing past. Herzog sees himself as a visionary, and perhaps his fans do too, but unlike other so-called "visionary" filmmakers (Bergman for example), Herzog rarely goes "close-up." He is not thoughtful, and he refuses to investigate. Herzog just films, and in this way, he is a passive filmmaker; he offers no depth to his images, because he passes no comment, and never tries to probe. What's more, without a zoom, things become static, they have no perspectival depth and begin to seem flat. The world no longer resembles itself, instead it is flattened to an image. As we shall see, this distancing is rejected by the Benjaminian cameraman who brings objects up close rather than pushes them away. Not only does the distancing of the image attempt to reinstate auratic concepts to the mechanically reproduced artwork, it also reintroduces a sense of time that is quite alien to modernity.

Modernity is constructed in a series of discontinuous moments; continuity and timeliness are impossible here. Any attempts for time must be deceitful, and this accusation would please Herzog, for his notoriety depends on his villainy.[3] Personal exploits aside, Herzog's deceit can also be framed in temporal terms. In regards to time, his films stand as attempts to circumvent the necessarily momentary presence of the cinematic image. Herzog does not give the spectator "moments" or "glimpses"; quite to the contrary, he draws everything out, and his camera is persistent. He holds his shots for a long time, so long that the spectator is forced to contemplate an image for longer than usual. In his fictional films, he stretches the image into something poetic or painterly; while in his documentaries he focuses on his subject until they have nothing left to say, making them fidget, and wish that the camera would stop rolling. Boredom steps in, and with boredom the modern moment is shattered. Adhering to a foreign stretch of time, images are dragged out and made alien to our modern sensibilities. When the image is prolonged and made to drift, our intellect becomes stunted and our captivation becomes boring. Herzog's films are too flat for engagement, but then on another level there is too much engagement to permit disinterest. What could be magnificent is dulled, and the spectator is rendered incapable of awe, but what is most peculiar, is that they are still captivated.

And yet, perhaps, this is not so peculiar at all. Reception is necessarily bound up in time. Though boredom and captivation appear to be polar opposites, from Benjamin's perspective, the bored spectator and the captivated spectator are both tied to the same stretch of time and tradition. In such profound states, the spectator remains subservient to a temporality that is bound up with what Benjamin calls the aura. The stretch of time and the distant limit, which define captivation and boredom, are very different from the discontinuous moment that creates Benjamin's distracted audience.

In 1932, Walter Benjamin said: "there is no longer any place for boredom in our lives."[4] The decline of boredom and the rise of what Benjamin called distraction, are not merely issues of lifestyle, modern man[5] does not choose distraction over boredom. It is rather the case that modern man has lost the capacity to be bored. No longer accessible, boredom belongs to another time, a time when experience was possible, and a time when these experiences could be made communicable. As Giorgio Agamben says, modern man's "incapacity to have and communicate experiences is perhaps one of the few self-certainties to which he can lay claim."[6] For thinkers of reason, the decline of experience and translatability must equate to the decline of art; and this is surely a matter of tragedy. Yet in Benjamin's most programmatic essay, "The Work of Art in the Age of Mechanical Reproducibility,"[7] the destruction of experience signals no calamity, instead, it is a cause for celebration. As we shall see, the success of a distracted mode of receptivity opens the possibility of collectivity and revolution in the mass audience. It is quite clear that a mode of bored receptivity is excluded from Benjamin's program for art. But then again, in all its clarity, Benjamin's theory of distraction is also deeply ambiguous. For although boredom is denied to modern subjects, Benjamin also hints at its return. This return never replaces distraction; it never inhabits the place of "true experience" either. Boredom returns to a place where it sits uncomfortably – where it barely sits at all.

In this essay Benjamin's ambiguity will be played out in a reading of Werner Herzog's style of cinema. From the outset Werner is Walter's worst enemy; words like "romantic," "sublime," or "auratic," attach themselves to Herzog easily. Moreover, he himself repeatedly proclaims that his films are "poetic" and "true."[8] These terms are all very dangerous in Benjamin's lexicon, they denote obsolete concepts, they let down the cause, and spell out fascism. On the side of the spectator, they never call Herzog's films exciting or distracting, they leave the theatre crying "boredom," or swooning with "intoxication" and "captivation."

At a recent conference on Herzog, Timothy Corrigan divided Herzog's critical audience into two different camps: "there are those that read Herzog's films as neo-romantic, even neo-fascist, visionary statements. And there are those that see them laced with a kind of irony, which undercuts that whole tradition."[9] Corrigan goes on to tell the story of when Herzog's *Lessons of Darkness* screened at the Berlin Film Festival. At the end of the screening, the whole audience rose up to boo him, all the while Herzog stood on stage, a madman, gesticulating wildly and shouting: "You're all wrong! You're all wrong!"[10] Whether the critics take Herzog's side, or whether they bow to consensus in disgust, *Lessons of Darkness* remains a deeply ambiguous film. It is made up of footage of the oil fires at the end of the first Iraq war, yet what seems be overtly political content, is transformed into something apolitical, more like science-fiction-poetry than critique. Thus while *Lessons of Darkness* is an extraordinarily beautiful film, as Corrigan says, it seems to "avoid or detour around the undeniable politics"[11] of his subject matter, and its message is less than clear. This obscurity is not unintentional, Herzog challenges clear-cut readings and despises "accountant's truths." As Thomas Elsaesser says, "Herzog retains (as a technique of *Verfremdung*) a 'stupid' eye, one that is merely curious rather than knowing or demonstrative."[12]

Herzog's stupid eye, his obscurity and his irony, need not be read as matters of ineffectuality; as Corrigan says, they can "undercut" and challenge tradition. Now Herzog is sounding more like a Benjaminian. A film can be political independently of its content – it may threaten tradition by virtue of some more formal qualities. Following the terms given by Benjamin in his essay on cinema, Herzog does, and does not, meet this challenge. This essay sets out to follow Herzog's shortcomings, and his triumph, from the perspective of the spectator, and what can be called their mode of receptivity. Auratic modes of receptivity are likely reactions to a Herzog film: boredom, contemplation, association, and continuity, all have a place within his audience. Yet these states are never complete, "laced with a kind of irony," they always arrive at ambiguity.

1.

Receiving images has never been so easy. It is modernity's privilege, and its poverty, that its visual field is never empty. One is continually surrounded by the image, wherever the modern subject goes, and even if they stay at home, their eyes are always engaged with the flicker. In what Patrice Petro calls "a founding text of critical theory,"[13] Georg Simmel describes the city dweller's perceptual field as being dominated by "the rapid crowding of changing images, the sharp discontinuity in the grasp of a single glance, and the unexpectedness of onrushing impressions."[14] *"Die Grossstadt und das Geistesleben"* (The Metropolis and Mental Life) was published in 1903 and as Petro points out, this essay had a "tremendous impact"[15] on the writing of Walter Benjamin and Siegfried Kracauer. In his essay, Simmel gives a phenomenological account of the city; it is an account in which vision presides over the other senses, and thus one where the image comes to govern over experience and subjectivity.

In every direction, the city dweller's perceptual field is determined by the "rapid telescoping of changing images;"[16] their fragmentation is violent, experience becomes an assault, and life becomes very different from what it was before. The discontinuous and fragmentary structure of the modern image limits it to the moment. Cutting through space and time, the modern image breaks with continuity, and pushes the urbanite's gaze away from timely experience and tradition. In contrast to the placid rural man whose gaze is met by a more consistent world, urban man becomes a creature of intense sensation. Outside of the city, our eyes are met by images which are more long lasting than a flickering screen, or a face in a moving crowd. Standing before regular and even sensory imagery, man's consciousness can relax, perception flows uninterrupted. In the city, on the other hand, the fragmentation of the image is always interrupting perception and experience-dislocation reigns, and continuity and rhythm are lost. Never at rest, the urbanite's gaze forever hurtles into the moment and becomes limited to this instant. With only a "now," "deeply felt and emotional relationships"[17] do not have a chance to develop, and tradition is lost to the "ever-new." Because the rural gaze is met by "the slower, more habitual, more smoothly flowing rhythm" of imagery, the peasant's consciousness is more receptive and more attentive. And in virtue of "the steady equilibrium of unbroken customs," rural folk have a relationship with the world which is "rooted in the more unconscious levels of the psyche."[18] These "unconscious levels of the mind" necessitate a way of looking at the world, which exists through time rather than purely in the moment. Once a timely gaze is lost to the blur of the city, the subject's ability to concentrate and associate is interrupted. Attention is limited to a disconnected glimpse, and with little more than a look, the human subject loses the ability to "receive" the time-warped images associated with custom and tradition. The urbanite is simply too distracted by the modern visual world to maintain a "steady equilibrium" with it.

Once defined in distraction, aesthetic reception has shifted, perhaps irrevocably, from an experience with an existence over time, to the singularity of a momentary event. This modern reception of the image must have the temporal structure of an "encounter," as opposed to that timeliness that defines the rural "experience." The image is now thrust upon the subject, so much so, that the subject no longer needs to "receive" an image – there is simply no time for reflection or assimilation because the image comes and goes in a moment. With only this moment, sensation takes over from older forms of perception that are associated with universality and knowledge; and the image becomes something that is lived through rather than received and experienced.

Benjamin refers to this mode of receptivity as distraction, it is the defining mood of modernity for him, and it signifies a change in the structure of experience.[19] *Erfahrung,* i.e. experience through time, is replaced by *Erlebnis,* experience limited to the moment. Stepping back in order to understand things, pre-modern "man" could actually integrate and assimilate their experience into tradition, he is wise, knowledgeable, and ahistorical. With cities, with photography, or with film, the fragmented image demands isolated sensation, experience is "lived through" rather than assimilated. We are losing time. Without *Erfahrung,* the modern subject "feels as though he has been dropped from the calendar. The big-city dweller knows this feeling on Sundays."[20]

Modern man has lost the ability to be bored. Because boredom requires a stretch of time which is denied to modernity, a modern Sunday is just another series of moments, disconnected ones. Though these Sundays might be devoid of human project or ambition, they are nevertheless full of distraction – and not boring at all. As I will elaborate on later, Benjamin has an ambivalent relationship to this mode of receptivity (as could be also argued for Kracauer).[21] This ambivalence can also be gleaned from Simmel's essay. The metropolis is undeniably a site of loss, things cannot be absorbed, wise men are cast into the countryside. And yet, at the same time, life in the city is undoubtedly stimulating, and the modern metropolis becomes the proper seat of sophistication, intellect, and power. Life is never boring, the "swift and uninterrupted change of outer and inner stimuli"[22] excites metropolitan man because "man is a differentiating creature. His mind is stimulated by the difference between a momentary impression and the one which preceded it."[23]

And yet over-stimulation does not always lead to excitement, it can also lead to a mood which leans toward boredom or even paralysis. In other words, a little indifference is needed to get through your modern day. What Simmel calls the "blasé attitude," quite obviously anticipates the Andy

Warhols who charm us today; and more implicitly, it is illustrative of Freud's analysis of consciousness as a barrier rather than a purely receptive faculty. As Simmel puts it, "the metropolitan type of man [...] develops an organ protecting him against the threatening currents and discrepancies of his external environment which would uproot him."[24] Thanks to this "protective organ," the blasé consciousness becomes adept "in the blunting of discrimination."[25] Simmel's blasé individual is not stupid, he can still perceive distinctions, only "the meaning and the differing values of things, and thereby the things themselves, are experienced as insubstantial."[26] This lack of interest in the differences between things will, according to Benjamin, find its revolutionary potential in the movie watcher. A blasé character, a mode of distracted receptivity, and a fragmented perceptual field, will be celebrated in Benjamin's essay on cinema. The reason for celebration will become clear later on, but for now, Simmel's blasé character must surely signify a crisis for the art-world. If the spectator is apathetic, and does not respond to distinctions, how are they supposed to appreciate an artwork? Everything looks the same, one experiences every art opening with indifference and disdain. The blasé character loses interest in the world, not because there are not enough interesting things in the world, but because there are too many. If this spectator is bored, it is a boredom without lack or poverty. It is not really boredom at all. The city, or the cinema, contain too many images, all too discontinuous and momentary for the stretch of boredom to cling to. But then again, this subject is all too boring as well. Neither the street corner nor the artwork can command a coherent interest from the spectator – let alone a span of concentration. Our eyes easily fall to banality, they cannot attach to one thing, they need only glance absentmindedly at the images passing by. These eyes are dulled, some would say, because they can no longer tap into a continuous body of knowledge, or have an "experience," which the image might once have offered.

Baudelaire, according to Benjamin, was the first to deal with this "crisis in spectatorship." Writing for an impatient audience who no longer had the time for lyric poetry, Baudelaire faced an impossible task. No one has patience enough for boredom any longer, as Benjamin says of Baudelaire's readers, "will power and the ability to concentrate are not their strong points. What they prefer is sensual pleasures; they are familiar with the 'spleen' which kills interest and receptiveness."[27] The modern subject inhales pleasure through an inherently distracted relationship to the image. By living through the image, by not receiving it in an "interested" fashion, and perhaps not even "experiencing" it at all, the modern spectator can nonetheless enjoy the image immensely. One desires the flicker, a continuity of image is not distracting enough, the modern spectator yawns as the image passes through time, for it does not change and it begins to look flat.

The proliferation of sensory stimuli that the modern subject faces not only produces a change in the spectator's choice of image. Because pure boredom becomes actually impossible for the modern man who cannot relax without constant stimuli, he chooses to immerse himself as much as possible, not in a single image, but in a constant chaotic blur of them. An empty screen freaks out the spectator, one cannot engage because one is asked to engage too much. Without "interest" or "receptiveness," the blasé spectator has no faculties with which to experience the imagery of emptiness.

In many ways, it is temporal structure of the empty image that makes it creepy. Impossible in the flicker, emptiness needs to adhere to the stretch of time, a time outside the fragmentation of modernity. An uneasiness with emptiness reflects its marked absence in "the age of mechanical reproducibility"; and in this way, the sensibility of the blasé character mimics the structure of the world around him and his own perception. Ironically for the modern spectator, this means that his distraction necessitates a bored and disinterested outlook; on the other hand, in temporal terms, the spectator neither has a chance to get bored, nor encounters the emptiness required for boredom. Distraction carries ambiguity in its form, this ambiguity is encapsulated by the German *Zerstreuung*: while Harry Zohn translates *Zerstreuung* as "distraction," in German it explicitly carries the contrary connotations of both absent-mindedness and alertness.

Just as Simmel's blasé character is constructed by the fragmentary material conditions of the city, Benjamin's distracted figure is constructed materially, with the advent of mechanical reproducibility. The discontinuous image is made possible only with technology, and the demise of the ability to experience goes hand in hand with the demise of traditional arts and crafts. Tradition is dissipating, and not only in human phenomenological experience. Most decisively, perhaps, technology liquidates continuity from the artwork. The demise of non-mechanical art forms is often mourned, and as will be addressed further on, even in Benjamin's own work there is a certain nostalgia for the craft of timely "passing on." However, for the moment, this nostalgia is quite absent from the Artwork Essay. In this essay, mechanical reproduction has radically revolutionary potentiality in its ability to cut through time. Benjamin's program is clear, but even so, there is ambiguity again in this achievement. As an agent in the decline of experience (as *Erfahrung*), the cinematic image is most certainly triumphant, but whether it strictly keeps its "eyes" in the moment is another question. Pushing these "timely" thoughts aside for now, the next section will focus on the cinematic experience (as *Erlebnis*) and outline a Benjaminian theory of cinematic "ballistics."

2.

Flashing at 24 frames per second, cinema mimics the fragmented visual field, which characterises Simmel's account of the metropolis. The "telescoping images" of the street corner, their structure and their temporality, are mirrored in the cinematic form: one image need not follow from the next, as the camera zooms in and out, then cuts, and changes, the spectator is assaulted by a continual shift in perspective. As Benjamin says, cinema arises as "a symptom of profound changes in apperception," its mimicry is reflective and representative of a "change in the structure of experience." But cinema is more than a symptom, it is also an agent. In its mimicry, cinema becomes a "true training ground [*Übungsinstrument*]" for the spectator. Cinema meets "a new and urgent need for stimuli," for, "in a film, perception conditioned by shock [*chockförmige Wahrnehmung*] was established as a formal principle. What determines the rhythm of production on a conveyer belt is the same thing that underlies the rhythm of reception in the film."[28] With cinema (Benjamin is talking about Mickey Mouse films in this instance!) "mankind makes preparations to survive civilisation."[29] Like the blasé character, the audience's consciousness acts as a buffer, "screening stimuli," that would otherwise be too much.[30] But while the blasé character seems to be of a passive and ineffectual nature, cinema (as opposed to the street corner) has revolutionary potential, and Benjamin's distracted audience is all but passive.

Quite the opposite of nonchalant, the distracted audience is of a destructive character. In 1931, Benjamin described the destructive character as one who "stands in the front line of traditionalists. Some people pass things down to posterity, by making them untouchable and thus conserving them; others pass on situations, by making them practicable and thus liquidating them. The latter is called destructive."[31] In 1936 with the Artwork essay, Benjamin claims that cinema revolutionises experience by making it "practicable" (it sharpens the consciousness' "screen against stimuli") and, then, it also possesses the power of liquidation. Cinema explodes our "prison-world with the dynamite of the split second,"[32] dislodging tradition, and actively perpetrating the demise of the spectator's experience of the world as *Erfahrung*.

Cinematic images are not "ballistic" merely in imitation, they participate in the destruction of the art-object itself. Using the metaphor of the surgeon, Benjamin describes the cameraman as cutting through the surface of reality, bringing objects closer, closing the distance that tradition creates. Thanks to technology, distance is eliminated from the artwork, it differs radically from traditional art forms because cinema cuts through the image it produces, eliminating any trace of what Benjamin calls the "aura." The painter, for example, "maintains in his work a natural distance from reality," while "the cinematographer penetrates deeply into its tissue." "By the laying-on of hands," the painter acts as a "magician,"[33] dragging the objects through time and into time, creating a distance from whence auratic values might flourish. Bringing the image closer, freeing it from the time of tradition and of the aura, cinema disposes with "a number of traditional concepts – such as creativity and genius, eternal value and mystery – which, used in an uncontrolled way (and controlling them is difficult today), allow factual material to be manipulated in the interests of fascism."[34] To avoid a fascist sensibility in the world of mechanical reproducibility, the traditional notions associated with a "true" experience of art must be shattered – and it is the camera that has such destructive powers of proximity and transience.

The notion of the "copy" also challenges the auratic notions of authenticity and originality: "the technology of reproduction detaches the reproduced object from the sphere of tradition. By replicating the work many times over, it substitutes a mass existence for a unique existence."[35] Once a "unique existence" in a particular point in time is dislodged, the reproduced object can "reach the recipient in his or her own situation," and the artwork becomes a matter of a collective reception. Of all the reproducible arts, the "most powerful agent is film. The social significance of film, even – and especially – in its most positive form, is inconceivable without its destructive, cathartic side: the liquidation of the value of tradition in the cultural heritage."[36] "Uniqueness and permanence" are untroubled by the painting or the religious icon, and these singular objects can develop an aura surrounding their "unique existence in space and time." In the copy, and with a scalpel, the mechanically reproduced object is blasé: to go back to Simmel, it is fundamentally indifferent toward the distinctions between things.[37] With this indifference, the artwork no longer has a singular existence, and uniqueness and distance are shattered. In Benjamin's words, "the stripping of the veil from the object, the destruction of the aura, is the signature of a perception whose "sense of sameness in the world" has so increased that, by means of reproduction, it extracts sameness even from what is unique."[38]

If we follow Agamben's reading of Benjamin, then the diminished temporality of the non-auratic art-work is of utmost importance, for as Agamben says, "the original task of a genuine revolution, therefore, is never merely to 'change the world,' but also, and above all, to 'change time.'"[39] The non-auratic artwork has the ability to change time in a double movement. Never "handling" the object over time, as a painter would, the camera captures the object up close, in the present moment. This closure of time and distance is further solidified in the advent of the copy: once the object's singularity is thwarted, the object is brought even closer, it can meet the spectator "in his own particular situation," and as a collective.

Without the shackles of outmoded concepts and a fixed existence in time, the film image jolts the spectator like a "missile."[40] Like the visual capacity of the city-dweller, the spectator's consciousness must respond to the shock of the cinematic image. The aura cannot be maintained in such an explosive instant, and nor can a span of attentiveness on the part of the spectator. Without the aura, and in only a frame, the cinematic image is obsolete as an object of contemplative immersion. Contemplation, as we learnt from Simmel, requires a relationship to time, which is unavailable to modernity. But the power of film does not exist in an attempt to resuscitate Simmel's "rural" capacities; to the contrary, it radically denies any possibility for the stasis of contemplation, or any train of associative thought. This distracted mode of spectatorship contrasts sharply with the one of painting – in Benjamin's words, "let us compare the screen [*Leinwand*] on which a film unfolds with the canvas of a painting. The painting invites the viewer to contemplation; before it, he can give himself up to his train of associations. Before a film image, he cannot do so. No sooner has he seen it than it has already changed. It cannot be fixed on."[41] The sharp discontinuity of the cinematic image continually interrupts the possibility of a thought outside of the present moment, the film-goer cannot think forwards or backwards, they are continually shocked into the present: "the train of associations in the person contemplating these images is immediately interrupted by new images. This constitutes the shock effect of film."[42]

Due to its reproducibility, the cinematic image "meets the spectator in their particular situation," and due to its shock effect, the situation is outside the self, in a collective audience. As Rodolphe Gasché puts it, the film spectator "is neither a substantial nor a formal centre that would ground its autonomy,"[43] and in this way, individualism is obstructed. Thus when Benjamin quotes Duhamel's cinema loathing words, "I can no longer think what I want to think. My thoughts have been replaced by moving images,"[44] Duhamel's antipathy is transformed into accolade: loss of individualism is now a site of potentiality.

3.

Benjamin's demand to interrupt individualism and its auratic foundations is never in question. What this essay intends to question, however, is the stylistic bias, which frames the above reading of Benjamin's essay on cinema. Considering the rhythm of the conveyer belt as a metaphor for cinema, considering its structural and affective ballistics, it would appear that Benjamin evokes a picture of cinema that revolves around speed, shock and penetration. Benjamin's "theory of cinema" is not supported by many examples; nevertheless, the examples he does use appear to evoke a certain style, or even genre, of cinema. Vertov and Chaplin are Benjamin's heroes, both directors are interested in the mechanisation of the human subject, and both directors exploit the mechanical apparatus of the camera to make their interests material. In Vertov and Chaplin, one could certainly evoke an "archetype" for Benjamin's film theory. This privileging would most surely be dangerous, and I think that Benjamin could sense this, not only would you exclude a large proportion of films, all flickering at 24 frames per second, but you would also ignore the more "enigmatic" side to cinematic ballistics.

This essay sets out to explore this "enigmatic" side in terms of temporality and the kind of receptivity, which is overcome in the modern command of the moment. The modern moment does not have the time to be bored, this much is certain, but even so, with this certainty, boredom remains enigmatic throughout Benjamin's work. Looking backwards in his essay on Leskov, Benjamin posits the storyteller as engaged in a timely activity, reaching through and passing on, the storyteller weaves and spins with continuity. On the side of the receiver, they are also weaving and spinning while they listen; and reception is thus linked to time outside the moment.

Listening to a story is boring, it involves a "process of assimilation, which takes place in the depths, requires a state of relaxation which is becoming rarer and rarer. If sleep is the apogee of physical relaxation, boredom is the apogee of mental relaxation."[45] Modernity cannot relax, and the proliferation of information and the rise of the novel, contribute to the increasing "poverty of experience" in the modern subject: "experience has fallen in value. And it looks as if it may fall into bottomlessness."[46] Though published only shortly after the Artwork Essay, it has often been suggested that the Leskov piece contains a radically different sentiment towards modernity's obliteration of time.[47] Benjamin's ambivalence is more and less a matter of sentiment, or rather it is not a matter of sentiment at all: time never leaves Benjamin's writing and when it is neither being mourned, or critiqued, it is returning. This return complicates Benjamin's theory of experience, it reintroduces time and exceeds the moment, and what I will question is whether it opens up the possibility for another site of potentiality, and another style of cinema.

There are many examples of modern cinema which react against the constructs of the "flicker," films that try to make associations, and draw out time from the present. Perhaps the emergence of slow cinema makes Benjamin's argument appear a little dated; or maybe these films project a false aura, reintroducing outmoded concepts into a form which has no time for such things. Whichever is the case, my analysis of Werner Herzog is directed toward neither of these conclusions. Whether Herzog dispenses with the aura or not (and it is safe to say that he does *and* he does not), my intentions remain only to illuminate another side to Benjamin's treatise on cinema. This "other side" marks a deep ambivalence that runs across all Benjamin's writing. It is easy to ignore, and as Miriam Hansen remarks, this ambiguity is concealed in a strictly Brechtian or Marxist interpretation of Benjamin: "the particular blend of Marxism and modernism that determined the reception of Benjamin's work, however, tended to obscure the more incongruous and ambivalent features of the Artwork Essay, not to mention its problematic status in relation to Benjamin's other writings."[48] Interest in Benjamin's obscure side is never a dismissal of Marxism or of Modernism, and neither is it a denial of Benjamin's "theory of shock and ballistics." To the contrary, the reappearance of time within the cinematic image is unabashedly reliant upon its creation in the ballistic moment.

In her essay "Benjamin, Cinema and Experience: The Blue Flower in the Land of Technology," Hansen argues that via his concept of the "optical unconscious," Benjamin "readmits dimensions of temporality and historicity into his vision of the cinema, against his own endorsement of it as the medium of presence and tracelessness."[49] In "A Small History of Photography" (1931), Benjamin poses the existence of an "optical unconscious" for the first time in relationship to the photograph:

> For it is another nature that speaks to the camera rather than to the eye: "other" above all in the sense that a space informed by human consciousness gives way to a space informed by the unconscious. [...] It is through photography that we first discover the existence of this optical consciousness, just as we discover the instinctual unconscious through psychoanalysis.[50]

In 1936, he repeats this formulation in relation to film:

> Clearly, it is another nature which speaks to the camera as compared to the eye. "Other" above all in the sense that a space informed by human consciousness gives way to a space informed by the unconscious. Whereas it is a commonplace that, for example, we have some idea what is involved in the act of walking (if only in general terms), we have no idea at all what happens during the split second when a person actually takes a step. We are familiar with the movement of picking up a cigarette lighter or a spoon, but know almost nothing of what really goes on between hand and metal, and still less how this varies with different moods. This is where the camera comes into play, with all its resources for swooping and rising, disrupting and isolating, stretching or compressing a sequence, enlarging or reducing an object. It is through the camera that we first discover the optical unconscious, just as we discover the instinctual unconscious through psychoanalysis.[51]

In these descriptions, the act of ballistics reappears as the camera surgically slices through reality, de-shelling the object, and capturing the space reserved for the unconscious. The object is reconfigured, "re-activated" Benjamin would say, in the moment when the familiar becomes unfamiliar. In this sense the appearance of the "optical unconsciousness" assists in the demolition of the auratic traces which the subject consciously perceives. Duhamel could be made to say, "I cannot think what I want to think, my mind is overtaken by its unconscious side." But there is another sense in which the "optical unconsciousness" propagates return of the auratic in the object. Just as Proust's *mémoire involontaire* came flooding back in the tasting of a madeleine cake, the auratic returns to the familiar object in the form of "unconscious optics." Benjamin makes this connection more explicit in his later work on Baudelaire, where he describes the aura as having the capacity to return the spectator's gaze:

> Experience of the aura thus arises from the fact that a response characteristic of human relationships is transposed to the relationship between humans and inanimate or natural objects. The person we look at, or who feels he is being looked at, looks at us in turn. To experience the aura of an object we look at means to invest it with the ability to look back at us.[52]

In this ability to return our gaze, the object is reinstated with a temporality outside the present moment. The cinematic image becomes decidedly un-modern. Once "a space informed by human consciousness gives way to a space informed by the unconscious,"[53] the modern "ballistic" of the moment flies into time and the object becomes infected with traces of the past and of the future. In this sense, the "optical unconscious" functions like Proust's *mémoire involontaire*: it is "a key to everything that happened before it and after it."[54] These floodgates to the unconscious effectively destabilise the presence of the cinematic image, defamiliarising it, but at the same time, making it return our gaze. This activation of unconscious data appears to reinstate the sort of continuity, which was previously reserved only for the peasant. Time outside of the instant returns in the gaze of the object; and for the spectator this must surely mean that some kind of receptivity and attentiveness also return. What does not return, however, is relaxation. The unconscious data of the *mémoire involontaire* or of the "optical unconscious" remains shocking. As Proust made clear, the aura around his madeleine cake sent him reeling, he felt no abiding sense of continuity with the involuntary memories that he experienced. Recognisable traits of the object do not return in this evocation of the auratic, all is unfamiliar, and the image retains its ability to dislodge the spectator, to use Gasché again, the spectator "is neither a substantial nor a formal centre that would ground its autonomy."[55] If Hansen is correct and the auratic experience does in fact return to cinema "through the backdoor of the 'optical unconscious',"[56] then it does not return to reinstate the tradition and continuity that define the "outmoded concepts" associated with the aura. Quite to the contrary, emerging from the shock of 24 frames per second, it only solidifies the discontinuity already at work.

Yet at the same time as the "optical unconscious" participates in the "destruction of the aura," it also readmits the aura through a "back-door." Benjamin defines the aura as "the unique apparition of a distance, however near it may be."[57] Belonging outside the present moment of consciousness, the traces found in the madeleine cake, or in the "optical unconscious," always carry this (proximate) distance. The introduction of a space and a time beyond the present moment complicates Benjamin's theory of cinema immensely. With the introduction of these "traces" outside the truth of the instant, it could be said that the cinematic image becomes post-modernised. For the spectator, this means the reintroduction of an associative capacity: past and future hurtle into the moment of a taste, and absence inhabits the defamiliarised object. And yet, unlike a traditional mode of association, time arrives like a "missile."[58] Experience is still "lived through," timeliness happens, with what Benjamin calls "a tactile [*taktisch*] quality."[59] Relaxation and spinning are still replaced by assault, and distance has an immediacy, which displaces the aura and tradition. Moreover, association has an absent-minded quality. As Benjamin says of Proustian remembrance: "is not the involuntary recollection, Proust's *mémoire involontaire*, much closer to forgetting than what is usually called memory?"[60] As we have seen, continuous experience (*Erfahrung*), must adhere to an object with a fixed place in space and time; the experience of the *mémoire involontaire*, on the other hand, is one of dispersal: "For an experienced event is finite – at any rate, confined to one sphere of experience; a remembered event is infinite, because it is merely a key to everything that happened before and after it."[61] The shock of Proustian forgetting only finds its translation in another shock-like moment, like the culmination of the surrealist project, the data of the involuntary moment can only be inscribed in a burst of "profane illumination" or a "now of recognisability." So while the presence of unconscious data seems to readmit a notion of temporality to Benjamin's theory of the artwork, it is a weightless time, dispersed and discontinuous.

But once more, there is ambiguity in this reading of the "'return of the aura." In the enigmatic closing lines of "Some Motifs in Baudelaire," Baudelaire's poetry is lived through and weightless, and yet it still carries the "weight of experience (*Erfahrung*)." To quote the entire passage:

> Baudelaire battled the crowd – with the impotent rage of someone fighting the rain or the wind. This is the nature of the immediate experience [*Erlebnis*] to which Baudelaire has given the weight of long experience [*Erfahrung*]. He named the price for which the sensation of modernity could be had: the disintegration of the aura in immediate shock experience [*Chockerlebnis*]. He paid dearly for consenting to this disintegration – but it is the law of his poetry. This poetry appears in the sky of the Second Empire as "a star without atmosphere."[62]

While Proust and the surrealists attempted to translate an experience founded in *Erlebnis* back into an equally ballistic art form, i.e. one without weight, Baudelaire took the shock experience (*Chockerlebnis*), and gave it a new form of solidity within the weightlessness of words (*Chockerfahrung*). This achievement was not founded upon anything auratic, for it was only in the destruction of traditional lyric poetry that Baudelaire was able to form to his impossible task.

Baudelaire's feat of translation has been introduced at this late stage, because he stands as an interesting, if somewhat obscure, counterpoint to the cinematic feats with which I began. Just as lyric poetry sits uncomfortably in Baudelaire's Paris, the poetic quality of Herzog's films sits uncomfortably in the structure of cinema. As we have learnt from Benjamin, "a weight of experience" is an impossible outcome for cinema; poetry is much better suited to such a pursuit. In his search for "poetic, ecstatic truth," and in his rejection of "the inadequate imagery of today's civilisation,"[63] it seems that Herzog has chosen the wrong profession. But Werner is terribly faithful to the movie camera, and the task he sets himself is different from Baudelaire's. Between Baudelaire and Herzog, the terms of their tasks are reversed. For while Baudelaire sets out to translate modernity into a traditional artwork, Herzog sets out to translate a strangely traditional world into a strictly, and self-consciously, modern art form.

Herzog is patently un-Benjaminian; he is no mimic of modernity. Unlike Vertov or Chaplin, Herzog's camera captures modernity in neither form nor content. The city is strikingly absent from Herzog's films, quite literally, it only appears once or twice over his entire oeuvre (and this amounts to nearly 50 films!).[64] Moreover, his characters are always outsiders, the masses are never represented, nothing is everyday, and modernity is cast aside. The individual re-emerges, and they are disconnected from their brothers. As Thomas Elsaesser says, Herzog's protagonists "invariably circle around limit states and try to define what is human. [...] Whether superheroes or victims, however, Herzog's protagonists are always extreme, marginal and outside, in relation to the centre which is the social world, the world of history, that of ordinary beings. The existential dimension of his characters always seems to take precedence over any social issue against which they might revolt or from which they might suffer."[65]

In terms of form, Herzog rejects the flicker, his films are far from ballistic. As one critic said, they are rather "celebrations of stasis."[66] Herzog's images do not appear to "kaleidoscope": they stretch out rather than fragment. In this way, these images perform a curious inversion of the "optical unconscious." Herzog makes frequent use of montage techniques, but instead of obeying the camera and producing modernist motions of jerks and shocks, Herzog stretches the fragment out, often producing an artificial appearance of continuity. One striking example is the 1969 film *Fata Morgana*. Ostensibly a travelogue, the film is made up of footage taken from a trip across Africa. But it is not really a journey that we see, the footage is highly edited, and the images do not actually appear in sequence. Continuity is illusionary, and though this travelogue begins appropriately with a plane touching down, *Fata Morgana* is less a travel document than a series of disconnected fragments edited together. What should result is a montage, and yet Herzog's ambitions are not avant-garde in this sense. Instead he is again deceitful, large parts of the film are taken up by the illusion of a continuous tracking shot, and the spectator gets a sense of rhythm and consistent movement. Remembering Benjamin's metaphor of the surgeon versus the magician, Herzog unrelentingly takes on both roles. Firstly, Herzog holds a scalpel, uncovering the "other side" of the image, de-shelling it, and removing its aura. Then he is at the same time a "magician," making every effort to cover over his incisions, creating distance, and bringing a sense of timelessness to the fore. Critics continually refer to these qualities, and yet as qualities, they are quite insincere. Continuity is created artificially, both bypassing tradition and embarrassing its avant-garde adversaries. Documentary becomes poetry, truth becomes farce.

Often reiterating Benjamin's sentiments of the Storyteller essay in interviews, Herzog displays a pointed nostalgia for a time exclusive of modernity and mechanical reproduction.[67] But, as one should probably interpret Benjamin's similarly nostalgic sentiments, there is no sense in which Herzog wants to go backwards: "one must dig like an archaeologist and search our violated landscape to find anything new. One must go to war, if need be, to find these unprocessed and fresh images."[68] Likewise, Benjamin said of the destructive character: "What exists he reduces to rubble – not for the sake of the rubble, but for that of the way leading through it."[69] Herzog and Baudelaire both "battled the crowd – with the impotent rage of someone fighting the rain or the wind;" [70] not for the sake of the rubble, but rather for the sake of something timely within a structure that cannot support time. For Baudelaire, this means the impossible task of bringing lyric poetry to an ambivalent audience who crave only sensation, who are only "familiar with the 'spleen' which kills interest and receptiveness."[71] Herzog's efforts to find "the poetic ecstatic truth"[72] are just as futile. Always insincere, his images are not only mechanically reproduced, they are also always tinged with enough irony to undermine his preposterous ambitions.

As Benjamin said, "Baudelaire wrote a book which from the very beginning had little prospect of becoming an immediate popular success."[73] Herzog too, it was suggested in the 1970s, "has not found a popular audience, and probably never will."[74] Both did, of course, gain standing and notoriety. But their successes are based upon, in the end, a kind of impropriety – both side with the time of boredom, in time arrested by distraction. Boring time is always alien to modernity, it can never return, yet if timeliness does return, it returns as something undecidable, a "star without atmosphere," weight within weightlessness.

NOTES

[1] Herzog repeatedly, and obsessively, refers to this "accountant's truth" as undercutting the potential for a "deeper form of truth in cinema." Cinema, he says, "like poetry, is inherently able to present a number of dimensions much deeper than the level of the so-called truth that we find in cinema verité and even reality itself, and it is these dimensions that are the most fertile areas for filmmakers," Werner Herzog, *Herzog on Herzog*, ed. Paul Cronin (London: Faber and Faber. 2002), p. 239.

[2] To quote the entire incident: "I couldn't sleep. I turned on the TV and again found the same thing on Italian TV as on Austrian, Dutch, Canadian, and U.S. TV. Documentaries are always the same sort of boring, uninspired stuff. So I tried to force myself to sleep but I couldn't and I turned the TV on again. There was a porno film on and I had the feeling, yes, even though it's just a physical performance, it comes closer to what I call truth. It was more truthful than those documentaries. I couldn't fall asleep, so I got up at three o'clock in the morning and, in this anger of not being able to sleep and seeing all these things on TV, I wrote down the manifesto, in fifteen minutes," A.G. Basoli, "The Wrath of Klaus Kinski: An Interview with Werner Herzog," *Cineaste* 24.4 (September 1999), pp. 34-35.

[3] As Thomas Elsaesser says: Herzog, "like so many other German directors, appears to be a craven seeker of headlines to satisfy an inflated ego," Thomas Elsaesser, *New German Cinema: A History* (Hampshire: Macmillan, 1989), p. 91. In Herzog's case, his notoriety is excessive: he has been accused of killing his Amazonian extras, threatening his actors with guns, and taking a few bullets himself – he has even eaten a shoe!

[4] Walter Benjamin, "The Handkerchief" (1932), in *Selected Writings*, edited by Marcus Bullock and Michael W. Jennings, Volume.2, (Cambridge, MA: Belknap Press, 1999), p. 658. All essays from the *Selected Writings* will henceforth be abbreviated as *SW*, with volume and page number following.

[5] I will use the phrase "modern man" throughout this essay, because the modern subject, of whom Benjamin and his fellows write, is precisely that, a man. As Patrice Petro writes, for Benjamin, Kracauer and Heidegger, "it is male spectatorship which remains the (unspoken) subject of theoretical exploration. Nevertheless, because they stress the historicity of experience, their writings unwittingly reveal how the coincidence of cinematic technology with the crisis of perception (where the subject becomes an object) is inseparable from the crisis of male authority and the emergence of women's demands for an equal share in German culture," Patrice Petro, "Modernity and Mass Culture in Weimar: Contours of a Discourse on Sexuality in Early Theories of Perception and Representation," *New German Critique* 40 (Winter 1987), Special Issue on Weimar Film Theory, p. 124.

[6] Giorgio Agamben, *Infancy and History: the Destruction of Experience*, trans. Liz Heron (London; New York: Verso, 1993.), p. 13.

[7] Henceforth referred to as the "Artwork Essay."

[8] Herzog is not in the least ashamed by his aspirations towards "outmoded concepts." He openly strives for a "deeper strata of truth in cinema," he is always calling for "a poetic, ecstatic truth," and has the self-professed ability to, "articulate images that sit deeply inside us, I can make them visible," Werner Herzog quoted in Gideon Bachmann, "The Man on the Volcano: A Portrait of Werner Herzog," *Film Quarterly* 31.1 (Fall 1977), p.7.

[9] Timothy Corrigan, et al. "Walking on Ice: Werner Herzog's Metaphysics of Filmmaking," Slought   Foundation   Online   Content.   [22   October   2007]. <http://slought.org/content/11373/>.

[10] Ibid.

[11] Ibid.

[12] Elsaesser, *New German Cinema*, p.166.

[13] Petro, "Modernity and Mass Culture in Weimar," p. 132.

[14] Georg Simmel, "The Metropolis and Mental Life," in *Readings in Social Theory: The Classic Tradition to Post-Modernism*, ed. James Farganis. (New York: McGraw Hill, 1993), p. 136.

[15] Patrice Petro, "After Shock/Between Boredom and History," in Patrice Petro (ed.), *Fugitive Images* (Bloomington: Indiana UP, 1995.), p. 273.

[16] Simmel, "The Metropolis and Mental Life," p. 136.

[17] Ibid.

[18] Ibid.

[19] *"Reception in distraction [Die Rezeption in der Zerstreuung] – the sort of reception which is increasingly noticeable in all areas of art and is a symptom of profound changes in apperception – finds in film its true training ground."* Walter Benjamin, "The Work of Art in the Age of Mechanical Reproduction," Third version, *SW*, vol 4, p. 269.

[20] Walter Benjamin, "On Some Motifs in Baudelaire," in *SW*, vol 4, p. 336.

[21] Cf. Heide Schlüpmann, "Phenomenology of Film: On Siegfried Kracauer's Writings of the 1920s," *New German Critique* 40 (Winter, 1987) Special Issue on Weimar Film Theory, pp. 97-114.

[22] Simmel, "The Metropolis and Mental Life," p. 136.

[23] Ibid.

[24] Ibid., p. 137.

[25] Ibid., p. 139.

[26] Ibid.

[27] Benjamin, "On Some Motifs in Baudelaire," p. 313.

[28] Ibid., p. 328.

[29] Walter Benjamin, "Mickey Mouse," in *SW*, vol 2, p. 545.

[30] Benjamin, "On Some Motifs in Baudelaire," p. 319.

[31] Walter Benjamin, "The Destructive Character," in *SW*, vol 2, p. 542.

[32] Benjamin, "The Work of Art in the Age of Mechanical Reproduction," p. 265.

[33] Ibid., p. 263.

[34] Ibid., p. 252.

[35] Ibid., p. 254.

[36] Ibid.

[37] "The essence of the blasé attitude consists in the blunting of discrimination. This does not mean that the objects are not perceived, as is the case with the half-wit, but rather that the meaning and differing values of things, and thereby the things themselves, are experienced as insubstantial," Simmel, "The Metropolis and Mental Life," p. 139.

[38] Benjamin, "The Work of Art in the Age of Mechanical Reproduction," pp. 255-6.

[39] Agamben, *Infancy and* History, p. 91

[40] Benjamin, "The Work of Art in the Age of Mechanical Reproduction," p. 267.

[41] Ibid.

[42] Ibid.

[43] Rodolphe Gasché, "Objective Diversions: On some Kantian Themes in Benjamin's 'The Work of Art in the Age of Mechanical Reproduction'," in Andrew Benjamin and Peter Osborne (eds.), *Walter Benjamin's Philosophy: Destruction and Experience*, (London: Routledge, 1994), p. 194.

[44] Benjamin, "The Work of Art in the Age of Mechanical Reproduction," p. 267.

[45] Walter Benjamin, "The Storyteller: Reflections on the works of Nickolai Leskov," in *SW*, vol. 3. p. 149

[46] Ibid., p. 143.

[47] One such commentator, Richard Wolin, claims: "a sudden and dramatic change of heart on Benjamin's part concerning the issue of modern technological methods versus traditional forms of life," Richard Wolin, *Walter Benjamin: An Aesthetic of Redemption*, (New York: Columbia University Press, 1982.), p. 224.

[48] Miriam Hansen, "Benjamin, Cinema and Experience: 'The Blue Flower in the Land of Technology'," *New German Critique* 40 (Winter, 1987), Special Issue on Weimar Film Theory, p. 180.

[49] Ibid., p. 217.

[50] Walter Benjamin, "A Small History of Photography," in *SW*, vol. 2, pp. 510-12.

[51] Benjamin, "The Work of Art in the Age of Mechanical Reproduction," p. 266.

[52] Benjamin, "On Some Motifs in Baudelaire," p. 338.

[53] Benjamin, "A Small History of Photography," p. 510.

[54] Walter Benjamin, "Image of Proust," in *SW*, vol. 2, p. 238.

[55] Gasché, "Objective Diversions," p. 194.

[56] Hansen, "Benjamin, Cinema and Experience," p. 212.

[57] Benjamin, "The Work of Art in the Age of Mechanical Reproduction," p. 255.

[58] Ibid., p. 267.

[59] Ibid.

[60] Benjamin, "Image of Proust," p. 238.

[61] Ibid.

[62] Benjamin, "On Some Motifs in Baudelaire," p. 343.

[63] Herzog, *Herzog on Herzog*, p. 66.

[64] Strosek is probably the most glaring exception. Set in a German city to begin with, the character's dream of moving to America comes true, but they do not end up in New York, reinstating Herzog's obsession with the excluded margins, they find themselves in a backwater trailer park.

[65] Elsaesser, *New German Cinema*, p. 218.

[66] Lawrence O'Toole, "The Great Ecstasy of Filmmaker Herzog," *Film Comment* 15.6 (November-December 1979), p. 34.

[67] Here is one such Herzogian rant: "I have often spoken of what I call the inadequate imagery of today's civilisation. I have the impression that the images that surround us today are worn out, they are abused and useless and exhausted. They are limping and dragging themselves behind the rest of our cultural evolution. When I look at the postcards in tourist shops and the images and advertisements that surround us in magazines, or I turn on the television, or if I walk into a travel agency and see those huge posters with that same tedious and rickety image of the Grand Canyon on them, I truly feel there is something dangerous emerging here. The biggest danger, in my opinion, is television because to a certain degree it ruins our vision and makes us very sad and lonesome. Our grandchildren will blame us for not having tossing hand-grenades into TV stations because of commercials. Television kills our imagination and what we end up with are worn out images because of the inability of too many people to seek out fresh ones," Herzog, *Herzog on Herzog*, p. 66.

[68] Ibid., p. 67.

[69] Benjamin, "The Destructive Character," p. 542.

[70] Benjamin, "On Some Motifs in Baudelaire," p. 343.

[71] Ibid., p. 313.

[72] Basoli, "The Wrath of Klaus Kinski: An Interview with Werner Herzog," p. 35.

[73] Benjamin, "On Some Motifs in Baudelaire," p. 313.

74 O'Toole, "The Great Ecstasy of Filmmaker Herzog," p. 34.

WORKS CITED

Agamben, Giorgio. *Infancy and History: the Destruction of Experience.* Trans. Liz Heron. London; New York: Verso, 1993.

Bachmann, Gideon. "The Man on the Volcano: A Portrait of Werner Herzog." *Film Quarterly* 31.1 (Fall 1977). 2-10.

Basoli, A.G. "The Wrath of Klaus Kinski: An Interview with Werner Herzog." *Cineaste* 24.4 (1999). 32-35

Benjamin, Walter. "The Destructive Character," *Selected Writings.* Ed. Marcus Bullock and Michael W. Jennings, Vol. 2. Cambridge, MA: Belknap Press, 1999. 541-42.

———. "The Handkerchief" *Selected Writings.* Ed. Marcus Bullock and Michael W. Jennings, Vol. 2. Cambridge, MA: Belknap Press, 1999. 658-61.

———. "Image of Proust," *Selected Writings.* Ed. Marcus Bullock and Michael W. Jennings, Vol. 2. Cambridge, MA: Belknap Press, 1999. 237-47

———. "Mickey Mouse," *Selected Writings.* Ed. Marcus Bullock and Michael W. Jennings, Vol. 2. Cambridge, MA: Belknap Press, 1999. 545-46.

———. "On Some Motifs in Baudelaire," *Selected Writings.* Ed. Marcus Bullock and Michael W. Jennings, Vol. 4. Cambridge, MA: Belknap Press, 1999. 313-55

———. "A Small History of Photography," *Selected Writings.* Ed. Marcus Bullock and Michael W. Jennings, Vol. 2. Cambridge, MA: Belknap Press, 1999. 507-30

———. "The Storyteller: Reflections on the works of Nickolai Leskov" *Selected Writings.* Ed. Marcus Bullock and Michael W. Jennings, Vol. 3. Cambridge, MA: Belknap Press, 1999. 143-66

———. "The Work of Art in the Age of its Technological Reproducibility," Third version. *Selected Writings.* Ed. Marcus Bullock and Michael W. Jennings, Vol. 4. Cambridge, MA: Belknap Press, 1999. 251-83.

Corrigan, Timothy et al. "Walking on Ice: Werner Herzog's Metaphysics of Filmmaking." Slought Foundation Online Content. [22 October 2007]. <http://slought.org/content/11373/>.

Elsaesser, Thomas. *New German Cinema: A History*. Hampshire: Macmillan, 1989.

Gasché, Rodolphe "Objective Diversions: On some Kantian Themes in Benjamin's 'The Work of Art in the Age of Mechanical Reproduction'," in Andrew Benjamin and Peter Osborne (eds.), *Walter Benjamin's Philosophy: Destruction and Experience*. London: Routledge, 1994. 183-204.

Hansen, Miriam. "Benjamin, Cinema and Experience: 'The Blue Flower in the Land of Technology'." *New German Critique* 40 (Winter 1987), Special Issue on Weimar Film Theory. 179-224.

Herzog, Werner. *Herzog on Herzog*. Ed. Paul Cronin. London: Faber and Faber, 2002.

O'Toole, Lawrence. "The Great Ecstasy of Filmmaker Herzog," *Film Comment* 15.6 (November-December 1979). 34-48.

Petro, Patrice. "After Shock/Between Boredom and History," in Patrice Petro (ed.), *Fugitive Images* Bloomington: Indiana UP, 1995. 265-84.

——. "Modernity and Mass Culture in Weimar: Contours of a Discourse on Sexuality in Early Theories of Perception and Representation." *New German Critique* 40 (Winter 1987), Special Issue on Weimar Film Theory. 115-46.

Schlüpmann, Heide, and Thomas Y. Levin. "Phenomenology of Film: On Siegfried Kracauer's Writings of the 1920s." *New German Critique* 40 (Winter 1987), Special Issue on Weimar Film Theory. 97-114.

Simmel, Georg "The Metropolis and Mental Life," in *Readings in Social Theory: The Classic Tradition to Post-Modernism*, ed. James Farganis. New York: McGraw Hill, 1993. 136-44.

Wolin, Richard. *Walter Benjamin: An Aesthetic of Redemption*. New York: Columbia University Press, 1982.

CHAPTER 8

The Digital Void:
e-NNUI and experience

Marco van Leeuwen

According to Walter Benjamin, the acceleration of urban life around the end of the 19th century had profound consequences for the ways in which people were able to experience the world. In his analysis, deep and singularly meaningful experiences were forced out by droves of repeated, superficial ones, *Erlebnis* ("momentary experience") thus replacing *Erfahrung* ("momentous experience"). Today, the increased (and still increasing) availability of information is claimed by some to have a similar effect on the value of *social exchange*. The lack of an embodied connection in *mediated social interaction* has the added downside of allowing a "do-it-yourself normativity," an underdetermination of ethical constraints in on-line interaction. These modern forms of communication, however, are not necessarily inferior to traditional embodied and direct forms of interaction. Instead, in mediated interaction there might even be room for certain *auratic* qualities, in a way close to Benjamin's use of the word.

1. Introduction

Walter Benjamin's keen eye and pen chronicled the kaleidoscope of transformations and transitions that took place at the end of the 19th and beginning of the 20th century.[1] His descriptions of the demise of storytellers and the devaluation of artistic depictions draw our attention to the shift that took place then, away from authentic, *auratic* and meaningful experience, and towards assembly-line reproductions and the crush of rapid-fire, content-free impressions encountered in the hustle and bustle of modern city life. In this environment, boredom became a strategy to cope, a numbness that remains when modern, urban impression-overload recedes.

There are many reasons to suppose that these developments have not halted – to say, rather, that they are still continuing, seen more often than ever but noticed less every day, ever faster in their asymptotic trajectory towards a horizon they will never quite reach. There are good reasons to claim that a recent (and rather effective) catalyst of this development is *media-immersion*. Postmodern artefacts such as television and (especially) Internet are capable of opening up many worlds (sometimes almost literally, in video games or the virtual, online society "Second Life"), but it is also the case that the selectivity of their focus withholds information and distorts perception. One way of putting this is as follows: when the window on the world becomes a computer screen, human phenomenology shifts from *experiencing* life and the world that comes from being an embodied and embedded agent, to *consuming* pre-processed impressions that comes from being a virtual presence with different personalities and properties, depending on the website, chatroom or game.

However, in this paper I will use Benjamin's insights about the loss of aura and the absence of meaningful experience in the society he described to support the claim that, despite appearances to the contrary, current trends of media-immersion might actually accommodate the *reclamation* of a kind of aura.

One of the reasons to adopt a "Benjamin-like" pessimism regarding the current omnipresence of multimedia involves the *boredom* it induces. That is: parallel, in a sense, to the desensitisation of the city-dweller from a century ago described by Benjamin, one consequence of this Postmodern technological development can be the emergence of a multimedia-induced apathy and callousness. The specific causes of this boredom are not just sensory overload (the immense quantities of information and impressions available at the click of a button), but also the fading of a focused self that results from assuming different identities in different virtual environment, and a detachment from the real phenomena via the filtering power that comes from being able to click to another website at a moment's notice: "reality," apparently, is not what it used to be.

I believe that boredom, in its essence, is about a failure to connect, about not fitting in, about not wanting or being able to interact. When we are bored, we cannot bring ourselves to care about something in particular (or anything at all), we do not feel that this thing that – or person who – we are confronted with is important enough to actually *connect* and *interact* with.

Connectedness, and what happens when the natural connections of everyday life fail, is the theme of this essay: this is an exploration of *detachment* as a deeper cause of boredom. And, so one could argue, it is exactly the direct, interactive social connection of embodied and embedded agents with one another that is severed when those agents start to communicate via keyboards and computer screens, rather than face-to-face.

I suppose it is not a rare occurrence that parents tell their children that they should turn off the computer, quit talking to their friends via MSN (a popular chat program), and actually go play outside with those very friends. Parental interventions like this are expressions of the idea that *mediated* social interaction (e.g. via the Internet or mobile phones) is diluted, less "real" and certainly less worthwhile than face-to-face interaction. Is this in fact the case?

As announced above, my claim in this paper will be that this pessimistic construal of how the development of multimedia technology affects the user's experience and sense of self is not wholly accurate. I *do* wish to claim that Benjamin's analysis of the late-19th century city supports an extrapolation into such a view on current developments in ICT and Internet, but I am by no means a Neo-Luddite: I will attempt to demonstrate that amongst the negative side effects that it *does* have, this new form of technology might accommodate the reclamation of a *social aura*.

That might sound like a surprising claim. If there is anything that would be able to alleviate the boredom that is due to an ever-increasing detachment, it would be *really* interacting with people. That is: not typing messages on a computer, but actually living together, talking and touching, and sharing experiences. Obviously, my claim cannot be that embodied and embedded social interaction does not have that special qualitative content; the absolute opposite is true. No, I wish to defend the possibly somewhat more controversial thesis that it is *not* the case that mediated social interaction *lacks* this property: it is there, but it is *different*.

The remainder of this paper contains two distinct parts. In section 2, I will take a look at the way Walter Benjamin fills in the notions *aura* and *experience*, and at the changes he sees accruing for these phenomena in modern society. Benjamin's philosophy is relevant here because changes in the ways we interact with each other due to the advent of modern technological marvels such as the Internet create a complex transitional dynamic in which these two important themes from his work meet. While discussing experience, I will also include ideas by Nietzsche and Dilthey. In this sense, this section can be said to be about detachment, desensitisation and estrangement as the deeper causes of a kind of boredom, a kind of numbness that, at least if one thinks along the lines set out by Benjamin, is an affliction typical for modernity.

In section 3, I will focus on the changes in social interaction due to the advent of modern information and communications-technology, the Internet in particular, and its purported contribution to the rise of social detachment in a literal sense – for people now interact via machines instead of in an unmediated fashion.

2. Aura and Bodily Experience

The process of increasing detachment as described above can be understood as a development in which we find less and less interesting and meaningful "content" in the objects, situations and persons that surround us. Benjamin conceptualises the loss of meaningfulness – something that, apparently, *was* present in certain forms of unmediated interaction – in several different ways in his essays. I will focus on his analyses of the loss of aura in the mechanical reproduction of art, and of the transformation of experience due to the pressure and velocity of modern city life. I will first discuss these two themes, starting with insights from Dilthey and Nietzsche and using those insights to ameliorate Benjamin's ideas, and after that (in section 3) I will build my own argument on the foundation thus provided.

2.1. A Different Phenomenology

Dilthey (1883/1990) famously articulates a distinction between *Geisteswissenschaft*, i.e. the humanities, and *Naturwissenschaft*, the mathematico-empirical science of nature. Included in the *Geisteswissenschaften* by Dilthey are political sciences, psychology and the study of history.[2] George Lakoff and Mark Johnson suggest that this chasm Dilthey perceived (and probably helped widen) in the structure of human understanding might be buttressed by a rather persistently maintained belief in the ontological autonomy of man.[3] This belief is most saliently expressed by the claim that the essence of the human in the Judeo-Christian tradition (obviously shaped by those cultures' religious doctrines) is believed to be the soul, that most notorious of evaders of the constraints formed by what are quite widely accepted to be rather immutable laws of nature. The depths of such an ephemeral entity would not be susceptible to being fathomed by the probing instruments and theories of natural science, necessitating the nurturing of a different kind of science, one focused on *interpretation* rather than *computation*.

But even when claims concerning the existence of "the soul" are relinquished, and the more scientific course of (for instance) psychology or philosophy of mind is followed, Dilthey's distinction remains in effect. In his *Grundprobleme der Phänomenologie* [The Fundamental Problems of Phenomenology], Heidegger describes the essence of phenomenology as "the origin-science of life." As such he amplifies the echoes of Dilthey's life-philosophy by anchouring the way things are given to us in experience in the immediacy embodied by the organic coherence of life (the living body in its environment), rather than attempting the more psychologically inclined approach of (re-)constructing the attunement of subject and object by mediation of consciousness (as the active and directional analysis and ascription of meaning and essence to mute objects).[4]

Whatever the genesis of Dilthey's distinction, neither a radical suspension of this antagony in favour of the acceptance of a materialist reduction of "the mind" – which one would assume to be the ultimate expression of the mindset associated by Dilthey with natural science – has not as yet yielded a satisfyingly workable explanation of cognition, nor has a strict application of

Geisteswissenschaftliche methods and theoretical notions resulted in an illumination of the question at hand to the joy and acquiescence of all. Apparently, something new is needed.

2.2. Nietzsche's *Leib*

Nietzsche is said to have provided a radicalisation of phenomenology – now, I will explore a small part of that project. In *Götzendämmerung* [Twilight of the Idols],[5] Nietzsche develops a fierce criticism of the primacy of reason espoused by the ancient Greek philosophers. He criticizes the fixation on ratio as the preferred tool of knowledge-acquisition most explicitly displayed by Socrates and his heirs: this fixation was extrapolated to such an extent that reason, in the Greeks' apprehension, ceased to be a mere tool, and was instead taken to constitute the very *essence* of man. Nietzsche describes this philosophical tendency of the ancient Greeks as an act of despair, intended to wrest away from the clutches of decay and subsequent oblivion the achievements of Greek culture. Quite tragically, this attempt to save the legacy of the Pre-Socratics turned out to be a strategy which clouded from view the true nature of man. The human and its actions, so Nietzsche claims, are governed by the will to power, by its instincts, drives, tendencies and subconscious dispositions – primal forces that exert their influence in and through the *body* – and reason is merely a tool. The *Leib* (body), then, is introduced by Nietzsche as the substrate of embodied experience.

In the analysis Nietzsche provides, embodied experience is – in an important measure – an expression of the subconscious action of many of our experiences. Every *Leib*-centered experience is singular and unique, and its content dissipates once it is named and consciously processed. Nietzsche rejected the Cartesian epistemology, which includes an abstract and artificial separation of mind and body, and suggested a focus on embodied experience as an alternative to that view.[6] Similarly, Dilthey stated that placing conscious experience (obviously, in the sense in which this phenomenon was thematised by philosophers of mind of his time) at center stage of any philosophy of cognition will shortchange the psychological totality of the *living self*. The vital importance of this totality to the character of embodied experience for Dilthey is expressed in his *Aufbau* [construction] (as reported by Visser), as he notes:

> *Im Erleben bin ich mir selbst als Zusammenhang da.*

> [While in the act of experiencing, I appear to myself as a coherence]

Being a "self" means being an embodied agent interacting with a dynamic environment, and *experiencing* this coherence as such.

Based on similar convictions, Nietzsche is in a position to reduce the *cogito ergo sum* – held by Descartes to be the epistemological primitive upon which all tenets comprising certain knowledge could be based – to embodied experience. By doing this, Nietzsche attempted to remove the sting from natural science's positivistic, ratio-based methodologies, re-instating the *Leib*-centered, organic unity that precedes the cognisant self once more to its (in his eyes) proper place of prominence. In other words, the *cogito* dissolves into a finite *life-coherence*, the dynamic interrelatedness of embodied and embedded experience.

Nietzsche continues with his deconstruction of positivistic natural science, as he traces the ontic and ocular back to a decidedly non-objective worldview: the fixation on the measurable thing (ontic), as observed from a supposed-to-be-detached but fundamentally situated vantage point (ocular), constitutes an a priori positioning and self-imposed narrowing of the horizon – the introduction of a foundational prejudice which makes orthodox positivistic science overshoot its goal of objectivity and land right back at a form of preconstructed subjectivism. The guiding principle Nietzsche offers consists of the instincts – that is, a reaffirmation of the importance of the *Leib* in embodied experience.

Nietzsche understands everything, that is including embodied experience, as a meeting of forces. The Will-to-Power, Nietzsche's central concept, is recast by Dilthey as *finitude*. This notion and its accompanying dynamic converges on the edge of body and world – embodied experience manifests itself in the experience of a pressure (of an unmistakeable presence), which means the world is understood as imposing onto the body certain boundaries as exerting force, as limiting the range of movement and expression of the human will: the outside-of-me is characterised by a certain measure of resistance inhibiting the free unfolding of my (embodied) drives and instincts.

In recent years, embodied experience has also emerged as a theme in *analytic* philosophy.[7] Some philosophers of cognition, for instance, increasingly express their discontent with the Cartesian and/or cognitivistic picture of the relationship between mind and body – and in fact the idea that there is to be talk of a *relationship* at all, this criticism coinciding with and feeding off the groundswell of theories proclaiming that mind and body are in actuality an inseparable unity. These theories of *embodied* cognition state that explaining the mind requires taking into account the way in which that mind controls the body, and how the properties of that body in turn enable and/or constrain the activities of the mind. Expanding upon this notion, many maintain that cognition is also *embedded*, meaning that properties of the environment (i.e. factors external to the organism) are relevant to the explanation of cognitive processes as well. In short, these analytic philosophers would agree with Nietzsche and Dilthey that through the *Leib*, there is an inescapable imperative to answer to the organic coherence of self and world.

2.3. Benjamin's Aura

It is possible to understand Benjamin's aura as a quality that emerges exactly when the constraints for true embodied and embedded existence are satisfied. Benjamin defines the aura in terms of "a unique appearance of a distance, however close it may be," as such attempting to illustrate this notion by referring to the semi-mystic phenomenology associated with the experience of the overwhelming beauty of nature:

> *Es empfiehlt sich den [...] Begriff der Aura an dem Begriff einer Aura von natürlichen Gegenständen zu illustrieren. Diese letztere definieren wir als einmalige Erscheinung einer Ferne, so nah sie sein mag. An einem Sommernachmittag ruhend einem Gebirgszug am Horizont oder einem Zweig folgen, der seinen Schatten auf den Ruhenden wirft – das hei't die Aura dieser Berge, dieses Zweiges atmen.* (GS 1.2:479)[8]

> The concept of the aura [...] can be usefully illustrated with reference to an aura of natural objects. We define the aura of the latter as the unique apparition of a distance, however near it may be. To follow with the eye – while resting on a summer afternoon – a mountain range on the horizon or a branch that casts its shadow on the beholder is to breathe the aura of those mountains, of that branch. (*SW* 4: 255)

Benjamin claims that a unique and authentic work of art is also capable of eliciting such experiences. It is this specific quality that somehow disappears in the case of a (mechanical) reproduction:

> *Noch bei der höchstvollendeten Reproduktion fällt eines aus: das Hier und Jetzt des Kunstwerks – sein einmaliges Dasein an dem Orte, an dem es sich befindet. An diesem einmaligen Dasein aber und nichts sonst vollzog sich die Geschichte, der es im Laufe seines Bestehens unterworfen gewesen ist. Dahin rechnen sowohl die Veränderungen, die es im Laufe der Zeit in seiner physischen Struktur erlitten hat, wie die wechselnden Besitzverhältnisse, in die es eingetreten sein mag.* (GS 1.2:475-76)

> In even the most perfect reproduction, *one* thing is lacking: the here and now of the work of art – its unique existence in a particular place. It is this unique existence – and nothing else – that bears the mark of the history to which the work has been subject. This history includes changes to the physical structure of the work over time, together with any changes in ownership. (SW 4:253)

The idea here is that the physical *presence* of the original, containing as it does all physical traces of its history, of the brush strokes of the artist and the handling by its subsequent owners, is something that cannot be reproduced, hence is absent in the reproduced object.

> *Die Umstände, in die das Produkt der technischen Reproduktion des Kunstwerks gebracht werden kann, mögen im übrigen den Bestand de Kunstwerks unangetastet lassen – sie entwerten auf alle Fälle sein Hier und Jetzt. [...] Was aber dergestalt ins Wanken gerät, das ist die Autorität der Sache. Man Kann , was hier ausfällt, im Begriff der Aura zusammenfassen und sagen: was im Zeitalter der technischen Reproduzierbarkeit des Kunstwerks verkümmert, das ist seine Aura. (GS 1.2:477)*

> The situations into which the product of technological reproduction can be brought may leave the artwork's other properties untouched, but they certainly devalue the here and now of the artwork. [...] And what is really jeopardized when the historical testimony is affected is the authority of the object. One might encompass the eliminated element within the concept of the aura, and go on to say: what withers in the age of the technological reproducibility of the work of art is the latter's aura. (*SW* 4:254)

This means that the reproduction lacks the specific "here and now" of the original, is not embedded in the tradition which the original is a part of, hence lacks a certain authoritative quality which the original *does* possess. The difference between the two, the thing that is missing from the reproduction, is what Benjamin calls the "aura."

Benjamin acknowledges that there have been shifts in the value of art throughout history, and that this, in a sense, has been a process of the progressive devaluation and diminishing of the artwork's aura. Initially, he claims, works of art possessed *cult-value*: a work of art had a specific role in a magical or religious ritual, and was, because of this role, embedded explicitly in the context of the tradition associated with this ritual. In the Renaissance, many works of art were no longer made and used with cult-value in mind, but instead acquired *exhibition-value* as they were displayed in a specific setting that was designed in a way that enabled the art to be viewed and admired.

With the advent of ever-improving reproductive techniques, in particular photography and film, it became possible to make copies of works of art. These copies exhibited a loss of uniqueness, and concurrently a loss of aura, as highlighted above in the quotes. In the case of photographs, the notion of an "original" became problematic: there is no clear *criterium* to distinguish between the various prints from a single negative (cf. *GS* 1.2:485-87/*SW* 4:257-59).

In the case of film, the disappearance of aura transpired not necessarily because of the reproductive power of the medium in itself, but because the speed of the reproduction made it possible for the reproduction to fall into step with reality, to re-create – for the first time – the movement-aspect of life and living things (cf. *GS* 1.2:474-75/*SW* 4:253). Here too the fact that so many aspects of something significant can be copied almost indefinitely diminishes the value of the depiction.

For Benjamin, the disappearance of aura is but one part of a much larger evolution, in which the very fabric of *experience* starts shifting and changing.

2.4. The Transformation of Experience

A scarlet thread woven through the fabric of Benjamin's philosophical program, as well that of Dilthey and also, in a sense, of the phenomenologists (two chief examples being Husserl and Merleau-Ponty), was the intent to extract the splinters of *genuine experience* from the desensitised flesh of the urbanised Westerner of the late 19th / early 20th century. These splinters were embedded there still as remnants of real experience, but long since hidden from view by the callouses that had developed to protect its bearers from the hustle and bustle of the street. The streets of the modern city, with its endless barrage of overwhelming signals offered explosive encounters that might, unwantedly, switch from anonymous to intensely intimate and back again in a matter of moments. Also, the streets with its waves upon waves of nearly identical engagements that one no longer derives fulfilment from: the eternal recurrence of the advertisement. It is these engagements that one wishes to ignore, run away from or be relieved of the longer one resides in such an environment. In this sense, Benjamin can be understood to have cleared the path for Heidegger's *das Man*, the estrangement that characterises modern man lost in the crowd.

An aesthetically pleasing and philosophically rich analysis of this type of urban massification, and the footholds the citizen would seek to remain standing in the social, political and cultural vortex of the modern metropolis, is developed by Benjamin in his "Über enige Motive bei Baudelaire" [On Some Motifs in Baudelaire]; the thematic veins run deep and dense in this piece. A semantic distinction central to this essay is the one between *Erfahrung* and *Erlebnis*.[9] English does not offer a proper way of isolating the meaning of one from the other in a single word, opting to translate either by utilising "experience." *Erfahrung*, for an important part based on the analysis offered by Bergson in his *Matiére et mémoire* [Matter and Memory][10] and the evocations of Proust in his *A la récherche du temps perdu* [Remembrance of Things Past],[11] is said to accommodate a form of remembrance heavily dependant on tradition and subconscious experience, the contents of which might emerge briefly in reaction to some sensory input (like how a familiar smell might trigger a memory of one's youth long considered lost in the murky and muddled depths of imperfect and incomplete recollection). This would involve the intensely meaningful and essentially personal and organic character of an individual, content-rich experience.

Erlebnis, on the contrary, is more shallow, repetitious or repeatable, more common but ultimately fleeting in nourishing content. Gerhard Schulze, a German sociologist, offers an analysis of what he calls the modern *Erlebnisgesellschaft* [*Erlebnis* society],[12] which is intended to denote the growing tendency of modern Westerners to collect ever more extreme experiences, to continuously strive for ways to approach and transcend boundaries of danger, emotion, sensation, privacy, bad taste and sheer intensity in order to once again experience something new and exciting, thus puncturing through the thick armour of complacency, numbness, *boredom* and indifference that emerged because of a long-suffered exposure to the unrelenting candour of the media, urban massification and the sublimation of random impulses and ceaselessly repeated momentary experiences in the form of shocks. In an attempt to capture these shades of meaning, I would therefore wish to offer the translations "momentary experience" for *Erlebnis*, and "momentous experience" for *Erfahrung* – it should be noted that for each a further passive (experience-as-knowledge) and active (experience-as-occurrent-process) form might be distinguished.

Momentous experience might be described as an expression of an organic and thoroughly experienced being-in-the-world that embodies an echo of the pre-cognitive embeddedness of man, but is quite radically transformed via intimate interactions with the vast array of consciously and subconsciously maintained memories, feelings, sensations and the resultant dispositional attitudes of the subject – a momentous experience is personal, unique and meaningful, and as such denotes the organic coherence of being-in-the-world in its natural form.

Momentary experience, as I approach it, would count as the constituting unit of what usually appears as an array or constellation of either encountered but not autonomically invited and/or processed impulses (leading to desensitisation or shock), or, in more recent decades, sometimes actively pursued in order to assuage the desire for momentous experiences misunderstood as cravings for extreme sensations. These sensations are ultimately non-nourishing and merely serve to stretch the sensation-threshold even further (like extreme sports and extreme violence or shamelessness in the media), and can, ultimately, engender the previously described callousness and boredom.

2.5. Embodiment and Aura

Now, as hinted at earlier (at the beginning of section 2.3), I wish to suggest that *embodied experience* and Benjamin's *aura* are closely related notions: something can have an aura for an agent in virtue of the fact that this agent is capable of embodied experience, i.e. is embodied as well as contextually and environmentally embedded in a specific way. It is no coincidence that Benjamin refers to experiences associated with the immersion in the beauty of nature to elucidate his notion aura; this kind of immersion is, in a sense, what many consider to be a natural state to be in, i.e. closest to who and what we are supposed to be. Or, conversely, and perhaps almost tautologically: truly meaningful embodied and embedded experience carries with it a particular aura. A possible hypothesis is that the estrangement and apathy, the *boredom* that comes from information- and impression-overload in modern society, is constituted by the inability to recognise this auratic quality, even in the items, situations or people that *do* (or *should*) still have it.

In the remainder of this essay, I will explore certain aspects of this idea (of embodied experience as a natural, authentic state) by focusing on the case of *mediated social interaction*. If there is any arena in which auratic qualities can linger the longest, one would suppose it would be face-to-face interaction, the practice of (intermittently) partaking in the meaningful coherence of another person's life. It is exactly this form of auratic interaction that now, for many (mostly young) people, is being absorbed into the technological realm, e.g. the Internet, and as such would run the risk of losing its auratic qualities.

3. Mediated Social Interaction

Recall (from section 2.4 above) Schulze's notion *Erlebnisgesellschaft* (the "experience-economy"), which incorporates the idea that modern Western society offers an ever-increasing array of experiences to its citizens; part of this is supplied by what we call the entertainment industry. It has come to the point where we can *purchase* and, in a sense, *consume* experiences, by going on a holiday in an exotic location, going sky-diving, watching a movie or going on the Internet to partake in things that are not directly available in real life.

The expansion of possibilities presented by the ongoing growth, development and re-invention of the *Erlebnisgesellschaft* leads to a precarious balance between boredom and insecurity: less insecurity, for instance by curtailing the risk inherent to a complete immersion in the experiences offered by the modern entertainment industry, means an increase in boredom, whereas diminishing boredom by seeking out danger and novelty increases the potential for insecurity.

Schulze's notion *Erlebnisrationalität* [*Erlebnis* rationality] indicates a particular approach to navigating this "experience economy". In this context, says Schulze, an experience is not an impression, but rather a process of digestion, of *using it up*. Experiences (*Erlebnisse*) are seen as merchandise, as objects one can purchase, own and use. Conversely, in this experience economy, *mass-produced objects* are often used to elicit experiences. This is intriguing, because normally *people* or (according to Benjamin) natural scenes or *unique* objects induce the most vivid experiences: we specifically seek out other people or visit especially beautiful destinations to be moved in special ways. Nonetheless, objects play an increasing role in our experiential life: we retrieve experiences via souvenirs (in line with the lush descriptions provided by Proust), we evoke experiences by reading books or watching movies (however, this usually involves experiences we have already had: we rarely sympathise with protagonists in novels who are completely unlike ourselves), and we generate experiences via, for instance, ICT-mediated social interaction.

And this is, perhaps, where certain problems arise. Consider the following quote:

> In our work, home, and social lives, we are saturated with data and stimulus. While our grandparents were limited by access to information and speed of communication, we are restricted largely by our ability to wade through it all. As with calories, we must work constantly to whittle down, prioritize, and pick out the choice nutritional bits. If we don't monitor our information diets carefully, our cerebral lives quickly become bloated. Attention gets diverted (sometimes dangerously so); conversations and trains-of-thought interrupted; skepticism short-circuited; stillness and silence all but eliminated. Probably the greatest overall threat is that so many potentially meaningful experiences can easily be supplanted by merely *thrilling* experiences.[13]

Benjamin could have written this, were he alive today. However, are there good reasons to suppose that what Shenk says here is correct? There might be. Even a decade ago, there was already a substantial body of research concerning the problem of information overload, an important part of that overload being attributed to the use of modern media.[14] Many colourful terms – amongst them *infoglut, data smog, analysis paralysis* and *information fatigue syndrome*[15] – have been devised to describe the phenomenon of having too much information available about too many topics, because of which it becomes extremely difficult to separate those choice bits of qualitatively appropriate data from mountains of nonsense. Klapp[16] drew attention to the possibility that, faced with such an overwhelming task, some people shut down and retreat into apathy: having grown *bored* and jaded, they lack the energy to process this information in a productive manner.

In addition to the danger of inducing boredom and apathy, some claim that multimedia also has the power to dilute the quality of "normal" social interaction. Consider the following less-than-flattering description of visitors of the Internet:

> Plugged into the Network of communications and computers, they seem to enjoy omniscience, and omnipotence: severed from their network, they turn

out to be insubstantial and disoriented. They no longer command the world as persons in their own right. Their conversation is without depth and wit; their attention is roving and vacuous; their sense of place is uncertain and fickle.[17]

In this vein, it is possible to highlight the idea that a progressive familiarity with the construal of virtual personalities harbours a destructive potential: the cyber-surfer is denied the possibility to bring his online swagger and (claims to) intellectual prowess into the real world, simply because real people and real objects impose many more constraints on the expression and realisation of one's desires than chatrooms and (online) computer games. That is, the real world is too viscous to permit the fluidity of identity the cyber-surfer has grown accustomed to.

In the remainder of this paper, I will focus my analysis on the matter of mediated social interaction, i.e. what consequences (if any) the use of the Internet has on the way we maintain relations with other people.

3.1. Connectedness

In a first analysis, one could say that declining to meet face-to-face, to instead interact via keyboards and computer screens, constitutes a turn for the worse: the latter case is somehow less real, less meaningful. In general it seems to be the case, and I suppose Benjamin would agree, considering his claim that he sees an aura return one final time in *portrait* photography, that person-to-person interaction has a *privileged* status, as opposed to other kinds of interaction.

Still, people seek out the Internet more and more often for their social engagements, and this development is disconcerting to some. What happens, so runs the argument, is that Internet users trade in embodied and embedded immersion for *connectedness*. Connectedness presupposes a natural separation or detachment, coupled with a freedom to choose *who* or *what* to connect to. The mediation of social interaction by computers epitomises this separation, and the freedom derives, in essence, from being disembodied, from being able to jump from one chatroom, with all the people that "reside" there, to another one at a moment's notice.

A classification of this new, mediated form of social interaction under the experiential mode described by Benjamin, i.e. as contributing to the intensification and acceleration of input, impulses and shocks, can be supported by noting the following properties:

(a) it involves, in the opinion of some, a *diluted* form of interaction;

(b) it is available in large amounts and great variety;

(c) it is easy to obtain or be confronted with, even if one is not actively looking for it;

(d) it provides a relatively easy satisfaction of needs and desires, i.e. it is not nearly as cumbersome as the more traditional forms of socialising (which would, at the very least, involve actually leaving the house).

Interesting to note is that these needs are, at least partially, manufactured or elicited by the availability of the technology and its supporting infrastructure: note how ten or fifteen years ago, no one suffered from "e-mail anxiety" (the need to check for new messages inordinately often). One specific characteristic of the technology, namely the anonymity it affords to its user, also affords the easier satisfaction of certain niche-based and/or socially undesirable needs.

3.2. Do-it-yourself Normativity

One aspect of the Internet that forms an especially poignant contribution to the advent of boredom (apart from the increase in impulses and shocks the excessive availability of information represented by this electronic medium), is that it engenders a *qualitative* change in informational streams, plus a (correlated) shift in the *value* of said information.

Formerly, information was most often monodirectionally divergent: one or few sources would serve many receivers, for instance via newspapers, radio or television. The Internet, rather, enables a different kind of structure: a polydirectional and diffuse stream, with people talking to other people in divergent, convergent or one-on-one relations.

This has a negative influence on the value of the information that is provided. This is because (it sometimes seems as if) everybody has an opinion, and (almost) nothing is accepted as undisputed fact. Because practically every home in western Europe, north America and the Pacific rim is connected to the Internet, everybody has the means to vent those opinions, and often it seems that what matters is not how well-reasoned and carefully researched an opinion is, but how effective that opinion's proprietor is in selling (in a figurative sense) or advertising his views to as many people as possible. That is, the postmodern fragmentation of narratives, communicative strategies and worldviews is almost tangibly instantiated in *cyberspace*.

I submit that this concatenation of factors leads to a desensitisation, a callousness to the voice of others that can lead to boredom: "Oh no, there you have *yet another* blogger who believes he knows the truth." In addition, this might cause one to view one's own opinion as merely one voice amongst many, thus adding to the aforementioned callousness: why bother fighting for a conviction when it either (apparently) is worth so little, or no one is prepared to afford it whatever value it might still have?

Hence, some of the properties of interaction via cyberspace have quite noticeable *ethical* consequences. The fact that people can partake of the Internet in relative anonymity, and that they (usually) cannot be confronted physically by irate discussion partners, results in an online morality that is looser than that of the real world. More than a few discussion forums and newsgroups are filled with posts that are marked by a greater coarseness, irascibleness and profanity than what (I have to assume) the authors would display in real life.

This is due to what I wish to call the *do-it-yourself normativity* present on the Internet. In a broader sense, by this I mean the inherent interpretationally and ontologically underdetermined, epistemologically open-ended nature of abstract systems (e.g. mathematics, basic physics, computer science). That is: a focus on pure quantity and/or form is often insufficient to lock in the *qualitative* features of a phenomenon under study. For instance, there is a case to be made for the claim that however detailed neuroscientific knowledge about the functioning of the brain gets, the qualitative features of phenomenal consciousness – the "what it is like" to experience pain and joy or taste sugar, and so on – are forever out of reach of the descriptive strategies of the natural sciences.[18] There is something essential that falls between the cracks of these scientific theories, because it is not the kind of thing that can be captured in formal and/or quantitative accounts.

Specific to the Internet, this point can be made as follows: the way in which one makes use of the Internet is underdetermined by the technology that helps constitute the medium. What falls out is the moral imperative that, in normal situations, comes from being confronted by another living, breathing human being. Most people would never dream of doing in real life what is almost second nature to them online, but because they are typing responses while sitting in front of a computer screen instead of engaging in embodied/embedded social interaction, divergent behavioural patterns are considered to be appropriate.

One of the central aspects of person-to-person interaction involves enforced normative constraints (e.g. a discussion partner responds immediately to incomprehensible or morally reprehensible exclamations). When conversing in an online chat room, this feedback is much less direct, and does not impose as strong a limitation on one's responses as it does in the real-life case. Furthermore, the freedom one has to migrate to another chatroom at the click of a button is, to an important extent, the freedom to *extract oneself* from the normative system that is in place in the initial chatroom: "I do not need this," or "these rules do not apply to me." The absence of many of the sanctions on misbehaviour that are available in real life tends to remove the ethical and social ("politically correct") filters from people's online dispositions towards communication.

3.3. The Value of Meaning

The detachment I see as the underlying cause of media-induced boredom involves a fundamental transformation of meaningful encounter. In the original situation, described by Benjamin, the meaning or meaningfulness of a beautiful landscape, a work of art, or another person emerges in dynamic interaction with that landscape, work of art or person. It involves actually *being there*, being submerged in the experiences that arise in embodied and embedded interaction. When this meaningfulness – this *aura* – recedes for whatever reason, a heavy burden is placed on the agent: meaning is to be deduced from or even injected into the world from a supposedly objective vantage point by the agent himself. In that case, we ruin into the problem of "do-it-yourself normativity" discussed above, i.e. the normative underdetermination of the media that might be used to regenerate the aura, e.g. the Internet.

Despite this, and here comes my positive claim, I maintain that mediated social interaction still retains a specific aura, i.e. is imbued with a modicum of meaningfulness and value, *exactly because it is social*. How can this be the case?

David Roberts underlines the fact that an auratic object possesses a certain humanising nature: the idea that beauty in nature or a work of art can "speak" to an observer, that such objects are invested with meaning (and meaningfulness) in a way that is similar to how a social encounter can be meaningful, is perhaps less of a metaphor than one might think.[19]

Recall that Walter Benjamin defines the aura of an authentic work of art in the following fashion: "*eine einmalige Erscheinung einer Ferne, so nah sie sein mag*" ["a unique appearance of a distance, however close it may be"] (cf. section 2.1). What he describes is an almost mystical experience that is associated with unique, authentic works of art. I submit that it is not surprising that, to many people, it is somehow thought to be appropriate to use metaphors like "this painting *speaks* to me" to characterise these experiences: the paradigmatic kind of situations in which something can be meaningful involves *social* interactions, and something resembling the "meaningfulness" from those social encounters is recognised in a particularly beautiful painting or sculpture.

Note that here we have this notion "meaning" (or "meaningfulness") again. I suggest that "meaning" is something that can emerge in an interactive process, and that such a process can take a number of different forms:

(a) Meaning in SOCIAL INTERACTION: recognising meaning (largely in terms of being disposed or evoked to react oneself) requires a particular *readiness*, and this readiness requires the agent to have a *history* – extracting meaning in this way is a diachronic process. This history entails being an embodied and contextually (environmentally and socially) embedded agent who has traversed a specific developmental (ontogenetic) trajectory, as well as being a member of a species that has traversed a particular evolutionary (phylogenetic) trajectory. The criterion for the readiness (the having-the-right-kind-of-history) is the success of social interaction: such judgments of success or failure are made in the social context, for instance in terms of to what extent a discussion partner is prepared to treat you with respect, as an equal deserving of his time and attention, and conversely to what extent you are prepared to spend time interacting with that other person. In that sense, the proof of the pudding is most definitely in the eating: what this social encounter means becomes clear in being immersed in that encounter.

(b) Meaning in SYMBOLIC INTERACTION: recognising meaning in the arrangement (of features or aspects of) the environment, for instance linguistic symbols, requires *knowledge*. This knowledge involves a suite of behavioural dispositions with a phenomenal component: "I *know* this, because in this situation, I *feel* that this is what I should *do*."

(c) Meaning in AURATIC INTERACTION: I suggest this as a way of providing a more general description of recognising *meaningfulness*, and this requires not merely "being there" or "being in the world," but "being *human* in *this* world," of being properly immersed in a suitable, human-specific niche. As this niche evolves, the kinds of dispositions an agent needs to possess or enact, the *work* this agent needs to perform to fulfil his half of the agent-world interaction dynamic will change as well: this agent will need to *adapt*. That is, where or how this agent recognises an aesthetic or social aura might change. Focusing on this social aura, the ability to engage in meaningful social interaction as *mediated by a machine* (be it telephone, e-mail, instant messaging via Internet), i.e. not in a classical face-to-face situation, would be an example of such an adaptation.

Above, I make a rather casual distinction between an aesthetic and a social aura. Is this a valid distinction, or is it merely an abstraction? That is, is the apprehension of an aura of a beautiful artefact or natural scene fundamentally different from the experience of uniqueness and meaningfulness that can emerge during a social encounter? My hypothesis is that the two are fundamentally intertwined; Roberts' description of the humanising nature of auratic objects or natural scenes, or when Marcuse or Bloch understand nature as a subject, appear to suggest something similar.[20] Conversely, I would claim, just as physical objects in the environment present affordances for specific forms of *bodily* action,[21] there is merit in viewing other agents as very special parts of the environment, namely as parts which instantiate affordances for *social* action. In both cases, something in the environment (either an object or another person) places certain demands on an agent, imposes constraints in some cases and enables specific action patterns in other cases, hence dictating (to an extent) what the agent should or is able to do. The main difference lies in the kinds of responses that are appropriate in a given instance: a coffee cup is for picking up and drinking from, and a person is for (amongst many other things) having a conversation with.

3.4. Conclusions: Mediated Social Aura

I do not see any conclusive reasons to suppose that the class of social affordances cannot arise in a mediated form, e.g. in Internet chatrooms, via e-mail and so on. Certainly, these affordances will be *different* than the kinds of social affordances prevalent in face-to-face interaction, but that does not automatically render them meaningless. After all, it is a defining characteristic of an affordance that it applies very specifically in a particular situation and for a particular agent, hence that it transforms along with changes in properties of the environment, the agent, or the relation between the two.

I submit that most of the difficulties involved in realising the appropriate adaptations, i.e. evolving along with the shift in social affordances (offered by the Internet, for instance), can be classified as a form of *horseless carriage syndrome.*[22] When the first cars appeared in the streets, some people attempted to conceptualise this new technological marvel in terms of what they were familiar with – horse-drawn carriages, but without the horses – thus failing to understand the car on its own terms, i.e. in terms of its suite of properties and possibilities. Similarly, when one understands the computer as a souped-up typewriter, perhaps embellished with some of the functions of the television and the CD-player, it is likely to be difficult to grasp the possibilities inherent to this new technology that cannot be described in terms of those older machines. One of these possibilities of the computer, if connected to the Internet, is the vast realm of affordances for social interaction in a way that did not exist before.

Amongst these new, Internet-specific affordances are the possibility to switch rather quickly between different social settings (e.g. different chatrooms), or to switch between different personalities (either by typing different kinds of answers during a chat than one would do in real life, or by actually assuming a different persona in a multi-user video game).

Horseless carriage syndrome is a fundamentally conservative affliction, but there is nonetheless room within it for an intriguing form of *progress.* Oosterling notes that throughout history, people have shown a tendency to romanticise the old and familiar as (part of) a reaction to overwhelming estrangement as elicited by a profoundly new development. When the Industrial Revolution transformed society, many turned to the unspoilt wilderness to find true, authentic aesthetic experience. The paradox here is that in order to reclaim "true experience" from an increasingly manufactured world, "nature" was redefined to be the aesthetic and ontological ideal in a way that seems quite *artificial*.[23] The interesting idea here is that what was once a source of feelings of estrangement, can come to be regarded as a source of authentic experience once something even newer comes along. Oosterling notes that there might be interesting insights to be gained from exploring the way in which *the machine* rose to prominence as a theme in twentieth-century avant-garde art (e.g. Marcel Duchamp's "readymades," or Jean Tinguely's kinetic sculptures), possibly as a response to the progressive "virtualisation" of our society. In the hands of those artists, "the machine" that had once been considered an expression of a decidedly non-natural, anti-auratic development, became an appropriate topic of artistic exploration, hence possibly the bearer of auratic qualities.[24]

I am not (yet) certain what stage is supposed to follow the "virtual" one, hence I cannot say what the contrast class is next to which current multimedia might turn out to be auratic after all. However, as an attempt to anticipate what might very well be an unavoidable development, I submit that that is exactly the case: there are new auratic forms that can evolve or emerge, with a social aura also emerging in mediated interaction. This auratic aspect of mediated social interaction is contingent (possibly even parasitic) upon the user's belief that another person (instead of, for instance, an advanced computer program) is the causal origin of a particular message. What is surprising, perhaps, is that the justified truth of this belief is not important; what suffices is the occurrence of the belief itself, regardless of whether or not the belief is warranted. The disposition towards forming such beliefs presupposes a natural and evolved capacity for social interaction – the whole "theory of mind"-discussion in the philosophy of mind is geared towards analysing how agents acquire knowledge of intentions and motivations of a discussion partner.

We can see how this new social aura fits in with the evolution of aura as described by Benjamin. De Mul highlights the idea that a nostalgic inclination might obscure the possibility that (some semblance of) an auratic quality of a work of art might continue to be present, even in the face of modern mechanical and even digital reproductive techniques.[25] Where the original work of art had *cult value* as it played a role in religious ritual, and it had *exhibition value* in the age of mechanical reproduction, digital representations can be claimed to possess *manipulation value*. The potential for profound interactivity of digital media allows sufficiently capable users of manipulating these representations, hence creating something new, of making a new "original work of art" rather than a copy. According to this idea, it is the potential for creation and the exertion of influence that elicits a new auratic quality.

However, there is a clarifying remark to be made in response to this line of argumentation. Cult value and exhibition value as contributors towards an aura are thought to be properties of the work of art, as is the aura itself. The manipulation value of digital representations means that acts of creation and transformation involving these representations have "auratic qualities," as De Mul puts it – *the acts* have these qualities, not so much the representations that are being manipulated.

With this in mind, we can wonder whether this new kind of aura would meet the criteria set forth by Benjamin. One could claim that the creative potential is to be understood as the appearance of a distance, an openness of possibilities. However, one could also claim that the "uniqueness"-aspect is diminished because just about anyone can partake in this creative process. To revisit an earlier example, one hundred years ago a published opinion (in a newspaper, for instance) had a certain status, because it was one of a very small number of published opinions: the technology available at the time simply did not allow everyone to have their say. Similarly, a work of art had an aura, because it was unique and special, and could not be created, reproduced, adapted or manipulated by just about anyone. In contrast, how much value do we attach to an opinion published on a weblog, when anyone can start up a blog and start "publishing"? How interesting is my neighbour's digital tinkering, when I have a harddrive filled with "creative excretions" of my own? Here, I think, we see the downside, at least in terms of the possibility of a digital representation having an aura, of the fact that the means to manipulate those digital representations are available to almost everybody. Perhaps we can still speak of digital representations having an aura, but that is a different kind of quality than what Benjamin recognised in unique works of art.

I think the transformations in social aura due to the emergence of modern communications technology are much less drastic. In fact, I think the basic properties of social aura in this multimedia-environment are the same as they always were. That is, first of all, because the capacity for experiencing those auratic properties is, to an important extent, hardwired into us. Consider the "mirror neurons" that have taken the neuroscience-community by storm over the past ten (or so) years, a vast industry of experiments, papers and conferences billowing up around them. Mirror neurons group together in neural regions that are oddly selective in becoming active when faced with input associated with conspecifics (e.g. sights or sounds caused by purposeful food-related action by an animal of the same species). Whatever reservations one might have about the panacea-like role attributed to mirror neurons in much current neuroscientific literature, the simple fact is that we humans are, by and large, evolutionarily predisposed to react along certain lines when confronted by an emoting conspecific, *regardless of the medium through which those emotions reach us*. A sad letter or e-mail can bring us to tears – why would that letter or e-mail not count as a meaningful social expression?

A second reason to suppose that a mediated social aura is highly similar to a normal social aura is that both face-to-face interaction and mediated interaction are *means* rather than *ends*. The bulk of the effectivity of a social aura is encapsulated in the *experiences* associated with interaction, rather than mainly or wholly in the "vehicles of interaction" (e.g. computers) themselves. Even when typing messages in a chatroom, a great deal of those experiences (excitement about finding a good friend, feeling remorse for being too harsh, being ashamed at revealing private thoughts) are highly similar to the experiences we might have during "normal" – that is, physical and face-to-face – interaction. Once again: why would those experiences be of lesser value?

Some might continue to argue that social interaction via Internet is a diluted form of "the real thing." However, a critical question then arises: disregarding the many occurrent and obvious differences in material realisation, is the auratic aspect of Internet-mediated social interaction actually qualitatively different from the aura of a hand-written letter? A letter might be forged, or may contain lies. A printed-out letter does not even contain the obvious idiosyncratic traces of the sender's handwriting, hence no obvious "natural" source of aura. My suggestion is as follows: the only thing ensuring the auratic character of such messages is the receiver's conviction that it originated with an authentic social partner capable of the accepted kinds of interaction. As suggested earlier, this belief about the origin of some message need not even be veridical for the auratic effect to take place.

Supposing that this is true is the only way I can understand a phenomenon I saw advertised on television recently: erotic instant text messaging. Instead of calling a telephone number and having an erotically tinted conversation with an actual person, it is now also possible to receive erotic text messages on your cell phone, which, as the advertisement wished to convey, comes directly from a scantily clad young lady who is waiting "just for you." This service is probably extremely easy to "fake" – these return messages can be generated automatically, and/or what is supposed to be a scantily clad young lady typing in answers can in reality be a very large, middle-aged man. Nonetheless, apparently people are ordering this service and are getting what they need from it – for some people, this brief message on a tiny cell-phone screen evokes the kinds of experience usually associated with real social interaction.

Obviously, this example is not very highbrow, but it does illustrate that face-to-face interaction is not a necessity for the occurrence of a social aura. Herein lie some dangers: we are all familiar with the horror stories of young children visiting chatrooms, conversing with people who turned out to have misrepresented themselves, sometimes with disastrous results. But the underlying truth is this: despite the continued and progressive manifestation of separation and detachment (geographically, as well as figuratively, due to "information overload") in cyberspace, mediated social interchange is on the rise, offering new ways for people to interact, ways of establishing trans-global connections that were not available twenty years ago. Perhaps this potentiality will offer contributions towards a cure for the ailments of modern society as Benjamin described them – that is, the continued shallowing of experience and the advent of boredom that we are confronted with. In any case, there is no need to assume a priori that mediated social interaction does not have this potential.

NOTES

[1] Many thanks to an anonymous referee for his/her very valuable comments.

[2] Cf. Wilhelm Dilthey, *Einleitung in die Geisteswissenschaften* (1883), in *Gesammelte Schriften*, vol. 1, (Göttingen: Vandenhoeck & Ruprecht, 9th edition: 1990).

[3] Cf. George Lakoff and Mark Johnson, *Philosophy in the Flesh: The Embodied Mind and Its Challenge to Western Thought* (London: HarperCollins, 1999).

[4] Cf. Martin Heidegger, *Die Grundprobleme der Phänomenologie*, Marburger Vorlesung (Sommersemester 1927), F.-W. von Herrmann (ed.), *Gesamtausgabe* vol. 24 (Frankfurt am Main: Vittorio Klostermann, 1975).

[5] Cf. Friedrich Nietzsche, *Götzendämmerung*, in *Sämtliche Werke*, vol. 6, eds. Giorgio Colli and Mazzino Montinari (Berlin: de Gruyter, 1988); English translation: *Twilight of the Idols, or, How to Philosophize with a Hammer*, trans. Duncan Large (Oxford; New York: Oxford University Press, 1998).

[6] Gerard Visser, "Dilthey und Nietzsche, unterschiedliche Lesarten des Satzes der Phänomenalität," in *Dilthey-Jahrbuch für Philosophie und Geschichte der Geisteswissenschaften*, vol. 10 (1996), pp. 224-245.

[7] Cf. Francisco J. Varela, Evan Thompson and Eleanor Rosch, *The Embodied Mind: Cognitive Science and Human Experience* (Cambridge, MA: The MIT Press, 1991); Andy Clark, *Being There: Putting Brain, Body, and World Together Again* (Cambridge, MA: The MIT Press, 1998); Antonio R. Damasio, *The Feeling of What Happens: Body and Emotion in the Making of Consciousness* (New York: Harcourt Brace, 1999); Evan Thompson, *Mind in Life: Biology, Phenomenology and the Sciences of Mind* (Cambridge, MA: Harvard University Press, 2007).

[8] All references to Benjamin's "Das Kunstwerk im Zeitalter seiner technischen Reproduzierbarkeit" (The Work of Art in the Age of Its Technological Reproducibility) are made parenthetically in the text; I provide both the German text of the *Gesammelte Schriften* (Collected Writings), ed. Rolf Tiedemann and Hermann Schweppenhäuser, 7 vols. in 15 (Frankfurt am Main: Suhrkamp, 1972–89), (hereafter cited as *GS*), and the English translation of the *Selected Writings*, ed. Marcus Bullock and Michael W. Jennings, 4 vols. (Cambridge, MA: Belknap Press of Harvard University Press, 1996–2003) (hereafter cited as *SW*).

[9] Cf. also Gerard Visser, *De Druk van de Beleving: Filosofie en Kunst in een Domein van Overgang en Ondergang* (Nijmegen: SUN, 1998); also available in German as *Erlebnisdruck: Philosophie und Kunst im Bereich eines Übergangs und Untergangs* (Würzburg: Königshausen & Neumann, 2005).

[10] Henri Bergson, *Matiére et mémoire* (1896), in *Oeuvres*, ed. André Robinet (Paris: Presses universitaires de France, 1959); English translation: *Matter and Memory*, trans. Nancy Margaret Paul and W. Scott Palmer (New York : Zone Books, 1988).

[11] Marcel Proust, *A la récherche du temps perdu*, ed. Jean-Yves Tadié (Paris: Gallimard, 1999).

[12] Gerhard Schulze, *Die Erlebnisgesellschaft: Kultursoziologie der Gegenwart* (Frankfurt an Main/New York: Campus, 1992).

[13] David Shenk, "The E Decade: Was I right about the Dangers of the Internet in 1997?," posted Wednesday, July 25, 2007, available at: http://www.slate.com/id/2171128/

[14] Cf. Angela Edmunds and Anne Morris, "The Problem of Information Overload in Business Organisations: a Review of the Literature," *International Journal of Information Management*, vol. 20 (2000), pp. 17-28.

[15] Cf. Ibid.

[16] Orrin E. Klapp, *Overload and Boredom: Essays on the Quality of Life in the Information Society* (Westport, CT: Greenwood Press, 1986).

[17] Albert Borgmann, *Crossing the Postmodern Divide* (Chicago: University of Chicago Press, 1992).

[18] Cf. Thomas Nagel, "What is it Like to Be a Bat?," *Philosophical Review* LXXXIII, issue 4 (1974), pp. 435-50.

[19] Cf. David Roberts, "On Aura and an Ecological Aesthetics of Nature," in *With the Sharpened Axe of Reason: Approaches to Walter Benjamin*, ed. Gerhard Fischer (Oxford/Washington DC: Berg, 1996).

[20] Quoted in Roberts "On Aura and an Ecological Aesthetics of Nature," p. 57.

[21] Cf. James J. Gibson, *The Ecological Approach To Visual Perception* (Boston: Houghton Mifflin, 1979).

[22] Cf. Jos de Mul, *Cyberspace Odyssee* (Kampen: Uitgeverij Klement, 2002).

[23] Henk Oosterling, "De Mens als Medium der Media – Radicalisering van een Middelmatig Denken," in Jos de Mul (ed.), *Filosofie in Cyberspace: Reflecties op de Informatie- en Communicatietechnologie* (Kampen: Uitgeverij Klement, 2002), pp. 292-328.

[24] Oosterling, "De Mens als Medium der Media, p. 312.

[25] de Mul, *Cyberspace Odyssee*, p. 124.

WORKS CITED

Benjamin, Walter. *Gesammelte Schriften*. Eds. Rolf Tiedemann and Hermann Schweppenhäuser. Frankfurt am Main: Suhrkamp, 1972–89. (cited as *GS* in the article).

———. *Selected Writings*. Eds. Marcus Bullock and Michael W. Jennings. Cambridge, MA: Belknap Press of Harvard University Press, 1996–2003. (cited as *SW* in the article).

Bergson, Henri. *Matiére et mémoire* (1896) in *Oeuvres*. Ed. André Robinet. Paris: Presses universitaires de France, 1959.

———. *Matter and Memory*. Trans. Nancy Margaret Paul and W. Scott Palmer. New York: Zone Books, 1988.

Borgmann, Albert. *Crossing the Postmodern Divide*. Chicago: University of Chicago Press, 1992.

Clark, Andy. *Being There: Putting Brain, Body, and World Together Again*. Cambridge, MA: The MIT Press, 1998.

Damasio, Antonio R. *The Feeling of What Happens: Body and Emotion in the Making of Consciousness*. New York: Harcourt Brace, 1999.

De Mul, Jos. *Cyberspace Odyssee*. Kampen: Uitgeverij Klement, 2002.

Dilthey, Wilhelm. *Einleitung in die Geisteswissenschaften* (1883), in *Gesammelte Schriften*, vol. 1, 9th edition. Göttingen: Vandenhoeck & Ruprecht: 1990.

Edmunds, Angela and Anne Morris. "The Problem of Information Overload in Business Organisations: a Review of the Literature." *International Journal of Information Management* vol. 20 (2000). 17-28.

Gibson, James J. *The Ecological Approach To Visual Perception*. Boston: Houghton Mifflin, 1979.

Heidegger, Martin. *Die Grundprobleme der Phänomenologie*. Marburger Vorlesung (Sommersemester 1927). *Gesamtausgabe* vol. 24. Ed. F.-W. von Herrmann. Frankfurt am Main: Vittorio Klostermann, 1975.

Klapp, Orrin E. *Overload and Boredom: Essays on the Quality of Life in the Information Society*. Westport, CT: Greenwood Press, 1986.

Lakoff, George and Mark Johnson. *Philosophy in the Flesh: The Embodied Mind and Its Challenge to Western Thought*. London: HarperCollins, 1999.

Nagel, Thomas. "What is it Like to Be a Bat?" *Philosophical Review* LXXXIII, issue 4 (1974). 435-50.

Nietzsche, Friedrich. *Götzendämmerung. Sämtliche Werke*, vol. 6. Eds. Giorgio Colli and Mazzino Montinari. Berlin: de Gruyter, 1988.

———. *Twilight of the Idols, or, How to Philosophize with a Hammer*. Trans. Duncan Large. Oxford & New York: Oxford University Press, 1998.

Oosterling, Henk. "De Mens als Medium der Media – Radicalisering van een Middelmatig Denken." In Jos de Mul (ed.). *Filosofie in Cyberspace: Reflecties op de Informatie- en Communicatietechnologie.* Kampen: Uitgeverij Klement, 2002. 292-328.

Proust, Marcel. *A la récherche du temps perdu.* Ed. Jean-Yves Tadié. Paris: Gallimard, 1999.

Roberts, David. "On Aura and an Ecological Aesthetics of Nature." *With the Sharpened Axe of Reason: Approaches to Walter Benjamin.* Ed. Gerhard Fischer. Oxford/Washington DC: Berg, 1996.

Schulze, Gerhard. *Die Erlebnisgesellschaft: Kultursoziologie der Gegenwart.* Frankfurt an Main/New York: Campus, 1992.

Shenk, David. "The E Decade: Was I right about the Dangers of the Internet in 1997?" http://www.slate.com/id/2171128/

Thompson, Evan. *Mind in Life: Biology, Phenomenology and the Sciences of Mind.* Cambridge, MA: Harvard University Press, 2007.

Varela, Francisco J., Evan Thompson, and Eleanor Rosch. *The Embodied Mind: Cognitive Science and Human Experience.* Cambridge, MA: The MIT Press, 1991.

Visser, Gerard. "Dilthey und Nietzsche, unterschiedliche Lesarten des Satzes der Phänomenalität." *Dilthey-Jahrbuch für Philosophie und Geschichte der Geisteswissenschaften,* vol. 10 (1996). 224-245.

———. *De Druk van de Beleving: Filosofie en Kunst in een Domein van Overgang en Ondergang.* Nijmegen: SUN, 1998.

———. *Erlebnisdruck: Philosophie und Kunst im Bereich eines Übergangs und Untergangs.* Würzburg: Königshausen & Neumann, 2005.

CHAPTER 9

The Devil Inside:
Boredom Proneness and Impulsive Behaviour

Joseph Boden

The experience of boredom has been linked to a wide range of impulsive and destructive behaviours, including criminal activity, violence, compulsive gambling and sexual activity, as well as other maladaptive behaviours. Research also suggests that individuals who engage in these maladaptive behaviours often share a certain personality trait in common: boredom proneness. The essay reviews the range of emotional states and behaviours that have been linked to boredom proneness. Further, it examines research that locates the trait of boredom proneness within established models of personality structure, and in particular links between boredom proneness and the major personality traits of neuroticism and extraversion. In addition, the links between boredom proneness and cognitive and neuropsychological phenomena are examined, including time perception, task absorption, and attention control. Finally, the essay examines possible causal pathways by which boredom proneness is linked to maladaptive behaviour.

1.1. Introduction

"Angry, bored, and unable to sleep, (name deleted) grabbed his Marksman slingshot and headed out of his foster home to destroy something that might bring him a degree of infamy that rivalled his rage, police said."

"A teenager charged in connection with last month's car arson spree allegedly bragged to friends about the fires – at one point autographing a newspaper with coverage of the event, according to an arrest warrant released Friday by [...] police. [...] On June 29, police interviewed another woman who overheard a conversation between (name deleted) and her boyfriend. (Name deleted) allegedly said he 'exploded a Dumpster and lit some cars on fire. [...] She said (name deleted) explained he lit papers from inside the cars on fire to start the fires [...] (he) was really drunk and did it because he was bored,' the affidavit said."

"A 'bored' teenager who threw a chain from a bridge over the M25 because he 'wanted to see a car's tyre pop' has been sentenced to 14 months in a young offenders' institution. (Name deleted) was out with friends when he saw a heavy link chain and decided to pick it up. After driving around, he

threw it off a bridge at about 4am. The chain struck a white van, shattering the windscreen and inflicting minor injuries on the driver, who was forced to pull over onto the hard shoulder. When questioned by police about why he threw the chain, the teenager initially said he did not know, then claimed that he just did not want to take it home with him. He added: 'I was just bored and causing trouble, I don't know, I was just bored.' Later he confessed he thought it might be fun to watch a car's tyre pop and that it would be more exciting to throw it off a motorway bridge than just into the verge."

The above stories are not uncommon in the news: a "bored" teenager has done something impulsive and dangerous, and has ended up in court. Of course, these kinds of news stories provide merely a sampling of the wide range of dangerous, impulsive, and destructive things that individuals do. But in many cases a single common denominator may be found amongst them: boredom. This anecdotal evidence is supported by the findings of a range of research studies examining the phenomenal experience of boredom. A number of studies have linked the experience of boredom to a wide range of impulsive and destructive behaviours, including criminal activity, violence, compulsive gambling and sexual behaviour, as well as other maladaptive behaviours. While the precise causal role of the experience of boredom in these behaviours remains unclear, what is clear is that individuals often attribute the motivations for engaging in these behaviours to boredom, and that the phenomenal experience of boredom is frequently followed by sensation-seeking behaviour that is maladaptive in some way.

Given the associations between the experience of boredom and maladaptive and violent behaviours, the question arises whether it may be possible to predict the extent to which individuals are at greater risk of experiencing boredom, and are thereby at greater risk of engaging in behaviours that are detrimental to their own or others' health and well-being. In recent years, a number of studies have examined a personality trait known as *boredom proneness* and its relationship to maladaptive behaviours.[1] Perhaps unsurprisingly, high levels of boredom proneness have been linked to increased risks of impulsive, maladaptive, and violent behaviour. In this essay, I will examine the research regarding the trait of boredom proneness. First, I will review the range of behaviours that have been linked to boredom proneness, and second examine research that locates the trait of boredom proneness within established models of personality structure. Then, I will examine the links between boredom proneness and underlying cognitive and neuropsychological phenomena, in order to elucidate possible causal pathways by which boredom leads to maladaptive behaviour. Finally, I will integrate these findings into an overall view of the phenomenon of boredom proneness, including its status as a dimension of personality, and indicate possible directions for future research.

2.1. What is boredom proneness?

Boredom proneness is a personality trait that has been linked to cognitive, attentional, and neuropsychological phenomena that are associated with an inability or a disinclination to focus attention on a task in the environment. While I will discuss the status of boredom proneness as a personality trait in more detail below (in sections 4 and 5), for the purposes of the present discussion we may consider the trait of boredom proneness as corresponding to a particular set of behavioural dispositions associated with boredom. Because boredom proneness is considered by some to be a personality trait, in could be argued that individuals have varying levels of dispositional boredom proneness, based on the extent to which they habitually display these behaviours. That is, individuals can be described as boredom prone, to the extent to which they habitually perceive, report, or are observed in a state of boredom.[2] More simply put, individuals who are more boredom prone are more likely to become bored, are less likely to shift themselves from a state of boredom to a state of interest, and may feel boredom more intensely than individuals who are less boredom prone.

The status of boredom proneness as a personality trait also entails that it may be possible to measure the construct. The Boredom Proneness Scale, a 28-item self-report questionnaire, was developed in order to assess the extent to which an individual reports: a lack of stimulation from or enthusiasm for work and other pursuits; restlessness; a lack of ideas; failure to persist at tasks; and perceiving situations as being tiresome or monotonous.[3] According to its authors, the Boredom Proneness Scale has adequate psychometric qualities, including moderate to high reliability, and strong correlations with other measures of boredom and the mental/emotional states associated with boredom (such as depression).[4] However, subsequent research has suggested that there may be at least five "sub-factors" within the Boredom Proneness Scale.[5] What this suggests is that the construct of boredom proneness may in fact be an amalgamation of a number of distinct facets of personality that may or may not be inter-related within the individual. For example, while the sub-factors referred to as "Time Perception" and "Constraint" may be indicators of boredom proneness, these indicators may not be sufficiently inter-correlated to conclude that they are measuring the same construct. I will examine the implications of these measurement issues in more detail below.

2.2. Behaviours and mental/emotional states associated with boredom proneness

Setting to one side issues of measurement, a number of research studies have examined the behaviours, mental states, and emotional states exhibited by individuals scoring at differing levels of the boredom proneness scale. In general, the studies described here were correlational in nature; that is, the studies tended to employ the questionnaire measure of boredom proneness mentioned previously, in conjunction with a variety of other self-report measures. These studies suggest that a number of different behaviours and emotional states are associated with higher levels of boredom proneness. For example, Sommers and Vodanovich reported that higher levels of boredom proneness were associated with higher scores on measures of depression, anxiety, interpersonal sensitivity, obsessive-compulsive behaviour, and somatization.[6] Similarly, Rupp and Vodanovich found that higher levels of boredom proneness were associated with higher levels of self-reported anger and aggression in everyday settings,[7] while Gana and colleagues found that higher levels of boredom proneness were linked with increased tendencies to engage in introspective behaviour and a greater likelihood of hypocondriasis.[8] Collectively, these findings suggest that boredom proneness is associated with a greater tendency to experience and express negative emotions, higher levels of inward-directed attention, greater sensitivity to bodily states and social situations, and compulsive behaviours.

A number of other behaviours have been associated with boredom proneness as well. For example, Ferrari found that boredom proneness was associated with a greater tendency to procrastinate.[9] Also, Kelly reported that both pathological and non-pathological worry were correlated with boredom proneness.[10] Kass and colleagues found that, in an organizational setting, those individuals high in boredom proneness were more likely to report job frustration and dissatisfaction, and had higher levels of absenteeism from work.[11] In addition, von Gemmingen et al. reported that boredom proneness was associated with higher levels of paranoia.[12] Here again, the evidence suggests that boredom proneness is related to a constellation of behaviours that suggest poor adaptation to the environment.

The collective results of these studies suggest that boredom proneness is associated with a range of negative emotional and behavioural states, including irritability, anxiety, hypochondriasis, and to some extent self-absorption. In addition, those high in boredom proneness tend to be less adapted to the work environment, and show increasing levels of worry and paranoia. The overall impression of the boredom-prone individual is a person who displays generally lower levels of adjustment in personal and professional life. As we will see in the next section, the maladaptive behaviours and emotional states associated with boredom proneness may lead to a variety of adverse, longer-term outcomes.

2.3. Outcomes associated with boredom proneness

While it is clear that the boredom prone individual may demonstrate adjustment difficulties in day-to-day behaviour, boredom proneness may also be linked to variety of adverse outcomes. A number of studies have reported associations between boredom proneness and maladaptive behavioural outcomes. As in the previously-cited studies of behaviour and emotional states, the studies cited below generally used self-report measures of maladaptive behaviour, and their statistical associations with boredom proneness were measured. For example, Blaszczynski and colleagues reported that boredom proneness scores were higher amongst a group of pathological gamblers, compared with controls.[13] Chaney and colleagues found that boredom proneness was associated with compulsive sexual behaviour, including sexual addiction, in a sample of gay men.[14] Also, Dahlen et al. reported that higher levels of boredom proneness were associated with increased risks of anger while driving, and aggressive and risky driving behaviour.[15] In addition, Newberry and Duncan found that higher boredom proneness scores were linked with a greater likelihood of juvenile delinquency.[16] Although these studies have not examined a particularly wide array of outcomes, it is clear that boredom proneness has been linked to a variety of adverse outcomes associated with a general lack of control over compulsive and risky behaviour.

In a sense, the links between boredom proneness and maladaptive behaviour are not surprising. Indeed, in several articles, the phenomenal state of boredom has been linked to criminal activity, violence, and delinquency.[17] For example, Baumeister and Campbell asserted that violence and aggression are ways in which the tedium of boredom may be reduced temporarily.[18] It stands to reason, therefore, that individuals with higher levels of boredom proneness may be more likely to engage in behaviours that attempt to reduce that state – including violent, aggressive, and criminal behaviours. However, the question arises as to what links the state of boredom, and by extension boredom proneness, to these behaviours. One possibility is that boredom proneness may be related to other factors that may increase the likelihood of engaging in maladaptive behaviours, including criminal offending. Impulsivity is a common factor in compulsive and addictive behaviour, as well as aggression and criminality. Like boredom proneness, impulsivity has been described as a dimension of personality.[19] To better understand the phenomenon of boredom proneness, it may prove useful to examine the relationships between boredom proneness and a range of personality constructs, including impulsivity. These are examined in the following section.

3.1. Boredom proneness and personality

As mentioned previously, boredom proneness is regarded as a dimension of personality, on which individuals differ in terms of the extent of their "traitedness." As such, the links between boredom proneness and other personality traits can be examined, in order to gain a greater understanding of the phenomenon. In this way, it may be possible to link boredom proneness with other personality traits and psychological processes, and in doing so to elucidate the links between boredom proneness and both short- and long-term tendencies to maladaptive behaviour.

In current personality theory, hierarchical models of personality suggest that all personality traits are linked, with hierarchical relationships between "lower order" traits (including such things as boredom proneness and impulsiveness) and "higher order" traits, with which the lower order traits are correlated. At the top of the hierarchy sit five major dimensions of personality.[20] Any proposed trait can be located within the existing structural models of personality simply by examining the statistical relationships between the measurement of the trait in question, and the measurement of (theoretically) related traits. This description overlooks the fact that some so-called personality traits are not particularly well defined, but part of the processes of research in personality is to examine the adequacy of various trait concepts, and the extent to which trait concepts describe unique aspects of personality. The adequacy of boredom proneness as a personality trait will be discussed further in section 5.

3.2. Associations between boredom proneness and other personality traits

Several studies have linked the trait of boredom proneness to other dimensions of personality. In particular, boredom proneness has been linked to the two major personality dimensions that correspond to emotional responding: neuroticism (also referred to as negative affectivity), and extraversion (also known as positive affectivity).[21] For example, Barnett and Klitzing found that boredom proneness was inversely related to both the major personality dimension of extraversion, and to intrinsic motivation, such that those individuals high in boredom proneness were low in extraversion and were less likely to be internally (intrinsically) motivated.[22] Vodanovich and colleagues reported a similar finding, with participants high in boredom proneness reporting higher levels of several negative emotional states, and lower levels of a number of positive emotional states. Gordon and colleagues reported that boredom proneness was inversely correlated with positive affectivity (extraversion), and in addition reported that boredom proneness was positively correlated with negative affectivity (neuroticism).[23] In addition, Culp found that at least one sub-factor of boredom proneness was inversely related to extraversion in a sample of college students.[24] While the fact that boredom proneness is related to both neuroticism and extraversion raises concerns about the status of boredom proneness as a unitary construct, the research cited above suggests that boredom proneness is strongly related to habitual patterns of emotional responding. The findings suggest that boredom prone individuals are more likely to experience and express negative affect, and are less likely to experience and express positive affect. This in turn suggests that it may be possible to view the behaviours arising from boredom (and boredom proneness) as being related to the experience of chronic negative emotional states.

In terms of other dimensions of personality, Watt and Vodanovich reported that boredom proneness was associated with impulsivity, with boredom prone individuals showing higher levels of impulsivity.[25] Gordon and Caltabiano found that boredom proneness was associated with higher levels of sensation seeking, a trait related to impulsiveness.[26] Similar findings were reported by Kass and Vodanovich.[27] McGiboney and Carter found that boredom proneness was related to a disregard for rules and social dependency (i.e. relying on others to organize social lives).[28] Similarly, Tolor reported that individuals higher in boredom proneness had lower scores on a measure of assertiveness, and higher scores on a measure of alienation.[29] Finally, Wink and Donahue found that boredom proneness was related to a measure of narcissism, with boredom prone individuals scoring higher on measures of narcissistic behaviour.[30] The results of these studies suggest that boredom proneness is related to impulsivity, dependency on others, and narcissism. In a general sense, the relationship between boredom proneness and these aspects of personality suggest that boredom proneness is an indicator of poor adjustment, and could serve as a risk marker for future adverse outcomes. More importantly, however, the links between boredom proneness and impulsivity/poor behavioural control may provide a means for understanding the associations between boredom proneness and maladaptive behaviour. That is, the route by which boredom proneness leads to adverse outcomes may be through poor behavioural control. These issues will be examined in more detail in section 5.

4.1. Boredom proneness and cognitive / neuropsychological phenomena

In addition to being linked with measures of personality, and with evidence of adverse outcomes, boredom proneness has also been linked with a number of cognitive and neuropsychological phenomena. This research has examined the cognitive states underlying boredom, and has studied whether the cognitive and neuropsychological functioning of individuals high in boredom proneness differs from that of individuals low in boredom proneness. Unlike studies that have been cited previously, which have used primarily correlational methods, most of the studies in this area have compared groups of individuals with high and low scores on boredom proneness, and measure the differential performance of these individuals on various tasks.

A number of studies have found links between boredom proneness and cognitive functioning. In particular, boredom proneness has been linked with differences in stimulus perception, time estimation, and the extent to which the individual is able to become engaged with a particular task. For example, Bornstein and colleagues reported that individuals high in boredom proneness demonstrated immunity from the "mere exposure effect," such that those participants high in boredom proneness did not report increased liking of figures that appeared more frequently.[31] Danckert and Allman found that individuals at differing levels of boredom proneness had differing perceptions of the passage of time; those individuals higher in boredom proneness perceived time as passing more slowly.[32] Watt also found that higher levels of boredom proneness were associated with estimations of time passing more slowly.[33] Harris[34] found that boredom prone individuals were less likely to experience a sense of flow,[35] in which absorption in a particular task takes place. In addition, Seib and Vodanovich found that boredom prone individuals reported significantly lower levels of absorption.[36] The range of evidence provided by these studies suggests that boredom proneness is associated with a bias in cognitive functioning that corresponds to a lower general interest level, such that those individuals with higher levels of boredom proneness seem less inclined and less able to engage fully in cognitive tasks.

In addition to lower levels of interest and attention to tasks, a number of studies have found that boredom proneness is related to poorer performance on tasks that require sustained attention. For example, Kass et al. found that boredom prone individuals performed more poorly than those low in boredom proneness at a vigilance task requiring attention.[37] Similar findings were reported by Sawin and Scerbo, who found that low boredom prone participants out-performed high boredom prone participants on a signal detection task.[38] In both cases, the tasks were described by the researchers as being of low interest (i.e. boring to the majority of participants), and in both cases boredom-prone participants were less likely to be able to perform the task efficiently, or to persist in the task. These findings suggest some interaction between the demands of the task and the characteristics of the individual.

The lower levels of interest, absorption, and subsequent performance on cognitive tasks suggest that boredom prone individuals demonstrate a bias in cognitive processing, such that they are less likely to engage in cognitive processing that requires effort and sustained attention. It appears to be the case that individuals high in boredom proneness are less inclined to undertake cognitive tasks, and are less likely to persist in completing them, or to sustain effort. Indeed, Watt and Blanchard reported that boredom prone individuals reported lower levels of need for cognition, indicating that there were less likely to engage in and enjoy effortful cognitive activities.[39] Collectively, the results of these studies indicate that boredom proneness is associated with a disinclination to engage in effortful, cognitive processing. In the next section, I will examine the possible means by which biases in cognitive functioning may increase the likelihood of boredom prone individuals engaging in maladaptive behaviour.

5.1. Integration – examining possible causal pathways in boredom, boredom proneness, and behavioural outcomes

The research cited above has shown that boredom proneness is associated with a range of adverse behavioural and emotional outcomes, both short- and long-term. In addition, boredom proneness has been linked with the major personality dimensions of negative and positive emotionality, such that those individuals high in boredom proneness are more likely to experience negative emotions and less likely to experience positive emotions. Boredom proneness was also linked with impulsivity, sensation-seeking, and narcissism. Finally, boredom proneness was linked with biases in cognitive processing, such that those higher in boredom proneness demonstrated lower levels of task engagement, persistence, and performance on cognitive tasks. The overall profile of the boredom prone individual is one who has difficulty engaging with tasks, has difficulties with impulse control and in interpersonal relations, has poorer day-to-day emotional and behavioural outcomes, and is at greater risk of engaging in maladaptive behaviours.

Despite the accumulated evidence, it remains unclear precisely why boredom, and in particular the tendency to experience boredom more often, would be associated with this range of behaviours and lead to such adverse outcomes. In the present section, I will examine possible causal pathways from boredom to adverse outcomes, and highlight some of the issues arising from the research on boredom proneness. Finally, I will examine some of the ways in which research on boredom and boredom proneness might be advanced.

5.2. Linking boredom proneness to adverse outcomes via emotions and emotion regulation

The most salient feature of boredom, as a phenomenal state, is the fact that it is psychologically aversive.[40] What this suggests is that individuals with high levels of boredom proneness are likely to be experiencing an aversive psychological state more often, and perhaps more intensely, than individuals with lower levels of boredom proneness. In one sense, it may seem quite reasonable to conclude that individuals who experience a greater level of aversive psychological states in their day-to-day lives are more likely to experience adverse outcomes. On the other hand, acknowledgement of this link does not explain the pathways by which increased levels of aversive states lead to poorer outcomes. In order to understand the causal pathway between the aversive state of boredom and outcomes, it may be useful to consider the possibility that adverse outcomes may be the result of a behavioural choice on the part of the boredom prone individual, in response to the (regular) experience of boredom.

One response to aversive psychological states – often accompanied (or defined) by the experience of negative affect – is emotion regulation. Gross defines emotion regulation as an individual's conscious or unconscious attempts to change an undesired emotional state into a more desirable emotional state.[41] On the thesis of hedonism, most emotion regulation will involve attempts at alleviating negative (aversive) emotional states, replacing these with neutral or positive states, with the experience of unpleasant affect being particularly apt to motivate attempts at emotion regulation.[42] It could be argued, therefore, that under the assumption of emotion regulation, most individuals will attempt to consciously or unconsciously alter their state of boredom, replacing that with a less aversive mental state.

This potential means of regulating boredom, however, is complicated by the fact that attempts to alter emotions and emotion-related mental states, without attending to the particular problem that caused these states, are often unsuccessful. Folkman and Lazarus' theory of emotion-focused coping suggests that attempts to control emotions alone are often doomed to failure, because the initial situation or conditions that caused the aversive state in the first instance will frequently still obtain.[43] This is particularly likely in the case of boredom, in which there appears to be no specific stimulus causing the aversive emotional state; it is, instead, defined by a lack of sufficient stimulation. Folkman and Lazarus also suggested that individuals who attempt to control their emotional state alone will oftentimes resort to maladaptive methods for doing altering their present mental state, including the use of alcohol or other drugs.[44] It would seem likely that the risks of many of the adverse outcomes associated with boredom proneness could be increased through alcohol or other drug intoxication.

A further difficulty in the regulation of boredom is that it is also a state accompanied by a perception of insufficient levels of interest and stimulation. What this suggests is that the regulation of boredom would also be accompanied by an attempt to change a state of low activation to a state of high activation. One means of doing this is through engaging in highly stimulating activities. This is another pathway by which boredom – and by extension boredom proneness – may be related to adverse outcomes. In an attempt to increase one's stimulation level, chronically bored individuals may attempt to invoke states of greater stimulation by engaging in highly stimulating, and perhaps even dangerously stimulating activities. As an example, the boredom prone individual may regard an act of violence as a good means of dispelling a state of boredom, in part because it is very exciting and stimulating. As pointed out previously, Baumeister and Campbell have noted that aggression and violence may be extreme examples of behaviours that serve the purpose of alleviating states of boredom.[45] While it is by no means certain that boredom prone individuals will choose dangerous or illegal activities to alleviate boredom, it may be speculated that this is one outlet for boredom prone individuals to alleviate their chronic aversive mental states.

We have already seen that boredom proneness is defined by the frequent experience of boredom and an apparent greater susceptibility to boredom, and that boredom proneness is accompanied by the chronic experience of negative emotional states and relative absence of positive emotional states. This would suggest that, for most boredom prone individuals, their attempts at dispelling the aversive state are largely unsuccessful, and that they have generally failed to find a reliable means for avoiding a state of boredom. This in turn implies that the processes described above are most likely a kind of vicious circle in which boredom prone individuals find themselves stuck. Thus, the path from boredom proneness to adverse outcomes may begin with a chronic inability to regulate the negative hedonic state of boredom.

5.3. Distorted cognition – the next step

In addition to the personality attributes and behaviours correlated with boredom proneness, we have also previously seen that boredom proneness is associated with a range of cognitive biases and distortions. The nature of these biases and distortions is such that, for boredom prone individuals, time seems to pass more slowly – increasing the perception that an activity or state is boring – and these individuals have lower levels of interest in, engagement with, and persistence with cognitive tasks. The weight of the evidence suggests that boredom prone individuals are unable to engage fully with tasks in their environment. It could be argued that, in a sense, these cognitive biases operate in a manner such that the boredom prone individual has a lower threshold for boredom. Under such an explanation, the boredom prone individual is likely to find boring tasks, states, and situations that other (low boredom prone) individuals do not find boring, thus increasing the likelihood that the boredom prone individual will experience an aversive mental state. Under normal conditions, the tasks and situations provided by the social environment are less absorbing for the boredom prone, due in part to the way in which they perceive, and fail to engage with tasks.

It could also be argued that the failure of attention, engagement, and interest evidenced in high boredom prone individuals will also make it more difficult for the individual to escape from the state of boredom once it ensues. Because the boredom prone individual finds it more difficult to engage with any task, the cycle of boredom might be that much more difficult to break, with a smaller range of tasks and situations available for the person to find relief from their aversive mental state. For example, the person low in boredom proneness might have a range of tasks to alleviate the occasional experience of boredom, such as watching television or reading a book. The person high in boredom proneness, on the other hand, would be more likely to consider such activities boring, because a much larger range of activities are boring to the person high in boredom proneness. The boredom prone individual will be less likely to put to use the panoply of behaviours with which he might combat the state of boredom when it occurs, simply for having never developed the set of behaviours.

However, the link from boredom proneness to adverse outcomes may also be due in part to the associations between boredom proneness and attention. The evidence suggests that boredom is, in part, a problem of attention, in that it is very difficult for the bored individual to focus his or her attention on a particular stimulus or task. It may be speculated that, while in a state of boredom, the judgement and behavioural choices of the boredom prone individual may be altered. It has been noted that, while in a state of boredom, the average individual may have some difficulty in imagining a task that might alleviate the boredom. This must surely be even more difficult for individuals with higher levels of boredom proneness. Boredom prone individuals have a smaller range of tasks and activities to choose from in the first instance (because they are more apt to find things boring), and will habitually experience difficulty in focusing their attention on solving the problem of boredom. Simply put, difficulties in focusing and maintaining attention will make it more difficult to choose to engage in the kinds of behaviours that will successfully alleviate boredom.

A further possibility is that, because of the inability to focus and maintain attention, boredom prone individuals may display impaired judgement in choosing activities or behaviours to alleviate boredom. It could be argued that a lack of attention and effortful processing could lead the individual to make rash, ill-considered choices concerning ways to alleviate boredom.[46] In addition, the links between boredom proneness and impulsivity, the antithesis of behavioural control, increases the likelihood that behavioural choice will be random, ill-considered, and maladaptive.[47] For example, the boredom prone individual may (rightly) believe that the thrill of engaging in petty vandalism may solve the immediate problem of boredom and may immediately (impulsively) choose this as a solution, failing to consider the longer-term consequences of boredom. Baumeister has shown that individuals will often use methods of escaping aversive mental states that are socially unacceptable, dangerous, or even injurious to one's reputation or one's health, and that one factor in choosing these behaviours is an alteration of judgement.[48] It seems reasonable to argue, then, that boredom prone individuals may also suffer from an impairment of judgement, linked to their persistent and chronic inability to focus attention and devote processing resources to cognitive tasks. The result may be poorly thought-out forays into thrilling, but dangerous behaviours, with potentially severe consequences.

5.3. The social side – boredom proneness and day to day behaviour

A further means by which boredom proneness may be linked to adverse outcomes is through the maladaptive day to day behaviours demonstrated amongst boredom prone individuals. As we have seen previously, boredom proneness was associated with increased levels of pathological worry, and paranoia, and an increased likelihood that the individual will experience a greater range and frequency of negative emotions and fewer positive emotions. This behavioural profile suggests the boredom prone individual as one who will have significant adjustment issues, not the least of which will involve social life and social interaction.

It is clear that a fulfilling social life is one important ingredient in a happy and well-balanced life for many individuals.[49] Most people desire and enjoy the company of family and friends, and rely on others emotionally to some extent. However, the maintenance of friendships, partnerships, and family relationships is based in part on being able to engage in appropriate interactions with other people.[50] Clearly, the boredom prone individual, with higher levels of paranoia, worry, and negative emotions, is going to find it more difficult to navigate within the social sphere. For example, the boredom prone individual may have more difficulty in finding and maintaining friendships, not only because he finds other people in general less interesting, but also because he has difficulty in relating to others in an appropriate manner. In this way, one major means of alleviating boredom, socialising, may be restricted for the boredom prone. Paradoxically, the worry, paranoia, and negative emotional states that accompany boredom proneness may serve as a kind of a self-fulfilling prophecy, creating recurring difficulties for the social life of the boredom prone individual, and perhaps in turn increasing not only boredom, but also worry, paranoia, and negative emotions. The vicious circle of impaired social interactions may therefore stand in the way of the individual being able to use a social network to escape the vicious circle of boredom proneness.

5.5. Issues arising

While the preceding account may describe possible pathways between boredom proneness and the maladaptive, destructive behaviour evidenced in the vignettes that opened the present chapter, it should also be acknowledged that these links are, at the moment, mere speculation. There is very little research concerning the causal pathways from boredom proneness to adverse outcomes. Indeed, the causal relationship between boredom proneness and maladaptive behaviours has not yet been established. While it seems reasonable to posit that boredom, and therefore boredom proneness, could increase the likelihood of engaging in behaviours with adverse outcomes, it could also be argued that the causal arrow in fact points in the opposite direction. Because the vast majority of the studies in this particular area have been correlational and cross-sectional in nature, it is impossible to ascertain whether boredom proneness is a causal factor in many of the behaviours reviewed here. Furthermore, it could also be argued that the observed links between boredom proneness and outcomes might arise due to the effects of confounding factors that are associated with both boredom proneness and outcomes. The links between boredom proneness and adverse outcomes could be examined more clearly using longitudinal data, in which measures of boredom proneness could be linked either prospectively or retrospectively to outcomes.

The limitations mentioned above regarding the inference of causality generally do not apply to laboratory studies that examine the relationship between boredom proneness and performance on various laboratory-based tasks (such as cognitive tasks). Under experimental conditions, it is possible to deduce causality, particularly when differences in behaviour are observed between individuals high and low in boredom proneness. However, in order to elucidate links between boredom proneness and cognitive/emotional states and behaviour, a wider range of research is needed. Presently, the laboratory-based research linking boredom proneness to outcomes is limited in scope, with relatively few studies addressing these issues. Given the links between boredom proneness and adverse long-term outcomes that have been surveyed in the present chapter, a better understanding of the processes by which boredom prone individuals arrive at their particular behavioural choices could play an important role in reducing adverse outcomes.

A further issue arising from the research on boredom proneness concerns the extent to which it may be considered a personality trait. The ongoing debates surrounding the psychometric properties of the boredom proneness scale may indicate that the construct is not comprised of a single dimension. If it were shown to be the case that boredom proneness was not uni-dimensional, its status as a personality trait would be somewhat in doubt.[51] In addition, the fact that boredom proneness is correlated with both neuroticism (negative affectivity) and extraversion (positive affectivity), two of the major dimension of personality, would suggest that boredom proneness does not easily fit within current models of the structure of personality. This in turn suggests the possibility that boredom proneness may be a description of a constellation of behaviours that fall under various dimensions of personality, but is not a personality trait *per se*. This may have very little impact on research on boredom proneness; indeed, there are thriving research endeavours on a number of measurable constructs that are not personality traits, such as self-esteem.[52] However, it could be argued that, if boredom proneness was found not to be a personality trait, it would be more difficult to arrive at a consensus definition of the construct, and in turn it may be more difficult to conduct a programme of research linking boredom proneness to outcomes. The example of research on self-esteem can be used here again; while there is a great deal of research on the topic, and it proves possible to measure self-esteem,[53] it is unclear precisely what the construct is comprised of, and there are vigorous debates about the potential causal role of self-esteem in a range of outcomes.[54] Further research is needed in clarifying the status of boredom proneness, and in refining its psychometric structure. The uncertain status of boredom proneness may relegate that construct as well to an uncertain position in the psychological landscape.

6.1. Conclusion

The vignettes that opened the present chapter illustrated the links between boredom proneness and adverse outcomes. A range of research studies have shown that individuals with higher levels of boredom proneness demonstrate biases in cognition and attention, have difficulties with adjustment and behaviour on a day-to-day basis, and are at greater risk of engaging in maladaptive behaviours with adverse longer-term outcomes. While the pathways linking boredom proneness and outcomes are not clear, it seems likely that boredom prone individuals have difficulties in regulating their internal states, and may engage in maladaptive behaviour as a means of escaping the aversive state of boredom. Furthermore, cognitive biases and problems of social interaction may exacerbate both boredom and the extent to which boredom prone individuals may be able to alleviate their distress. In addition, while there are issues arising from the body of research on boredom proneness, future research may be useful in clarifying the nature of the boredom proneness construct, and in elucidating the pathways leading from boredom proneness to the adverse outcomes described in the opening to this chapter.

It is abundantly clear that boredom, and boredom proneness, poses a problem that can be measured in damage, destruction, and a range of other adverse outcomes. The solution to this problem lies in a better understanding of the causes and correlates of boredom and boredom proneness, and an understanding of the links between boredom proneness and later outcomes.

NOTES

[1] Richard Farmer and Norman D. Sundberg, "Boredom Proneness: The Development and Correlates of a New Scale," Journal of Personality Assessment 50.1 (1986), pp. 4-17.

[2] Individuals with high levels of boredom proneness are sometimes described as *boredom prone* (as they are frequently described in the context of the present text), but this can be somewhat misleading in the context of a discussion of personality traits. In the strictest sense, *everyone* is boredom prone, but some more so than others.

[3] Farmer and Sundberg, "Boredom Proneness."

[4] Measured using one-week test retest methods, and through a measure of internal consistency (coefficient alpha).

[5] Stephen J. Vodanovich and Steven J. Kass, "Age and Gender Differences in Boredom Proneness," *Journal of Social Behavior & Personality* 5.4 (1990), pp. 297-307.

[6] Jennifer Sommers and Stephen J. Vodanovich, "Boredom Proneness: Its Relationship to Psychological- and Physical-Health Symptoms," *Journal of Clinical Psychology* 56.1 (2000), pp. 149-55.

[7] Deborah E. Rupp and Stephen J. Vodanovich, "The Role of Boredom Proneness in Self-Reported Anger and Aggression," *Journal of Social Behavior & Personality* 12.4 (1997), pp. 925-36.

[8] Kamel Gana, Benedicte Deletang, and Laurence Metais, "Is Boredom Proneness Associated with Introspectiveness?" *Social Behavior and Personality* 28.5 (2000), pp. 499-504; and Kamel Gana, et al. "The Relationship between Boredom Proneness and Hypochondriacal Tendencies in a Nonclinical Adult Sample," *European Review of Applied Psychology/Revue Europeenne de Psychologie Appliquee* 51.4 (2001), pp. 267-72.

[9] Joseph R. Ferrari, "Procrastination and Attention: Factor Analysis of Attention Deficit, Boredomness, Intelligence, Self-Esteem, and Task Delay Frequencies," *Journal of Social Behavior & Personality* 15.5 (2000), pp. 185-96.

[10] William E. Kelly, "Some Evidence for Nonpathological and Pathological Worry as Separate Constructs: An Investigation of Worry and Boredom," *Personality and Individual Differences* 33.3 (2002), pp. 345-54.

[11] Steven J. Kass, Stephen J. Vodanovich, and Anne Callender, "State-Trait Boredom: Relationship to Absenteeism, Tenure, and Job Satisfaction," *Journal of Business and Psychology* 16.2 (2001), pp. 317-27.

[12] Mitchell J. von Gemmingen, Bryce F. Sullivan, and Andrew M. Pomerantz, "Investigating the Relationships between Boredom Proneness, Paranoia, and Self-Consciousness," *Personality and Individual Differences* 34.6 (2003), pp. 907-19.

[13] Alex Blaszczynski, Neil McConaghy, and Anna Frankova, "Boredom Proneness in Pathological Gambling," *Psychological Reports* 67.1 (1990), pp. 35-42.

[14] Michael P. Chaney and Andrew C. Blalock. "Boredom Proneness, Social Connectedness, and Sexual Addiction among Men Who Have Sex with Male Internet Users," *Journal of Addictions & Offender Counseling* 26.2 (2006), pp. 111-22; and Michael P. Chaney and Catherine Y. Chang, "A Trio of Turmoil for Internet Sexually Addicted Men Who Have Sex with Men: Boredom Proneness, Social Connectedness, and Dissociation," *Sexual Addiction & Compulsivity* 12.1 (2005), pp. 3-18.

[15] Eric R. Dahlen, et al., "Driving Anger, Sensation Seeking, Impulsiveness, and Boredom Proneness in the Prediction of Unsafe Driving," *Accident Analysis & Prevention* 37.2 (2005), pp. 341-48.

[16] Angela L. Newberry and Renae D. Duncan, "Roles of Boredom and Life Goals in Juvenile Delinquency," *Journal of Applied Social Psychology* 31.3 (2001), pp. 527-41.

[17] For example, Roy F. Baumeister and W. Keith Campbell, "The Intrinsic Appeal of Evil: Sadism, Sensational Thrills, and Threatened Egotism," *Personality and Social Psychology Review* 3.3 (1999), pp. 210-21, and Tamar Horowitz and David Tobaly, "School Vandalism: Individual and Social Context," *Adolescence* 38.149 (2003): 131-9.

[18] Cf. Baumeister and Campbell, "The Intrinsic Appeal of Evil."

[19] Estibaliz Arce and Carmen Santisteban, "Impulsivity: A Review," *Psicothema* 18.2 (2006), pp. 213-20.

[20] The most well-known model uses the following five dimensions: neuroticism, extraversion, openness to experience, conscientiousness, and agreeableness. Other models use very similar dimensions that correspond to these, but have different names (e.g. Surgency, Agreeableness, Conscientiousness, Emotional Stability, Intellect). Cf. Robert R. McCrae and Paul. T. Costa, *Personality in adulthood* (New York: The Guildford Press, 1990), and Lewis R. Goldberg, "The Structure of Phenotypic Personality Traits," *American Psychologist*, 48 (1993), pp. 26-34.

[21] David Watson and Lee Anna Clark, "Negative Affectivity: The Disposition to Experience Aversive Emotional States," *Psychol Bull* 96.3 (1984), pp. 465-90, and David Watson, Lee Anna Clark, and Greg Carey, "Positive and Negative Affectivity and Their Relation to Anxiety and Depressive Disorders," *J Abnorm Psychol* 97.3 (1988), pp. 346-53.

[22] Lynn A. Barnett, "Measuring the Abcs of Leisure Experience: Awareness, Boredom, Challenge, Distress," *Leisure Sciences* 27.2 (2005), pp. 131-55.

[23] Anne Gordon et al., "The Psychometric Properties of the Boredom Proneness Scale: An Examination of Its Validity," *Psychological Studies* 42.2-3 (1997), pp. 85-97. The fact that boredom proneness was positively related to one major personality dimension (neuroticism) and negatively related to another (extraversion) suggests that the boredom proneness trait may in fact consist of more than one trait. Cf. Gordon et al, "The Psychometric Properties of the Boredom Proneness Scale."

[24] Neil A. Culp, "The Relations of Two Facets of Boredom Proneness with the Major Dimensions of Personality," *Personality and Individual Differences* 41.6 (2006), pp. 999-1007.

[25] John D. Watt and Stephen J. Vodanovich, "Relationship between Boredom Proneness and Impulsivity," *Psychological Reports* 70.3, Pt 1 (1992), pp. 688-90.

---

[26] In this particular study, boredom proneness was measured via an alternative measure, the "Leisure Boredom Scale." Cf. Winsome Rose Gordon and Marie Louise Caltabiano, "Urban-Rural Differences in Adolescent Self-Esteem, Leisure Boredom, and Sensation Seeking as Predictors of Leisure-Time Usage and Satisfaction," *Adolescence* 31.124 (1996), pp. 883-901.

[27] Steven J. Kass and Stephen J. Vodanovich, "Boredom Proneness: Its Relationship to Type a Behavior Pattern and Sensation Seeking," *Psychology: A Journal of Human Behavior* 27.3 (1990), pp. 7-16.

[28] Garry W. McGiboney and Clifford Carter, "Boredom Proneness and Adolescents' Personalities," *Psychological Reports* 63.3 (1988), pp. 741-42.

[29] Alexander Tolor, "Boredom as Related to Alienation, Assertiveness, Internal-External Expectancy, and Sleep Patterns," *Journal of Clinical Psychology* 45.2 (1989), pp. 260-65.

[30] Paul Wink and Karen Donahue, "The Relation between Two Types of Narcissism and Boredom," *Journal of Research in Personality* 31.1 (1997), pp. 136-40.

[31] The mere exposure effect involves the development of a preference (liking) for stimuli that are presented more frequently than others, when all stimuli are presented at speeds below the threshold for recognition; cf. William. R. Kunst-Wilson and Robert. B. Zajonc, "Affective Discrimination of Stimuli That Cannot Be Recognized," *Science* 207.4430 (1980), pp. 557-8.

[32] James A. Danckert and Ava-Ann A. Allman, "Time Flies When You're Having Fun: Temporal Estimation and the Experience of Boredom," *Brain and Cognition* 59.3 (2005), pp. 236-45.

[33] John D. Watt, "Effect of Boredom Proneness on Time Perception," *Psychological Reports* 69.1 (1991), pp. 323-27.

[34] Mary B. Harris, "Correlates and Characteristics of Boredom Proneness and Boredom," *Journal of Applied Social Psychology* 30.3 (2000), pp. 576-98.

[35] Mihaly Csikszentmihalyi and Judith LeFevre, "Optimal Experience in Work and Leisure," *Journal of Personality and Social Psychology* 56.5 (1989), pp. 815-22.

[36] Hope M. Seib and Stephen J. Vodanovich, "Cognitive Correlates of Boredom Proneness: The Role of Private Self-Consciousness and Absorption," *Journal of Psychology: Interdisciplinary and Applied* 132.6 (1998), pp. 642-52.

[37] Steven J. Kass et al., "Watching the Clock: Boredom and Vigilance Performance," *Perceptual and Motor Skills* 92.3, Pt 2 (2001), pp. 969-76.

[38] David A. Sawin and Mark W. Scerbo, "Effects of Instruction Type and Boredom Proneness in Vigilance: Implications for Boredom and Workload," *Human Factors* 37.4 (1995), pp. 752-65.

[39] John D. Watt and Michael J. Blanchard, "Boredom Proneness and the Need for Cognition," *Journal of Research in Personality* 28.1 (1994), pp. 44-51.

[40] Fisher defined boredom as "an unpleasant, transient affective state in which the individual feels a pervasive lack of interest in and difficulty concentrating on the current activity," Cynthia D. Fisher, "Boredom at work: A neglected concept," *Human Relations*, 46 (1993), p. 396.

[41] James J. Gross, "Emotion Regulation: Affective, Cognitive, and Social Consequences," *Psychophysiology* 39.3 (2002), pp. 281-91.

[42] Cf. Gross "Emotion Regulation."

[43] Susan Folkman, "Personal Control and Stress and Coping Processes: A Theoretical Analysis," *Journal of Personality and Social Psychology* 46.4 (1984), pp. 839-52; and Susan Folkman and Richard S. Lazarus, "Coping as a Mediator of Emotion," *Journal of Personality and Social Psychology* 54.3 (1988), pp. 466-75; and S. Folkman and R. S.

Lazarus, "The Relationship between Coping and Emotion: Implications for Theory and Research," *Social Science and Medicine* 26.3 (1988), pp. 309-17.

[44] Cf. Folkman, "Personal Control and Stress and Coping Processes," and Folkman and Lazarus "Coping as a Mediator of Emotion" and "The Relationship between Coping and Emotion."

[45] Baumeister and Campbell, "The Intrinsic Appeal of Evil."

[46] Cf. Serena Chen, Kimberly Duckworth, and Shelly Chaiken, "Motivated heuristic and systematic processing," *Psychological Inquiry* 10 (1999), pp. 44-49, for a discussion of these issues.

[47] Peter G. Enticott, James R.P. Ogloff, and John L. Bradshaw, "Associations between laboratory measures of executive inhibitory control and self-reported impulsivity," *Personality and Individual Differences,* 41 (2006), pp. 285-294.

[48] Roy F. Baumeister, *Escaping the Self: Alcoholism, Spirituality, Masochism, and Other Flights from the Burden of Selfhood* (New York: Basic Books, 1991).

[49] Lynn Bloomberg, James Meyers, and Marc T. Braverman, "The Importance of Social Interaction: A New Perspective on Social Epidemiology, Social Risk Factors, and Health," *Health, Education, & Behavior* 21.4 (1994), pp. 447-63.

[50] John B. Neziek, "Causal Relationships between Perceived Social Skills and Day-to-Day Social Interaction: Extending the Sociometer Hypothesis," *Journal of Social and Personal Relationships* 18.3 (2001), pp. 386-403.

[51] It could be argued that the issues concerning the dimensionality of boredom proneness are related to the measurement of the construct, rather than the construct itself. It may be possible to resolve these issues through refinement of the instruments used to measure it.

[52] Bernice Andrews, "Self-Esteem," *Psychologist* 11.7 (1998), pp. 339-42.

[53] James Blascovich and Joe Tomaka, "Measures of Self-Esteem," in *Measures of Personality and Social Psychological Attitudes: Measures of Social Psychological Attitudes*, eds. John P. Robinson and Phillip R. Shaver. Vol. 1 (San Diego, CA: Academic Press, 1991), pp. 115-60.

[54] Roy F. Baumeister et al., "Does High Self-Esteem Cause Better Performance, Interpersonal Success, Happiness, or Healthier Lifestyles?" *Psychological Science in the Public Interest* 4. (2003), pp. 1-44; and Roy F. Baumeister, Laura Smart, and Joseph M. Boden, "Relation of Threatened Egotism to Violence and Aggression: The Dark Side of High Self-Esteem," *Psychological Review* 103.1 (1996), pp. 5-33; and Joseph .M. Boden, David M. Fergusson, and L John Horwood, "Does Adolescent Self-Esteem Predict Later Life Outcomes? A Test of the Causal Role of Self-Esteem," *Development and Psychopathology*, 20.1 (2008), pp. 319-39.

WORKS CITED

Andrews, Bernice. "Self-Esteem." *Psychologist* 11.7 (1998). 339-42.

Arce, Estibaliz., and Carmen. Santisteban. "Impulsivity: A Review." *Psicothema* 18.2 (2006). 213-20.

Barnett, Lynn A. "Measuring the Abcs of Leisure Experience: Awareness, Boredom, Challenge, Distress." *Leisure Sciences* 27.2 (2005). 131-55.

Baumeister, Roy. F., and W. Keith. Campbell. "The Intrinsic Appeal of Evil: Sadism, Sensational Thrills, and Threatened Egotism." *Personality and Social Psychology Review* 3.3 (1999). 210-21.

Baumeister, Roy. F., Laura Smart, & Joseph M. Boden, "Relation of Threatened Egotism to Violence and Aggression: The Dark Side of High Self-Esteem." *Psychological Review* 103.1 (1996). 5-33.

Baumeister, Roy. F. *Escaping the Self: Alcoholism, Spirituality, Masochism, and Other Flights from the Burden of Selfhood*. New York: Basic Books, 1991.

Baumeister, Roy. F., et al. "Does High Self-Esteem Cause Better Performance, Interpersonal Success, Happiness, or Healthier Lifestyles?" *Psychological Sciences in the Public Interest* 4.1 (2003). 1-44.

Blascovich, James, and Joe Tomaka. "Measures of Self-Esteem." *Measures of Personality and Social Psychological Attitudes: Measures of Social Psychological Attitudes*. Eds. John P. Robinson and Phillip R. Shaver. Vol. 1. San Diego, CA: Academic Press, 1991. 115-60.

Blaszczynski, Alex, Neil McConaghy, and Anna Frankova. "Boredom Proneness in Pathological Gambling." *Psychological Reports* 67.1 (1990). 35-42.

Bloomberg, Lynn, James Meyers, and Marc T. Braverman. "The Importance of Social Interaction: A New Perspective on Social Epidemiology, Social Risk Factors, and Health." *Health Education & Behavior* 21.4 (1994). 447-63.

Boden, Joesph .M., David M. Fergusson, and L John Horwood. "Does Adolescent Self-Esteem Predict Later Life Outcomes? A Test of the Causal Role of Self-Esteem." *Development and Psychopathology* 20 (2008). 319-39.

Chaney, Michael P., and Andrew C. Blalock. "Boredom Proneness, Social Connectedness, and Sexual Addiction among Men Who Have Sex with Male Internet Users." *Journal of Addictions & Offender Counseling* 26.2 (2006). 111-22.

Chaney, Michael P., and Catherine Y. Chang. "A Trio of Turmoil for Internet Sexually Addicted Men Who Have Sex with Men: Boredom Proneness, Social Connectedness, and Dissociation." *Sexual Addiction & Compulsivity* 12.1 (2005). 3-18.

Chen, Serena, Kimberly Duckworth, and Shelly Chaiken. "Motivated Heuristic and Systematic Processing." *Psychological Inquiry* 10.1 (1999). 44 - 49.

Csikszentmihalyi, Mihaly., and Judith. LeFevre. "Optimal Experience in Work and Leisure." *Journal of Personality and Social Psychology* 56.5 (1989). 815-22.

Culp, Neil A. "The Relations of Two Facets of Boredom Proneness with the Major Dimensions of Personality." *Personality and Individual Differences* 41.6 (2006). 999-1007.

Dahlen, Eric R., et al. "Driving Anger, Sensation Seeking, Impulsiveness, and Boredom Proneness in the Prediction of Unsafe Driving." *Accident Analysis & Prevention* 37.2 (2005). 341-48.

Danckert, James A., and Ava-Ann A. Allman. "Time Flies When You're Having Fun: Temporal Estimation and the Experience of Boredom." *Brain and Cognition* 59.3 (2005). 236-45.

Enticott, Peter.G. , James R.P. Ogloff, and John L. Bradshaw. "Associations between Laboratory Measures of Executive Inhibitory Control and Self-Reported Impulsivity." *Personality and Individual Differences* 41 (2006). 285-94.

Farmer, Richard., and Norman. D. Sundberg. "Boredom Proneness--the Development and Correlates of a New Scale." *Journal of Personality Assessment* 50.1 (1986). 4-17.

Ferrari, Joseph R. "Procrastination and Attention: Factor Analysis of Attention Deficit, Boredomness, Intelligence, Self-Esteem, and Task Delay Frequencies." *Journal of Social Behavior & Personality* 15.5 (2000). 185-96.

Fisher, Cynthia D. "Boredom at Work: A Neglected Concept." *Human Relations* 46.3 (1993). 395-417.

Folkman, Susan. "Personal Control and Stress and Coping Processes: A Theoretical Analysis." *Journal of Personality and Social Psychology* 46.4 (1984). 839-52.

Folkman, Susan., and Richard. S. Lazarus. "Coping as a Mediator of Emotion." *Journal of Personality and Social Psychology* 54.3 (1988). 466-75.

———. "The Relationship between Coping and Emotion: Implications for Theory and Research." *Social Science and Medicine* 26.3 (1988). 309-17.

Gana, Kamel, Benedicte Deletang, and Laurence Metais. "Is Boredom Proneness Associated with Introspectiveness?" *Social Behavior and Personality* 28.5 (2000). 499-504.

Gana, Kamel, et al. "The Relationship between Boredom Proneness and Hypochondriacal Tendencies in a Nonclinical Adult Sample." *European Review of Applied Psychology/Revue Europeenne de Psychologie Appliquee* 51.4 (2001). 267-72.

Goldberg, Lewis R. "The Structure of Phenotypic Personality Traits." *American Psychologist* 48 (1993). 26-34.

Gordon, Anne, et al. "The Psychometric Properties of the Boredom Proneness Scale: An Examination of Its Validity." *Psychological Studies* 42.2-3 (1997). 85-97.

Gordon, Winsome Rose, and Marie Louise Caltabiano. "Urban-Rural Differences in Adolescent Self-Esteem, Leisure Boredom, and Sensation Seeking as Predictors of Leisure-Time Usage and Satisfaction." *Adolescence* 31.124 (1996). 883-901.

Gross, James. J. "Emotion Regulation: Affective, Cognitive, and Social Consequences." *Psychophysiology* 39.3 (2002). 281-91.

Harris, Mary B. "Correlates and Characteristics of Boredom Proneness and Boredom." *Journal of Applied Social Psychology* 30.3 (2000). 576-98.

Horowitz, Tamar, and David Tobaly. "School Vandalism: Individual and Social Context." *Adolescence* 38.149 (2003). 131-9.

Kass, Steven J., and Stephen J. Vodanovich. "Boredom Proneness: Its Relationship to Type a Behavior Pattern and Sensation Seeking." *Psychology: A Journal of Human Behavior* 27.3 (1990). 7-16.

Kass, Steven J., Stephen J. Vodanovich, and Anne Callender. "State-Trait Boredom: Relationship to Absenteeism, Tenure, and Job Satisfaction." *Journal of Business and Psychology* 16.2 (2001). 317-27.

Kass, Steven J., et al. "Watching the Clock: Boredom and Vigilance Performance." *Perceptual and Motor Skills* 92.3, Pt 2 (2001). 969-76.

Kelly, William E. "Some Evidence for Nonpathological and Pathological Worry as Separate Constructs: An Investigation of Worry and

Boredom." *Personality and Individual Differences* 33.3 (2002). 345-54.

Kunst-Wilson, W. R., and R. B. Zajonc. "Affective Discrimination of Stimuli That Cannot Be Recognized." *Science* 207.4430 (1980). 557-8.

McCrae, Robert R., and Paul T. Costa. *Personality in Adulthood.* New York: Guilford Press, 1990.

McGiboney, Garry W., and Clifford Carter. "Boredom Proneness and Adolescents' Personalities." *Psychological Reports* 63.3 (1988). 741-42.

Newberry, Angela L., and Renae D. Duncan. "Roles of Boredom and Life Goals in Juvenile Delinquency." *Journal of Applied Social Psychology* 31.3 (2001). 527-41.

Neziek, John B. "Causal Relationships between Perceived Social Skills and Day-to-Day Social Interaction: Extending the Sociometer Hypothesis." *Journal of Social and Personal Relationships* 18.3 (2001). 386-403.

Rupp, Deborah E., and Stephen J. Vodanovich. "The Role of Boredom Proneness in Self-Reported Anger and Aggression." *Journal of Social Behavior & Personality* 12.4 (1997). 925-36.

Sawin, David A., and Mark W. Scerbo. "Effects of Instruction Type and Boredom Proneness in Vigilance: Implications for Boredom and Workload." *Human Factors* 37.4 (1995). 752-65.

Seib, Hope M., and Stephen J. Vodanovich. "Cognitive Correlates of Boredom Proneness: The Role of Private Self-Consciousness and Absorption." *Journal of Psychology: Interdisciplinary and Applied* 132.6 (1998). 642-52.

Sommers, Jennifer, and Stephen J. Vodanovich. "Boredom Proneness: Its Relationship to Psychological- and Physical-Health Symptoms." *Journal of Clinical Psychology* 56.1 (2000). 149-55.

Tolor, Alexander. "Boredom as Related to Alienation, Assertiveness, Internal-External Expectancy, and Sleep Patterns." *Journal of Clinical Psychology* 45.2 (1989). 260-65.

Vodanovich, Stephen J., and Steven J. Kass. "Age and Gender Differences in Boredom Proneness." *Journal of Social Behavior & Personality* 5.4 (1990). 297-307.

von Gemmingen, Mitchell J., Bryce F. Sullivan, and Andrew M. Pomerantz. "Investigating the Relationships between Boredom Proneness, Paranoia, and Self-Consciousness." *Personality and Individual Differences* 34.6 (2003). 907-19.

Watson, David, and Lee Anna Clark. "Negative Affectivity: The Disposition to Experience Aversive Emotional States." *Psychological Bulletin* 96.3 (1984). 465-90.

Watson, David, Lee Anna Clark, and Greg Carey. "Positive and Negative Affectivity and Their Relation to Anxiety and Depressive Disorders." *Journal of Abnormal Psychology* 97.3 (1988). 346-53.

Watt, John D. "Effect of Boredom Proneness on Time Perception." *Psychological Reports* 69.1 (1991). 323-27.

Watt, John D., and Michael J. Blanchard. "Boredom Proneness and the Need for Cognition." *Journal of Research in Personality* 28.1 (1994). 44-51.

Watt, John D., and Stephen J. Vodanovich. "Relationship between Boredom Proneness and Impulsivity." *Psychological Reports* 70.3, Pt 1 (1992). 688-90.

Wink, Paul, and Karen Donahue. "The Relation between Two Types of Narcissism and Boredom." *Journal of Research in Personality* 31.1 (1997). 136-40.

CONTRIBUTORS

Joseph Boden is a Senior Research Fellow in the Department of Psychological Medicine, University of Otago, Christchurch School of Medicine and Health Sciences (New Zealand).

Matthew Boss is a postgraduate research student in the Department of Philosophy of the University of Sydney. His research is on Heidegger's interpretation of Kant's critical philosophy.

Barbara Dalle Pezze holds a PhD in Philosophy from The University of Hong Kong. After teaching at The Chinese University of Hong Kong, she is now working as Head of Cultural Studies Department at "Fondazione G. Toniolo" (Italy). She is the author of *Martin Heidegger and Meister Eckhart: A Path towards Gelassenheit* (Lewiston, NY: The Edwin Mellen Press, 2009).

Isis I. Leslie is an Assistant Professor of Political Science in the Honours College at Texas Tech University (USA).

William McDonald is a Senior Lecturer in Philosophy in the School of Humanities at the University of New England (Australia). He is the author of numerous articles on Kierkegaard, including those in *The Stanford Encyclopedia of Philosophy*, *The Internet Encyclopedia of Philosophy*, and *The Literary Encyclopedia*, and has translated Kierkegaard's *Prefaces: Light Reading for Certain Classes as the Occasion May Require, By Nicolaus Notabene* (Tallahassee: Florida University Press, 1989).

James Phillips is an ARC Australian Research Fellow in the School of History and Philosophy at the University of New South Wales and the author of *Heidegger's Volk: Between National Socialism and Poetry* (Stanford: Stanford University Press, 2005) and *The Equivocation of Reason: Kleist Reading Kant* (Stanford: Stanford University Press, 2007).

Carlo Salzani is a Research Associate in the Centre for Comparative Literature and Cultural Studies at Monash University (Australia), presently working as an Alexander von Humboldt Research Fellow in the Institut für Germanistik, Vergleichende Literatur- und Kulturwissenschaft at the Rheinische Friedrich-Wilhelms-Universität Bonn (Germany). He's the author of *Constellations of Reading: Walter Benjamin in Figures of Actuality* (Oxford: Peter Lang, 2009).

Rachel June Torbett has recently completed a PhD in the Centre for Comparative Literature and Cultural Studies at Monash University (Australia).

Marco van Leeuwen conducted his PhD-research (philosophy of cognition) at Radboud University Nijmegen, and is currently teaching philosophy at Breda University of Applied Sciences (The Netherlands).